# ITALIAN/EN
# BUSINESS GL

In the same series

*French Business Correspondence*
Stuart Williams and Nathalie McAndrew-Cazorla

*German Business Correspondence*
Paul Hartley and Gertrud Robins

*Italian Business Correspondence*
Vincent Edwards and Gianfranca Gessa Shepheard

*Spanish Business Correspondence*
Michael Gorman and María-Luisa Henson

*French Business Situations**
Stuart Williams and Nathalie McAndrew-Cazorla

*German Business Situations**
Paul Hartley and Gertrud Robins

*Italian Business Situations**
Vincent Edwards and Gianfranca Gessa Shepheard

*Spanish Business Situations**
Michael Gorman and María-Luisa Henson

*Manual of Business French*
Stuart Williams and Nathalie McAndrew-Cazorla

*Manual of Business German*
Paul Hartley and Gertrud Robins

*Manual of Business Italian*
Vincent Edwards and Gianfranca Gessa Shepheard

*Manual of Business Spanish*
Michael Gorman and María-Luisa Henson

*French/English Business Glossary*
Stuart Williams and Nathalie McAndrew-Cazorla

*German/English Business Glossary*
Paul Hartley and Gertrud Robins

*Spanish/English Business Glossary*
Michael Gorman and María-Luisa Henson

* Accompanying cassettes available

# ITALIAN/ENGLISH BUSINESS GLOSSARY

Vincent Edwards
and
Gianfranca Gessa Shepheard

London and New York

**Vincent Edwards** is Head of Research at the Business School, Buckinghamshire College (A College of Brunel University).

**Gianfranca Gessa Shepheard** is a freelance translator.

First published 1997
by Routledge
11 New Fetter Lane, London EC4P 4EE

Simultaneously published in the USA and Canada
by Routledge
29 West 35th Street, New York, NY 10001



Typeset in Rockwell and Univers by Routledge
Printed and bound in Great Britain by TJ International Ltd, Padstow, Cornwall



*British Library Cataloguing in Publication Data*
A catalogue record for this book is available from the British Library

*Library of Congress Cataloguing in Publication Data*
A catalogue record for this book is available from the Library of Congress

ISBN 0–415–16041–3

# Business Glossary

# Key to glossary

Grammatical abbreviations

| | |
|---|---|
| abbr | abbreviation |
| adj | adjective |
| adv | adverb |
| conj | conjunction |
| det | determiner |
| n | noun |
| nf | feminine noun |
| nfpl | plural feminine noun |
| nm | masculine noun |
| nmpl | plural masculine noun |
| pp | past participle |
| pref | prefix |
| prep | preposition |
| vb | verb |

Symbols

* denotes slang term
(US) term particular to USA
(GB) term particular to Great Britain

NB: Contexts are given in parentheses after term and part of speech or before multiple translations

Parts of speech are provided for all headwords and for translations where appropriate. Subterms are only supplied with parts of speech where it is considered necessary to indicate gender or to avoid ambiguity

# Italian–English

**abbandonare** *vb* abandon *vb* **abbandonare un impiego** quit *vb*
**abbandono** *nm* waiver *n*
**abbassare** *vb* (price, interest rate) bring down *vb*, lower *vb*
**abbonamento** *nm* season ticket *n*
**abbondanza** *nf* abundance *n*
**abbreviare** *vb* abbreviate *vb*
**abbreviato** *adj* abbreviated *adj*
**abbreviazione** *nf* abbreviation *n*
**abbuono** *nm* allowance *n*
**abile** *adj* **abile nell'uso dei computer** computer literate *adj*
**abilità** *nf* ability *n*, skill *n*
**abitudine** *nf* **abitudini del consumatore** consumer habits *npl*
**abolire** *vb* abolish *vb*
**abolizione** *nf* abolition *n* **abolizione delle tariffe** elimination of tariffs
**abrogare** *vb* (offer) revoke *vb*
**abusare di** *vb* abuse *vb*
**abuso** *nm* **abuso di autorità/ di fiducia** abuse of power/confidence
**accaparramento** *nm* takeup *n*
**accaparrare** *vb* forestall *vb*
**accedere a** *vb* access *vb*
**accelerare** *vb* accelerate *vb*, expedite *vb*
**accelerazione** *nf* acceleration *n*
**accendere** *vb* (machine) turn on *vb*
**accentramento** *nm* centralization *n*
**accentrare** *vb* centralize *vb*
**accertamento** *nm* assessment *n*
**accertare** *vb* assess *vb*
**accessibilità** *nf* accessibility *n*
**accesso** *nm* access *n*
**accessorio** *adj* auxiliary *adj*
**accettazione** *nf* **accettazione condizionata** qualified acceptance **accettazione del consumatore** consumer acceptance **accettazione da parte del mercato** market acceptance **mancata accettazione** non-acceptance **presentarsi al banco di accettazione** (airport) check in *vb*
**accludere** *vb* enclose *vb*
**accomiatarsi** *vb* take leave of sb *vb*
**accompagnatore** *nm* **accompagnatore turistico** courier *n*
**acconsentire a** *vb* consent *vb*
**acconto** *nm* down payment, part payment
**accordo** *nm* (agreement) arrangement *n* treaty *n*, understanding *n* **accordo commerciale** trade agreement **accordo di compensazione di cambio** exchange clearing agreement **accordo di contingente** quota agreement **accordo formale** formal agreement **accordo tra gentiluomini** gentleman's agreement **accordo internazionale** international agreement **accordo di mantenimento dei prezzi** fair-trade agreement **Accordo Monetario Europeo (AME)** European Monetary Agreement (EMA) **accordo operativo** working agreement **accordo di prezzo imposto** fair-trade agreement **accordo salariale** wage agreement **accordo di scambio** barter agreement **accordo verbale** verbal agreement **mettersi d'accordo** agree *vb* **raggiungere un accordo** make a treaty **per tacito accordo** by tacit agreement **venir meno ad un accordo** break an agreement **violare un accordo** break an agreement
**accreditare** *vb* accredit *vb* **accreditare un conto di una somma** credit sth to an account
**accredito** *nm* credit *n* **nota di accredito** credit note
**accrescere** *vb* (value) enhance *vb*
**accumulare** *vb* accumulate *vb*, hoard *vb*
**accumularsi** *vb* accumulate *vb*
**accumulato** *adj* accumulated *adj*
**accumulazione** *nf* accrual *n* **saggio di accumulazione** rate of accrual
**accusare** *vb* charge sb with sth *vb*
**acquirente** *nmf* vendee *n*
**acquisire** *vb* acquire *vb* **acquisire il controllo** (company) take over *vb*
**acquisitivo** *adj* acquisitive *adj*
**acquisizione** *nf* acquisition *n* **acquisizione di controllo** takeover *n*

**acquistare** *vb* acquire *vb*, purchase *vb* **acquistare in blocco** buy in bulk **acquistare all'ingrosso** buy sth wholesale, buy in bulk **acquistare di seconda mano** buy sth second hand
**acquisto** *nm* acquisition *n*, purchase *n* **acquisto in blocco** buy-out *n* **acquisto fittizio** fictitious purchase **acquisto di terreni** land purchase
**acume** *nm* **acume in affari** business acumen
**adattare** *vb* (adapt) tailor *vb*
**addebitamento** *nm* **addebitamento diretto** direct debiting
**addebitare** *vb* (account) debit *vb* **addebitare un onorario/ una tassa/ un compenso** charge a fee **addebitare in più** overcharge *vb* **addebitare la provvigione** charge commission **addebitare una somma su un conto** charge sth to an account
**addebito** *nm* debit *n* **nota di addebito** debit note
**addestramento** *nm* training *n* **addestramento avanzato** advanced training **addestramento di base** basic training **addestramento del personale** employee training **centro di addestramento** training centre **corso di addestramento** training course
**addestrare** *vb* (staff) train *vb*
**addetto** *nm* **addetto agli acquisti** buyer *n* **addetto all'ufficio spedizioni** dispatcher *n*
**addizionale** *adj* extra *adj*
**adeguamento** *nm* adjustment *n*
**aeroporto** *nm* airport *n*
**affare** *nm* bargain *n* **affare a condizioni poco vantaggiose** hard bargain **affari** *npl* business *n* **è un buon affare** it's a bargain **fare affari con** trade with sb **Affare fatto!** it's a deal! **i grossi affari** big business **nuovi affari** new business **parlare d'affari** talk business
**affarista** *nm* profiteer *vb*
**affidabile** *adj* reliable *adj*
**affidabilità** *nf* reliability *n*
**affidare** *vb* commit *vb*
**affiliante** *nm* franchisor *n*, franchise outlet *n*
**affiliato** *nm* franchisee *n*
**affiliazione** *nf* **affiliazione commerciale** franchise *n*
**affittare** *vb* (house, office) let *vb*, rent *vb*
**affitto** *nm* **dare in affitto** let *vb*, rent *vb* **prendere in affitto** rent *vb*, hire *vb*
**affittuario** *nm* occupant *n*, occupier *n*
**affrancare** *vb* frank *vb*
**agente** *nm* agent *n* **agente di assicurazioni** insurance agent, insurance salesperson **agente del credere** del credere agent **agente finanziario** fiscal agent **agente generale** free agent, general agent **agente immobiliare** estate agent, realtor (US) **agente importatore** import agent
**agenzia** *nf* **agenzia di cambiavalute** bureau de change **agenzia di collocamento** employment agency **agenzia di compravendita** brokerage firm **agenzia immobiliare** estate agency, real estate agency (US) **agenzia di informazioni commerciali** credit agency **agenzia d'intermediazione** brokerage firme **agenzia di pubblicità** advertising agency **agenzia di spedizioni** forwarding agency **agenzia di spedizioni per espresso** express agency **agenzia di stampa** news agency **agenzia per la vendita di biglietti** ticket agency **agenzia di viaggi** travel agency **agenzie di assicurazioni generali**, general agencies (US)
**aggiornare** *vb* (records) update *vb*
**aggiornato** *adj* up to date **tenersi aggiornato** (events) keep up with *vb*
**aggirare** *vb* bypass *vb*
**aggravarsi** *vb* escalate *vb*
**agribusiness** *nm* agribusiness *n*
**agricolo** *adj* agrarian *adj*
**agricoltura** *nf* agriculture *n*, farming *n*
**agronomo** *nm* agronomist *n*
**aiuto** *nm* **aiuto all'estero** foreign aid
**albergo** *nm* hotel *n* **albergo cinque stelle** five-star hotel
**alfanumerico** *adj* alpha-numeric *adj*
**aliquota** *nf* **aliquota fiscale** tax threshold **aliquota fissa** flat rate **aliquota d'imposta** tax rate
**allegare** *vb* enclose *vb*
**allegato** *nm* enclosure *n*, schedule *n*
**alloggio** *nm* accommodation *n* **alloggio in albergo** hotel accommodation **assegno integrativo d'alloggio** accommodation allowance
**alternativa** *nf* option *n*
**alto** *adj* **alto reddito** high-income **verso l'alto** upward
**altolocato** *adj* high-ranking *adj*
**alzare** *vb* **alzare il prezzo di** mark up *vb*
**ambasciata** *nf* embassy *n*
**ammanco** *nm* (accounts) shortage *n*
**ammenda** *nf* forfeit *n* **fare ammenda** make amends

**amministrare** *vb* administer *vb*, govern *vb*, manage *vb*

**amministratore** *nm* administrator *n*, director *n* **amministratore delegato** managing director **amministratore fiduciario** trustee **amministratore giudiziale** (bankruptcy) receiver, administrator (US) **amministratore rappresentante i lavoratori** worker-director **ufficio amministratori fiduciari** (bank) trustee department

**amministrazione** *nf* administration *n*, management *n* **amministrazione fiduciaria** trusteeship **amministrazione pubblica** civil service **avere l'amministrazione di fuduciaria** hold sth in trust **cattiva amministrazione** misconduct **proprietà tenuta in amministrazione fiduciaria** trust estate **studi di amministrazione aziendale** business studies

**ammodernamento** *nm* modernization *n*, refurbishment *n*

**ammontare** *nm* amount *n* **ammontare in arretrato** outstanding amount **ammontare della copertura** extent of cover **ammontare lordo** gross amount **ammontare netto** net, nett amount

**ammortamento** *nm* depreciation *n*, amortization *n*, redemption fund *n*

**ammortare** *vb* amortize *vb*, redeem *vb*

**ammortizzare** *vb* amortize *vb*

**ampliamento** *nm* (of contract) extension *n*

**ampliare** *vb* enlarge *vb* **ampliare la capacità** expand capacity **ampliare la gamma** extend the range

**analisi** *nf* analysis *n* **analisi dei costi e dei benefici** cost-benefit analysis **analisi economica** economic analysis **analisi funzionale** functional analysis **analisi delle mansioni** job analysis **analisi numerica** numerical analysis **analisi orizzontale** horizontal analysis **analisi dei sistemi** systems analysis **analisi stratificata delle cifre** breakdown of figures **analisi di tendenza** trend analysis

**analista** *nm* **analista di sistemi** systems analyst

**analizzare** *vb* analyze *vb*

**anno** *nm* year *n* **all'anno** per annum **anno commerciale** trading year **anno contabile** financial year **anno finanziario** financial year, fiscal year **anno fiscale** tax year

**annotare** *vb* make a note of sth *vb*, write down *vb*

**annullamento** *nm* annulment *n*, cancellation *n*

**annullare** *vb* **annullare un ordine** cancel an order

**annunciare** *vb* give notice of sth

**annuncio** *nm* **annuncio economico** classified advertisement **annuncio pubblicitario** advertisement

**anticipare** *vb* (salary) advance *vb*

**anticipo** *nm* (on salary) advance *n* **anticipo in contanti** cash advance

**antifortunistica** *nm* **responsabile dell'antifortunistica** safety officer

**anzianità** *nf* **anzianità di servizio** seniority *n*

**anziano** *adj* senior *adj*

**appaltatore** *nm* contractor *n* **appaltatore edile** building contractor

**appalto** *nm* **dare in appalto** farm out **offerta di appalto** tender *n*

**appello** *nm* appeal *n* **fare appello a** appeal to *vb*

**appianare** *vb* **appianare una lite** (dispute) settle *vb*

**applicare** *vb* (policy) enforce *vb*

**applicazione** *nf* enforcement *n*

**appoggiare** *vb* **appoggiare un'impresa rischiosa** back a venture

**appoggio** *nm* backing *n*

**apprendere** *vb* come to the notice of sb *vb*

**apprendista** *nmf* apprentice *n*, trainee *n*

**apprendistato** *nm* apprenticeship *n*

**appropriarsi** *vb* **appropriarsi indebitamente di** embezzle *vb*

**appropriazione** *nf* appropriation *n* **appropriazione indebita** embezzlement *n*, misappropriation *n*

**approssimativamente** *adv* approximately *adv*

**approssimativo** *adj* approximate *adj*

**approvare** *vb* approve *vb*

**approvazione** *nf* approval *n*

**approvvigionamento** *nm* supply *n*

**appuntamento** *nm* appointment **prendere un appuntamento** make an appointment **tenere un appuntamento** keep an appointment

**appunto** *nm* note *n* **prendere appunti su** make a note of sth

**aprire** *vb* open *vb* **aprire un conto** open an account **aprire il mercato** (market) open up *vb*

**arbitraggio** *nm* arbitrage *n*, arbitration *n*

**arbitrare** *vb* arbitrate *vb*

**arbitrario** *adj* arbitrary *adj*

**arbitrato** *nm* arbitration *n* **arbitrato industriale** industrial arbitration
**arbitro** *nm* arbitrator *n*, referee *n*
**archiviare** *vb* file *vb*
**archivio** *nm* file *n*
**area** *nf* **area commerciale** trading area **area fabbricabile** building site **area di libero scambio** free trade area **area valutaria** currency zone
**aria** *nf* **ad aria condizionata** air-conditioned *adj*
**aritmetica** *nf* arithmetic *n*
**arrestare** *vb* (inflation) halt *vb*
**arresto** *nm* holdup *n*
**arretrato** **1.** *adj* accumulated *adj* **2.** *nm* **arretrati** *nmpl* arrears *npl* **arretrati di paga** back pay *n* **in arretrato** in arrears *adv* **essere in arretrato** fall/get into arrears *vb*
**articolo** *nm* item *n* **articoli** *nmpl* wares *npl* **articoli casalinghi** household goods, housewares (US) **articoli d'importazione** imports **articoli di rapida vendita** fast-selling goods **articolo civetta** loss leader **articolo in omaggio** giveaway, free gift
**artificiale** *adj* synthetic *adj*
**aspettativa** *nf* expectation *n*, leave (of absence) *n* **aspettative dei consumatori** consumer expectations
**assediare** *vb* blockade *vb*
**assedio** *nm* blockade *n*
**assegnare** *vb* assign *vb*
**assegnatario** *nm* assignee *n*
**assegnazione** *nf* (patent) grant *n*
**assegno** *nm* cheque *n*, check (US) **assegno annuale** annuity **assegno aperto** open cheque **assegno in bianco** blank cheque **assegno circolare** bank draft, treasurer check (US) **assegno di comodo** exchange cheque **assegni familiari** family allowance **assegno non incassato** uncleared cheque **assegno incrociato** exchange cheque **assegno non onorato** unpaid cheque **assegno non passato alla stanza di compensazione** uncleared cheque **assegno al portatore** bearer cheque, open cheque **assegno sbarrato** crossed cheque **assegno scoperto** bad cheque, dud cheque **assegno per la somma di 100 sterline** a cheque for the amount of £100 **assegno trasferibile** negotiable cheque **assegno turistico** traveller's cheque, traveler's check (US) **assegno a vuoto** dud cheque **bloccare un assegno** stop a cheque **compensare un assegno** clear a cheque **firmare un assegno** sign a cheque **incassare un assegno** cash a cheque **mettere un fermo ad un assegno** stop a cheque **pagare con assegno** pay by cheque **restituire un assegno all'emittente** refer a cheque to drawer **scrivere un assegno** make out a cheque
**assemblea** *nf* (shareholders) meeting *n* **assemblea generale degli azionisti** annual general meeting (AGM) **assemblea generale ordinaria** ordinary general meeting **assemblea straordinaria** extraordinary meeting
**assente** **1.** *adj* absent *adj* **2.** *nmf* absentee *n*
**assenteismo** *nm* absenteeism *n*
**assenza** *nf* non-attendance *n*
**assicurabile** *adj* **non assicurabile** uninsurable *adj*
**assicurare** *vb* insure *vb*
**assicurato** *nm* policy holder
**assicuratore** *nm* insurance underwriter, underwriter
**assicurazione** *nf* insurance *n* **assicurazione auto** car insurance **assicurazione per il bagaglio personale** luggage insurance **assicurazione per il caso di sopravvivenza** endowment insurance **assicurazione collettiva** group insurance **assicurazione-credito nel commercio estero** export credit insurance **assicurazione contro i danni** indemnity insurance **assicurazione contro la disoccupazione** unemploment insurance **assicurazione di fedeltà** fidelity insurance **assicurazione contro l'incendio** fire insurance **assicurazione malattie** medical insurance **assicurazione contro le malattie** health insurance, medical insurance **assicurazione marittima** marine insurance **assicurazione mista** endowment insurance **assicurazione contro la responsabilità civile** third party insurance **assicurazione sulla responsabilità civile** third-party insurance **assicurazione contro la responsabilità civile del datore di lavoro** employer's liability insurance **assicurazione sullo scafo** hull insurance **assicurazione contro tutti i rischi** all-risks insurance, comprehensive insurance **assicurazione viaggi** travel insurance **assicurazione sulla vita** life assurance/insurance **assicurazioni sociali** national insurance (NI) (GB)
**assistenza** *nf* **assistenza alla clientela**

after-sales service **assistenza finanziaria** financial aid

**associazione** *nf* **associazione dei datori di lavoro** employer's federation

**assoluto** *adj* absolute *adj*

**assorbire** *vb* **assorbire le rimanenze** absorb surplus stock

**assumere** *vb* recruit *vb*, undertake *vb*

**assumersi** *vb* **assumersi l'impegno di** undertake *vb*

**assunzione** *nf* **campagna di assunzione** recruitment campaign **domanda d'assunzione** letter of application

**asta** *nf* auction *n* **vendere all'asta** auction *vb*, sell sth at auction *vb*

**attendere** *vb* (on phone) hang on *vb*, hold on *vb*, be on hold *vb*

**attendibile** *adj* reliable *adj*

**attendibilità** *nf* reliability *n*

**attenersi** *vb* **attenersi alle regole** comply with the rules

**Attenzione!** *nf* handle with care

**attestare** *vb* certificate *vb*, certify *vb*

**attestato** *nm* attestation *n*, certificate *n*, reference *n* **attestato di buona condotta** testimonial *n* **attestato di posizione creditizia** credit reference

**attestazione** *nf* attestation *n*

**attitudinale** *adj* vocational *adj*

**attività** *nf* asset *n* **attività congelate** frozen assets **attività di consulenza** consultancy work, consulting work (US) **attività correnti** floating assets **attività fisse** fixed assets **attività fittizie** fictitious assets **attività illegali per estorcere denaro** racketeering **attività immateriali** intangible assets **attività di non immediato realizzo** frozen assets **attività liquide** liquid assets **attività materiali** tangible assets **attività mineraria** mining **attività nette** net, nett assets **attività nominali** nominal assets **attività occulta** hidden assets **attività di pronto realizzo** quick assets **sospendere ogni attività** (informal) shut up shop **svolgere attività commerciale come** trade as

**attivo** *nm* asset *n* **attivi finanziari** financial assets

**atto** *nm* certificate of ownership **atto di cessione** bill of sale, deed of transfer **atto di compravendita** deed of sale **atto di procura** power of attorney **atto scritto** (law) deed *n* **atto di vendita** bill of sale

**attore** *nm* claimant *n*

**attraccare** *vb* moor *vb*

**attrattive** *nfpl* amenities *npl*

**attrezzatura** *nf* equipment *n* **attrezzature portuali** harbour facilities

**attribuzione** *nf* accrual *n*

**attuabilità** *nf* viability *n*

**attualità** *nf* topicality *n* **d'attualità** up to date

**attuario** *nm* actuary *n*

**aumentare** *vb* escalate *vb*, rise *vb* **aumentare i prezzi** bump up prices **aumentare di prezzo** (rise in value) appreciate **aumentare la produzione** boost production **aumentare le vendite** boost sales

**aumento** *nm* rise *n* **aumento del capitale** expansion of capital **aumento del carovita** increase in the cost of living **aumento di paga** pay rise **aumento dei prezzi** price increase **aumento salariale** wage increase **aumento di valore** (in value) appreciation **aumento delle vendite** sales growth **richiesta di aumento salariale** wage demand

**ausiliare** *adj* auxiliary *adj*

**autenticare** *vb* certify *vb*

**autenticazione** *nf* attestation *n*

**autofinanziamento** *nm* self-financing *adj*

**autogestione** *nf* self-management *n*

**automatico** *adj* automatic *adj*, built-in *adj*

**automazione** *nf* automation *n*

**autonomo** *adj* autonomous *adj*, self-employed *adj*

**autorità** *nf* (official) authority *n*

**autorizzare** *vb* authorize *vb*, license *vb*

**autorizzazione** *nf* licence *n*, permit *n*

**autostazione** *nf* bus station

**autosufficienza** *adj* self-sufficient *adj*

**autotassazione** *nf* self-assessment *n*

**avallante** *nm* backer *n*

**avanzare** *vb* (research, project) progress *vb*

**avanzo** *nm* **avanzo di bilancio** budget surplus

**avaria** *nf* average *n*, damage *n* **avaria generale** general average

**avente** *nm* **avente causa** assignee *n*

**avere** *nm* credit *n*

**avveduto** *adj* well-advised *adj*

**avvertire** *vb* **avvertire qualcuno di non fare qualcosa** warn sb against doing sth

**avviamento** *nm* goodwill *n*, start-up *n* **codice di avviamento postale statunitense**, zip code (US)

**avviare** *vb* (company) set up *vb* **avviare un'azienda** set up in business

**avvisare** *vb* notify *vb*

**avviso** *nm* advice note **debito avviso** due

warning **fino a nuovo avviso** until further notice **ultimo avviso** final notice
**avvocato** *nm* barrister *n*, solicitor *n*, lawyer (US)
**azienda** *nf* company *n* **azienda affiliata** affiliated company **azienda che assume lavoratori indipendenti** open shop **azienda in attività** going concern **azienda avviata** going concern **aziende statali** state-owned enterprises **nuova azienda** new business
**aziendale** *adj* corporate *adj*
**azionariato** *nm* **azionariato di maggioranza** majority holding **azionariato di minoranza** minority holding
**azione** *nf* (stock exchange) share *n* **azione industriale** industrial action **azione nominativa** registered share **azione ordinaria** equity share, ordinary share, ordinary stock (US) **azione al portatore** bearer share **azioni quotate in borsa** quoted shares, quoted stocks (US)
**azionista** *nm* shareholder *n*, stockholder *n* **azionista intestatario** nominee shareholder **azionista prestanome** nominee shareholder
**bacheca** *nf* bulletin board
**bacino** *nm* (for berthing) dock *n* **entrare in bacino** dock *vb* **mettere in bacino** dock *vb*
**baco** *nm* (listening device) bug *n*
**bagaglio** *nm* luggage *n* **bagaglio depositato** left luggage **bagaglio in eccedenza** excess luggage **deposito bagagli** left-luggage locker **ufficio deposito bagagli** left-luggage office
**balla** *nf* bundle *n*
**ballotaggio** *nm* strike ballot *n*
**banca** *nf* bank *n* **banca affiliata alla stanza di compensazione** clearing bank **banca centrale** central bank **banca commerciale** commercial bank **banca di credito ordinario** commercial bank **banca dati** data bank **banca di emissione** bank of issue **banca emittente** issuing bank **banca estera** foreign bank **Banca europea degli investimenti (BEI)** European Investment Bank (EIB) **banca mercantile** merchant bank **Banca Mondiale** World Bank **banca di risparmio** savings bank
**bancaria** *nf* **rete bancaria** banking network
**bancario** *nm* **il mondo bancario** banking circles
**banchiere** *nm* banker *n*
**banchina** *nf* quay *n* **diritti di banchina** quayage
**banco** *nm* **banco informazioni** information desk
**banconota** *nf* banknote *n*
**banditore** *nm* auctioneer *n*
**baracca** *nf* **mandare avanti la baracca** keep the business running
**barattare** *vb* barter *vb*
**baratto** *nm* barter *n*
**barone** *nm* **barone della stampa** press baron
**barriera** *nf* **barriera commerciale** trade barrier **barriera doganale sull'importazione** import barrier **barriera al libero scambio** trade barrier **barriera tariffaria** tariff barrier, tariff wall
**base** *nf* **base dati** database **base operaia** shopfloor **base razionale** rationale
**basilare** *adj* basic *adj*
**basso** *adj* (price) low *adj*
**battuta** *nm* **errore di battuta** typing error
**bene** *nm* asset *n* **bene economico basilare** basic commodity **bene d'esportazione** export **bene informato** knowledgeable
**benefattore** *nm* benefactor *n*
**beneficenza** *nf* charity *n*
**beneficiare** *vb* benefit *vb*
**beneficiario** *nm* payee *n*
**beneficio** *nm* benefit *n* **benefici accessori** fringe benefits **benefici aggiuntivi** fringe benefits
**benessere** *nm* welfare *n*
**benestare** *nm* approval *n*, consent *n*
**beni** *nmpl* goods *npl* **beni abbandonati** abandoned goods **beni capitali** capital goods **beni deperibili** perishable goods **beni non deperibili** durable goods **beni indiretti** capital goods **beni mobili** chattels **beni strumentali** capital goods **beni a termine** future goods
**benservito** *nm* testimonial *n*
**biennale** *adj* biennial *adj*
**biglietteria** *nf* ticket office
**biglietto** *nm* ticket *n* **biglietto di andata e ritorno** return ticket, round-trip ticket (US) **biglietto di sola andata** (rail/flight) single/one-way ticket **biglietto da visita** business card **prezzo del biglietto** price ticket
**bilancia** *nf* **bilancia commerciale** balance of trade, trade balance **bilancia commerciale attiva** favourable balance of trade **bilancia commerciale passiva** adverse balance of trade **bilancia dei pagamenti** balance of payments

**bilancio** *nm* **bilancio finanziario** financial balance, fiscal balance **bilancio fiscale** fiscal balance **bilancio patrimoniale** balance sheet **bilancio preventivo** budget **fare il bilancio dei libri contabili** balance the books

**bimensile** *adj* biweekly *adj*, bimonthly *adj*

**bimestrale** *adj* bimonthly *adj*

**bisogno** *nm* **avere bisogno di** call for *vb* **bisogni materiali** material needs

**bloccare** *vb* (prices, wages) freeze *vb*

**blocco** *nm* (on prices, wages) freeze *n*

**bocciare** *vb* **bocciare un progetto** kill a project

**boicottaggio** *nm* boycott *n*

**boicottare** *vb* boycott *vb*

**bolla** *nf* **bolla di consegna** delivery note **bolla di merce esente** free entry, entry for free goods

**bollettino** *nm* bulletin *n*, newsletter *n* **bollettino di spedizione** forwarding note

**bonifica** *nf* **bonifica urbana** urban renewal

**bonifico** *nm* credit transfer **bonifico bancario** bank transfer

**boom** *nm* **boom della domanda** boom in demand

**borsa** *nf* **borsa dei contratti a termine** futures exchange **borsa nera** black market **borsa valori** Stock Exchange **Borsa Valori di New York** NYSE (New York Stock Exchange) **intensa attività di borsa** heavy trading

**bottega** *nf* **chiudere bottega** (informal) shut up shop

**botteghino** *nm* (ticket office) box office

**bracciante** *nm* labourer *n*

**breve** *adj* **breve distanza** short-haul *adj*

**brevettato** *adj* patented *adj*

**brevetto** *nm* patent *n*

**britanniche** *adj* **le Isole Britanniche** British Isles

**broker** *nm* broker, money trader **broker di assicurazioni** insurance broker

**brokeraggio** *nm* brokerage *n*

**budget** *nm* budget *n* **avere un budget limitato** be on a tight budget **budget fisso** fixed budget **budget flessibile** flexible budget **budget degli investimenti di capitale** capital budget **budget promozionale** promotional budget **budget pubblicitario** advertising budget **budget rigido** fixed budget

**buono** *nm* coupon *n*, voucher *n* **buono frazionario** scrip *n* **buono d'ordine** order form **buono del tesoro (BOT)** Treasury bill

**buonuscita** *nf* golden handshake

**burocrate** *nm* bureaucrat *n*

**burocratico** *adj* bureaucratic *adj*

**burocrazia** *nf* bureaucracy *n*, red tape *n*

**business** *nm* **business ad alto livello** big business

**busta** *nf* **busta paga** wage packet, salary package (US)

**bustarella** *nf* backhander* *n*

**cabina** *nf* booth *n* **cabina telefonica** telephone box, phone booth (US)

**CAD (Design assistito da calcolatore)** *nm* CAD (computer-aided or assisted design) *abbr*

**calare** *vb* (reduce) cut *vb*

**calce** *nm* **in calce** at the bottom

**calcolare** *vb* calculate *vb*, tally up *vb*

**calcolatrice** *nf* calculator *n*

**calcolo** *nm* calculation *n*

**calmiere** *nm* (on prices) ceiling *n*

**calo** *nm* decrease *n*

**CAM (produzione assistita dal calcolatore)** *nf* CAM (computer-aided manufacture)

**cambiale** *nf* bill of exchange **cambiale di comodo** accommodation bill **cambiale di credito** finance bill **cambiale finanziaria** finance bill **cambiale insoluta** unpaid bill **cambiale trasferibile** negotiable bill **prima copia di cambiale** first bill of exchange

**cambiamento** *nm* **cambiamento repentino** turnabout *n*

**cambiare** *vb* (market) turn *vb*

**cambiavalute** *nm* foreign exchange dealer *n*

**cambio** *nm* exchange rate, rate of exchange **in cambio di** in return for **cambio di acquisto** buying rate **cambio estero** foreign exchange **cambio favorevole** favourable exchange **corso del cambio** rate of exchange

**camera** *nf* **camera di commercio** Chamber of Commerce **camere d'albergo** hotel accommodation

**campagna** *nf* **campagna indirizzata a un settore specifico** targeted campaign **campagna pubblicitaria** advertising campaign, publicity campaign **campagna di vendita** sales campaign **fare una compagna** run a campaign **intraprendere una campagna** wage a campaign

**campionamento** *nm* sampling *n* **campionamento proporzionale** quota sampling

**campionare** *vb* sample *vb*

**campionatura** *nf* sampling *n*
**campione** *nm* sample *n*
**cancellare** *vb* (debts) write off *vb*
**cancellazione** *nf* cancellation *n*
**cancelliere** *nm* **Cancelliere dello Scacchiere** chancellor of the exchequer (GB)
**candidato,a** *nm,f* candidate *n*
**canone** *nm* **canone di affitto** rental *n* **canoni di fitto** hire charges **canoni di nolo** hire charges
**cantiere** *nm* **cantiere edilizio** building site **cantiere navale** dockyard, shipyard
**CAP - codice di avviamento postale** *nm* post code, zip code (US)
**capacità** *nf* ability *n*, power *n*, skill *n* **capacità contributiva** ability to pay **capacità di credito** creditworthiness **capacità industriale** industrial capacity, manufacturing capacity **capacità inutilizzata** idle capacity **capacità di magazzinaggio** storage capacity **capacità di pagare** ability to pay **capacità di reddito** earning power, earning capacity
**capitale** *nm* capital *n* **capitale annacquato** watered capital **capitale azionario** risk capital **capitale azionario annacquato** watered stock **capitale di esercizio** trading capital **capitale fisso** capital assets, fixed capital **capitale d'impianto** initial capital **capitale iniziale** start-up capital **capitale interamente versato** paid-up capital **capitale investito** fixed capital, invested capital **capitale limitato** limited capital **capitale liquido** liquid capital **capitale a lunga scadenza** long capital **capitale netto** equity, equity capital **capitale netto di esercizio** working capital **capitale obbligazionario** debenture capital, debenture stock (US) **capitale di rischio** venture capital **capitale di risparmio** earned surplus **capitale sociale in circolazione** outstanding stock **capitale sociale nominale** registered capital **capitali vaganti** hot money **trasferimento di capitale** capital transfer **ad uso intensivo di capitale** capital-intensive
**capitalismo** *nm* capitalism *n*
**capitalista** *nm* capitalist *n*
**capitalizzare** *vb* capitalize *vb*
**capitano** *nm* **capitano d'industria** tycoon *n*
**capite** **pro capite** per head
**capitolato** *nm* (bid) specification *n*
**capo** *nm* boss *n* **a capo di** at the head of **capo di governo** head of government **capo reparto** foreman/forewoman *n* **essere a capo di** be head of
**capofamiglia** *nmf* householder *n*
**capufficio** *nm* head of department *n*
**carattere** *nm* **carattere corsivo** italic type **carattere numerico** numeric character **caratteri grandi** large type **caratteri piccoli** small type
**carenza** *nf* shortage *n*
**carica** *nf* (position) office *n* **carica di grande responsabilità** hot seat **essere in carica** hold office **ricoprente una carica** office holder
**caricare** *vb* load *vb*
**caricatore** *nm* shipper *n*
**carico** *nm* cargo *n*, load *n* **carico a massa** bulk cargo **carico pagante** (of vehicle) payload **carico remunerativo** (of vehicle) payload **carico alla rinfusa** bulk cargo
**caro** *adj* expensive *adj* **far pagare troppo caro** overcharge *vb*
**carovita** *nm* cost of living *n*
**carriera** *nf* career *n*
**carta** *nf* **carta di addebito** charge card **carta assegni** cheque card **carta commerciale** commercial paper **carta di credito** bank card, credit card **carta d'identità** identity card **carta intelligente** smart card **carta intestata** headed notepaper **carta-moneta inconvertibile** forced currency **carta di prim'ordine** first-class paper **carta verde** green card
**cartamoneta** *nf* paper currency *n*
**cartellino** *nm* ticket *n* **cartellino del prezzo** price ticket
**cartello** *nm* cartel *n*
**casa** *nf* **casa editrice** publishing house **casa madre** parent company **casa di vendita per corrispondenza** mail-order house
**casaccio** *nm* **a casaccio** at random
**casella** *nf* **casella postale** PO box
**casellario** *nm* filing cabinet *n*
**cash flow** cash flow **cash flow attualizzato** discounted cash flow (DCF) **cash flow negativo** negative cash flow
**cassa** *nf* cash desk **cassa automatica** automatic cash machine/dispenser **cassa di risparmio** savings bank
**cassiere, -a** *nm,f* cashier *n*, teller *n* **cassiere capo** chief cashier
**casuale** *adj* hit-or-miss
**catasto** *nm* land register *n*
**categoria** *nf* **categoria fiscale** tax bracket **categorie socioeconomiche** socio-economic categories

**catena** *nf* **catena alberghiera** hotel chain **catena di montaggio** assembly line **catena di negozi** chain of shops **catena di negozi al dettaglio** retail chain
**causa** *nf* lawsuit *n*, litigation *n* **causa legale che serve a creare un precedente** test case **intentare una causa** take legal action **parte in causa** litigant **le parti in causa** the contracting parties
**causare** *vb* **causare danni ingenti** cause extensive damage
**cauzione** *nf* bail, caution money
**CE (Comunità Europea)** *abbr* EC (European Community) *abbr*
**CECA (Comunità europea del carbone e dell'acciaio)** *abbr* ECSC (European Coal and Steel Community) *abbr*
**cedere** *vb* assign *vb* **cedere la proprietà** (ownership) transfer *vb*
**cedibile** *adj* transferable *adj*
**cento** *nm* hundred *n* **per cento** per cent **cento per cento** one hundred per cent
**centralinista** *nmf* switchboard operator
**centralino** *nm* switchboard *n*
**centralizzare** *vb* centralize *vb*
**centralizzazione** *nf* centralization *n*
**centro** *nm* centre *n*, center (US) **centro di calcolo** computer centre **centro cittadino** town centre **centro commerciale** business centre, shopping centre, shopping mall **centro di costi** cost centre **centro informatico** computer centre
**certificare** *vb* certificate *vb*, certify *vb*
**certificato** *nm* certificate *n* **certificato di assicurazione** insurance certificate **certificato azionario** share certificate, stock certificate (US) **certificato di lavoro** certificate of employment **certificato di matrimonio** marriage certificate **certificato di nazionalità** certificate of ownership **certificato obbligazionario** bond certificate **certificato di origine** certificate of origin **certificato di servizio** testimonial
**cessare** *vb* quit *vb* **cessare l'attività** break up *vb*
**cessionario** *nm* assignee *n*
**cessione** *nf* assignment *n*
**chiamare** *vb* call *vb*
**chiamata** *nf* telephone call
**chiarire** *vb* (agreement, policy) thrash out *vb*
**chilowatt** *nm* kilowatt *n*
**chilowattora** *nm* kWh *abbr*
**chiudere** *vb* **chiudere un'azienda** close a business **chiudere la cassa** cash up *vb* **chiudere un conto** close an account
**chiuso** *adj* closed *adj*
**chiusura** *nf* **chiusura di un'azienda** closure of a company
**ciclo** *nm* **ciclo economico** economic cycle, trade cycle
**cif (costo, assicurazione e nolo)** *abbr* cif (cost, insurance and freight) *abbr*
**cifra** *nf* numeric character **cifre consolidate** consolidated figures
**circa** *adv* approximately *adv*
**circolante** *nm* hard cash *n*
**circolare** 1. *nf* (letter) circular *n* 2. *vb* (document) circulate *vb* **far circolare** (document) circulate *vb*
**circolazione** *nf* **in circolazione** in circulation **circolazione stradale** road traffic
**circostanza** *nf* circumstance *n* **a causa di circostanze impreviste** due to unforeseen circumstances **circostanze al di fuori del nostro controllo** circumstances beyond our control **circostanze impreviste** unforeseen circumstances
**circuito** *nm* **circuito integrato molto miniaturizzato** microchip *n*
**citazione** *nf* **citazione in giudizio** writ *n* **emettere una citazione in giudizio** issue a writ
**classe** *nf* **classe business** (plane) business class **classe di merci** product line **prima classe** first class
**clausola** *nf* (in contract) clause *n* **clausola d'esclusione** exclusion clause **clausola di opzione** option clause **clausola di protezione**, hedge clause (US) **clausola di storno** escape clause **clausole del contratto** the terms of the contract
**cliente** *nm* client *n*, customer *n* **cattivarsi dei clienti** win customers **cliente abituale** regular customer **cliente regolare** regular customer **essere clienti di** trade with sb **guadagnarsi dei clienti** win customers **perdere clienti** lose custom **primo cliente** first customer
**clientela** *nf* clientele *n*, patronage *n*
**coda** *nf* queue *n*
**codice** *nm* **codice di avviamento postale** postcode, zip code (US) **codice fiscale** tax code
**coerente** *adj* **essere coerente** (argument) hang together *vb*
**cofirmatario** *nm* cosignatory *n*
**cogliere** *vb* **cogliere l'occasione** seize an opportunity

**collaborare** *vb* collaborate *vb*
**collaboratore** *nm* **collaboratore in affari** associate *n*
**collega** *nmf* colleague *n*, workmate *n*
**collettivamente** *adv* jointly *adv*
**collettivo** *nm* collective *n* **collettivo operaio** workers' collective
**colletto** *nm* **colletti bianchi** white-collar worker **colletto blu** blue-collar worker
**collo** *nm* package *n*
**collocamento** *nm* **ufficio di collocamento** Jobcentre (GB) *n*
**colloquio** *nm* interview *n* **fare un colloquio** hold an interview **presentarsi ad un colloquio** attend for interview
**colpa** *nf* fault *n* **colpa grave** gross negligence **concorso di colpa** contributory negligence
**colpito** *pp* **colpito duramente** hard-hit **essere duramente colpiti da** be hard hit by
**comandare** *vb* be in charge *vb*
**comando** *nm* **prendere il comando** take the lead
**comitato** *nm* committee *n* **comitato consultivo** advisory committee **comitato esecutivo** executive committee
**comma** *nm* (in contract) clause *n*
**commento** *nm* comment *n*
**commerciabile** *adj* marketable *adj* **non commerciabile** unmarketable *adj*
**commerciale** *adj* commercial *adj*
**commercialista** *nmf* chartered accountant
**commercializzazione** *nf* **commercializzazione globale** global marketing
**commerciante** *nmf* merchant *n*, trader *n*
**commerciare** *vb* merchandise *vb*, trade *vb*
**commercio** *nm* commerce *n*, trade *n* **commercio bilaterale** bilateral trade **commercio al dettaglio** retail trade **commercio di esportazione** export trade **commercio con l'estero** overseas trade **commercio estero** foreign trade **commercio internazionale** international trade
**commessa** *nf* order *n* **commessa permanente** standing order **stabilire i costi di commessa** cost a job
**commesso** *nm* shop assistant **commesso viaggiatore** commercial traveller, commercial traveler (US)
**commettere** *vb* commit *vb*
**commissionario** *nm* (buyer of debts) factor *n* **commissionario di borsa valori** commission broker
**commissione** *nf* commission *n*, committee *n* **Commissione delle comunità europee** European Commission **commissioni bancarie** bank charges
**comodo** *nm* (banking) accommodation *n*
**compagnia** *nf* company *n* **compagnia di assicurazione** insurance company **compagnia commerciale** trading company
**comparato** *adj* comparative *adj*
**compartecipazione** *nf* **piano di compartecipazione agli utili** profit-sharing scheme
**compatibile** *adj* compatible *adj*
**compensare** *vb* compensate for *vb*
**compensazione** *nf* compensation *n*
**compenso** *nm* compensation *n*
**compera** *nf* purchase *n*
**competente** *adj* experienced *adj*, expert *adj*
**competenza** *nf* expertise *n* **competenza di commissione** commission fee **competenze bancarie** bank charges
**competere** *vb* compete *vb*
**competitività** *nf* competitiveness *n*
**competitivo** *adj* competitive *adj*
**compilare** *vb* complete *vb*
**compimento** *nm* accomplishment *n*
**compito** *nm* assignment *n*, task *n*
**complessivo** *adj* total *adj*
**complesso** **1.** *adj* complex *adj* **2.** *n* complex *n* **complesso urbano** housing complex, housing estate, housing tenement (US)
**completare** *vb* complete *vb*
**completo** **1.** *adj* comprehensive *adj* **2.** *nm* business suit
**comprare** *vb* bribe *vb*, purchase *vb* **comprare a credito** buy sth on credit **comprare a prezzo alto** buy sth at a high price
**compratore** *nm* buyer *n* **compratore nazionale** home buyer **mercato del compratore** buyer's market
**compravendita** *nf* buying and selling *n* & *n*
**compromesso** *nm* compromise *n* **raggiungere un compromesso** come to an accommodation **venire a un compromesso** reach a compromise
**comproprietà** *nf* joint ownership *n*
**computer** *nm* **computer portatile** portable computer
**comunicare** *vb* give notice of sth **riuscire**

**a comunicare con qualcuno** (phone) get through to sb
**comunicato** *nm* bulletin *n*
**comunicazione** *nf* communication *n* **mettere in comunicazione** (phone) put sb through (to sb)
**comunità** *nf* community *n* **Comunità Europea (CE)** European Community (EC)
**concedere** *vb* grant *vb*
**concernente** *adj* regarding *prep*
**concernere** *vb* (be of importance to) concern *vb*
**concessionario** *nm* **concessionario di licenza** licensee *n*
**concessione** *nf* (patent) grant *n*
**concessore** *nm* **concessore di licenza** licensor *n*
**concludere** *vb* **concludere un affare** clinch a deal, close a deal
**concordare** *vb* concur *vb* agree *vb*
**concordato** **1.** *adj* agreed *adj* **2.** *nm* agreement *n*, arrangement *n*
**concorrente** *nm* competitor *n*, competing company
**concorrenza** *nf* competition *n* **concorrenza estera** foreign competition **concorrenza internazionale** international competition **concorrenza leale** fair competition **concorrenza del mercato** market competition **concorrenza sleale** unfair competition **concorrenza spietata** cut-throat competition, tough competition **fare concorrenza a** compete with
**concorrenziale** *adj* competitive *adj*
**concorrere** *vb* compete *vb* **concorrere ad un appalto** tender for a contract
**condirettore** *nm* associate director
**condizione** *nf* condition *n*, term *n* **condizioni di acquisto** conditions of purchase **condizioni del contratto** the terms of the contract **condizioni di credito** credit terms **condizioni finanziarie** financial position **condizioni di lavoro** working conditions **condizioni di pagamento rigorosamente nette** terms strictly net(t) **condizioni vantaggiose** favourable terms **condizioni di vendita** conditions of sale **condizioni di vita** living conditions **senza condizioni** unconditional *adj*
**condotta** *nf* **cattiva condotta** misconduct *n*
**condurre** *vb* manage *vb*, run *vb*
**conduzione** *nf* (of business) operation *n* **cattiva conduzione** mishandling *n*
**conferenza** *nf* conference *n* **conferenza del personale addetto alle vendite** sales conference **conferenza stampa** press conference
**conferire** *vb* **conferire la laurea** graduate *vb*
**conferma** *nf* confirmation *n*
**confermato** *adj & pp* **non confermato** unconfirmed *adj*
**confezione** *nf* packaging *n*
**confidenziale** *adj* **in via strettamente confidenziale** in strictest confidence
**confisca** *nf* forfeit *n*, forfeiture *n* **confisca di azioni** forfeit of shares
**confiscare** *vb* impound *vb*
**conflitto** *nm* **conflitto industriale** industrial dispute
**conformemente** *adv* **conformemente alle vostre esigenze** in accordance with your requirements
**conformità** *nf* **in conformità con** in accordance with
**conforts** *nmpl* amenities *npl*
**congedo** *nm* leave, leave of absence, furlough (US) **concedere il congedo a** furlough (US) *vb* **congedo per malattia** sick leave **prendere congedo** take leave
**congegnato** *pp* **essere ben congegnato** (argument) hang together *vb*
**congelamento** *nm* (on prices, wages) freeze *n*
**congelare** *vb* (prices, wages) freeze *vb*
**congiunto** *adj* joint *adj*
**congiuntura** *nf* **congiuntura bassa** slump *n*
**conglomerata** *nf* conglomerate *n*
**conglomerato** *nm* **conglomerato di aziende** conglomerate *n*
**congresso** *nm* congress *n*
**conguaglio** *nm* adjustment *n*
**coniare** *vb* mint *vb*
**conoscenza** *nf* knowledge *n* **conoscenza di base** knowledge base **conoscenza discreta** working knowledge **fare la conoscenza di** make the acquaintance of sb
**conoscere** *vb* **conoscere in profondità** have a thorough knowledge of sth
**conquista** *nf* breakthrough *n*
**consegna** *nf* delivery *n* **consegna a domicilio** home delivery **consegna per espresso** express delivery **consegna franco spese** free delivery **consegna futura** future delivery **consegna il giorno dopo** overnight delivery **consegna gratuita** free delivery **consegna registrata con ricevuta di ritorno** recorded delivery

**mancata consegna** non-delivery **ricevere in consegna** accept delivery
**consegnare** *vb* hand over *vb*, turn over *vb*
**consegnatario** *nm* consignee *n*
**conseguenza** *nf* consequence *n*
**conseguimento** *nm* achievement *n* **conseguimenti** *nmpl* track record *n*
**conseguire** *vb* achieve *vb*
**consenso** *nm* consent *n* **per mutuo consenso** by mutual agreement
**conservarsi** *vb* (goods) keep *vb*
**conservazione** *nf* **conservazione del titolo** retention of title
**considerazione** *nf* (for contract) consideration *n* **prendere in considerazione** take sth into account
**consigliare** *vb* **consigliare qualcosa a qualcuno** advise sb on sth
**consigliere** *nm* adviser/advisor *n* **consigliere economico** economic adviser
**consiglio** *nm* advice *n* **consiglio di amministrazione** board of directors **consiglio comunale** town council **consiglio direttivo** supervisory board **Consiglio europeo** Council of Europe **consiglio di fabbrica** factory board, workers' council **consiglio di gestione** works council **consiglio di supervisione** supervisory board
**consociata** *nf* **consociata controllata nella misura del 100 per cento** wholly-owned subsidiary
**consolato** *nm* consulate *n*
**console** *nm* consul *n*
**consolidamento** *nm* funding *n*
**consolidare** *vb* consolidate *vb*
**consorella** *nf* sister company
**consorzio** *nm* cartel *n*, consortium *n* **consorzio industriale** syndicate *n*
**consulente** *nm* adviser/advisor *n*, business consultant *n*, consultant *n* **consulente di direzione e organizzazione** management consultant **consulente finanziario** investment adviser, financial consultant
**consulenza** *nf* consultancy *n*, consulting (US) **consulenza finanziaria** financial consultancy
**consultare** *vb* consult *vb* **vogliate consultare il nostro ufficio centrale** we refer you to our head office
**consultivo** *adj* advisory *adj*
**consumarsi** *vb* **da consumarsi entro** best-before date
**consumatore** *nm* consumer *n* **consumatore finale** end consumer **gran consumatore** heavy user
**consumerismo** *nm* consumerism *n*
**consumo** *nm* **consumo globale** world consumption
**contabile** *nm* accountant *n*, book-keeper *n*
**contabilità** *nf* book-keeping *n* **contabilità finanziaria** financial accounting **contabilità generale** general accounting **contabilità gestionale** management accounting **tenere la contabilità** keep the books
**contante** *nm* cash *n* **in contanti** for cash **contanti all'ordinazione** cash with order
**contare** *vb* tally up *vb*
**contatore** *nm* meter *n*
**contattare** *vb* contact *vb*
**contatto** *nm* **contatti di affari** business contacts **contatto nel mondo degli affari** business acquaintance **mettersi in contatto con** get in contact with sb
**contenere** *vb* retain *vb*
**contenitore** *nm* container *n*
**contestare** *vb* litigate *vb*
**contingente** *nm* quota *n* **contingente d'importazione** import quota **contingente tariffario d'importazione** tariff quota
**conto** *nm* account *n* **aprire un conto** open an account **conguagliare i conti** adjust the figures **conti bloccati** blocked account **conto bancario** bank account **conto congiunto** joint account **conto corrente** current account **conto di credito** charge account **conto creditori diversi** accounts payable **conto debitori diversi** accounts receivable **conto economico operativo** operating statement **conto esercizio commerciale** trading account **conto merci** trading account **conto a più firme** joint account **conto profitti e perdite** profit and loss account **conto profitti e perdite operativo** operating statement **conto di risparmio** savings account **conto scoperto** overdraft, overdrawn account **conto spese** expense account **numero di conto** account number **nuovo conto** new account **rettificare i conti** adjust the figures **che sa far di conto** numerate *adj* **saldare un conto** settle an account **saper far di conto** numeracy *n* **tenere in conto** take sth into account **tenuto a rendere conto** accountable *adj*
**contrabbandare** *vb* smuggle *vb*

**contraente** *adj* **le parti contraenti** the contracting parties
**contraffare** *vb* counterfeit *vb*
**contraffazione** *nf* counterfeit *n*, forgery *n*
**contrarre** *vb* (stock) shrink *vb*
**contrassegno** *nm* COD (cash on delivery) *abbr.*, (collect on delivery) (US)
**contrattare** *vb* bargain *vb*, negotiate *vb*
**contrattazione** *nf* dealing *n*, trading (US) **abilità di contrattazione** negotiating skills **contrattazione collettiva** collective bargaining **contrattazione a termine** futures marketing **contrattazioni tariffarie** tariff negotiations **volume delle contrattazioni** trading volume
**contratto** *nm* contract *n* **contratti a termine** futures *npl* **contratto di assicurazione** insurance contract **contratto di assicurazione di fedeltà** fidelity bond **contratto di cambio per consegna differita** forward contract **contratto collettivo di lavoro** collective agreement **contratto formale** formal contract **contratto di lavoro** employment contract **contratto di nolo** hire contract **contratto preliminare** draft contract **contratto a premio** share option, stock option (US) **contratto a termine** futures contract **contratto tipo** standard agreement
**contravvenire** *vb* **contravvenire a** contravene *vb*
**contravvenzione** *nf* contravention *n*
**contrazione** *nf* (economic) downturn *n*
**contribuente** *nm* taxpayer *n*
**contribuire** *vb* contribute *vb*
**contributivo** *adj* contributory *adj* **non-contributivo** non-contributory *adj*
**contributo** *nm* contribution *n* **contributi previdenziali** social security contributions
**controfirmare** *vb* countersign *vb*
**controllare** *vb* check *vb*, inspect *vb*, tally *vb*
**controllo** *nm* **controllo dei cambi** exchange control **controllo dei conti** audit **controllo del credito** credit control **controllo doganale** customs check **controllo finanziario** financial control **controllo sulle importazioni** import control **controllo del livello delle scorte** inventory control, stock control **controllo della produzione** production control **controllo della qualità** quality control **controllo delle spese** expense control
**controllore** *nm* **controllore di volo** air traffic controller
**controversia** *nf* **controversia sindacale** labour dispute
**convalidare** *vb* validate *vb*
**conveniente** *adj* (price) keen *adj*
**convenire** *vb* agree *vb*
**convenuto** *adj* agreed *adj*
**convenzione** *nf* covenant *n*
**convertibile** *adj* **non convertibile** non-convertible *adj*
**convocare** *vb* **convocare un'assemblea** call a meeting, convene a meeting **convocare una riunione** call a meeting
**copertura** *nf* backing *n* **copertura assicurativa** insurance cover **nota di copertura** cover note
**copia** *nf* copy *n* **copia autenticata di testamento** probate **copia della fattura** duplicate invoice **copia fotostatica** photocopy **in triplice copia** in triplicate
**copiare** *vb* copy *vb*, photocopy *vb*
**corona** *nf* **corona danese** (Danish) krone *n* **corona norvegese** (Norwegian) krone *n* **corona svedese** (Swedish) krona *n*
**corrente** *adj* current *adj* **al corrente** well-informed *adj*
**correttezza** *nf* **correttezza commerciale** fair trade practice, fair trading
**corriere** *nm* courier *n* **tramite servizio di corrieri** by courier service
**corrispondente** *nmf* opposite number
**corrispondenza** *nf* correspondence *n* **ordinazione per corrispondenza** mail order *n*
**corrispondere** *vb* **corrispondere a** tally with *vb*
**corrompere** *vb* bribe *vb*
**corruzione** *nf* bribery *n*, corruption *n*
**corso** *nm* course *n* **in corso** in hand **corso di acquisto** buying rate **corso del cambio** exchange rate **corso a termine** futures price
**corte** *nf* court *n* **Corte d'Appello** Court of Appeal, Court of Appeals (US) **Corte di giustizia europea** European Court of Justice (ECJ) **Corte Internazionale di Guistizia** World Court
**costituire** *vb* amount to *vb*
**costituzione** *nf* (of company) formation *n*
**costo** *nm* cost *n* **costi comuni** overheads, overhead costs **costi correnti** running costs **costi di esercizio** operating cost, operating expenses **costi di fabbricazione** factory costs **costi fissi** fixed costs **costi di funzionamento** variable costs **costi generali** overhead costs **costi di trasporto** carriage costs **costi variabili** variable costs **costo aggiuntivo** extra cost **costo di capitale** capital cost **costo**

**indiretto** indirect cost **costo marginale** marginal cost **costo netto** net, nett cost **costo originario** original cost **costo pieno** full cost **costo di rescissione** cancellation charge **costo di trasporto** haulage, freight (US) **costo unitario** unit cost **costo di utilizzazione** carrying cost

**costruttore** *nm* builder *n*

**costruzione** *nf* building *n*, construction *n* **construzioni navali** shipbuilding *n*

**cottimo** *nm* piecework *n*

**credenziale** *nf*, treasurer check (US)

**credito** *nm* credit *n* **crediti congelati** frozen credits **in credito** in credit **credito aperto in conto corrente**, open note (US) **credito in bianco** open credit, unsecured credit **credito al consumo** consumer credit **credito all'esportazione** export credit **credito finanziario** financial loan **credito fisso** fixed credit **credito non garantito** unsecured credit **credito illimitato** unlimited credit **credito inesigibile** bad debt **credito a lunga scadenza** long credit **credito passivo** borrowing **credito scoperto** open credit **credito allo scoperto** bank overdraft **essere in credito** be in the black **fornire a credito** supply sth on trust **ottenere credit** obtain credit **vendere a credito** sell sth on credit

**creditore** *nm* covenantee *n*, creditor *n*

**crescere** *vb* thrive *vb*

**crescita** *nf* growth *n* **crescita economica** economic growth **crescita indotta dalle esportazioni** export-led growth **crescita del mercato** market growth **tasso di crescita** rate of growth

**crisi** *nf* **crisi economica** economic crisis **crisi finanziaria** financial crisis **entrare in crisi** (economic) slump *vb*

**criterio** *nm* **criterio basilare di accertamento** basis of assessment

**criticare** *vb* find fault with *vb*

**crollare** *vb* slump *vb*

**crollo** *nm* **crollo del mercato finanziario** collapse on stock market

**cronaca** *nf* news coverage

**crumiro** *nm* scab* *n*, strikebreaker *n*

**cura** *nf* **prendersi cura di** take charge of sth

**curatore** *nm* (bankruptcy) receiver *n*, administrator (US)

**curricolo** *nm* curriculum vitae (CV) *n*, resumé (US)

**curva** *nf* **curva di esperienza** experience curve

**danneggiare** *vb* damage *vb*

**danno** *nm* damage *n* **chiedere il risarcimento dei danni** claim compensation **danni alle merci in transito** damage to goods in transit **danni nominali** nominal damages **danni a proprietà** damage to property **danno accidentale** accidental damage **pretendere il risarcimento dei danni** claim for damages **risarcire i danni** pay compensation **stabilire l'entità del danno** adjust claim **tenuto a risarcire i danni** liable for damages

**darsena** *nf* dockyard *n*

**data** *nf* **data di consegna** delivery date **data obiettivo** target date **data di scadenza** expiry date, expiration date (US) **data di spedizione** date of dispatch **data traguardo** target date

**datato** *adj* dated *adj*

**dati** *nmpl* data *npl* **dati di prova** test data **dati riservati** classified information **dati tabulati** tabulated data

**datore** *nm* **datore di lavoro** employer *n*

**dattilografa** *nf* typist *n*

**dattilografare** *vb* type *vb*

**dattilografo** *nm* typist *n*

**dazio** *nm* (customs) duty *n* **dazio d'esportazione** export tax **dazio d'importazione** import duty **esente da dazio** duty free

**debito** *nm* debt *n* **debiti insoluti** outstanding debt **debito aziendale** corporate debt **debito fondato** funded debt **debito nazionale** national debt **essere in debito di** owe *vb* **riconoscimento di un debito** acknowledgement of debt

**debitore** *nm* covenantor *n*, debtor *n*

**decidere** *vb* resolve *vb*, establish *vb* **decidere di fare qualcosa** resolve to do sth

**decisione** *nf* **prendere una decisione** make a resolution, decision

**declino** *nm* decline *n* **declino economico** economic decline

**decrescere** *vb* decrease *vb*

**dedurre** *vb* deduct *vb*

**deficit** *nm* deficit *n* **deficit della bilancia commerciale** adverse balance of trade, trade gap **deficit della bilancia dei pagamenti** balance of payments deficit **deficit di bilancio** budgetary deficit **essere in deficit** be in the red

**deflatorio** *adj* deflationary *adj*

**deflazione** *nf* deflation *n*

**deflazionistico** *adj* deflationary *adj*

**defraudare** *vb* defraud *vb*
**degno** *adj* **degno di nota** noteworthy *adj*
**degradare** *vb* (employee) demote *vb*
**delega** *nf* (power) proxy *n*
**delegare** *vb* delegate *vb*
**delegato, -a** *nm,f* delegate *n* **delegato di fabbrica** shop steward
**delibera** *nf* decision *n*, resolution *n* **adottare una delibera** make a resolution
**democrazia** *nf* **democrazia industriale** industrial democracy
**demografia** *nf* demography *n*
**demolizione** *nf* breakup *n*
**denaro** *nm* money *n* **denaro caro** dear money **denaro liquido** cash **denaro pubblico** public money **denaro a richiesta** call money **denaro scottante** hot money **ottenere denaro liquido** raise money **spendere bene il proprio denaro** get value for one's money
**denigrare** *vb* disparage *vb*, knock *vb*
**depositare** *vb* deposit *vb*
**depositario** *nm* depository *n*
**deposito** *nm* deposit *n* **deposito per container** container depot **deposito franco** bonded warehouse, customs warehouse, entrepôt **deposito a lunga scadenza** long deposit **deposito a risparmio** deposit account
**deposizione** *nf* **deposizione giurata** affidavit *n*
**depressione** *nf* (economic) depression *n*
**deprezzamento** *nm* depreciation *n*
**deprezzare** *vb* depreciate *vb*, undervalue *vb*
**deputato** *nm* Member of Parliament (MP) (GB) **deputato del Parlamento Europeo** Member of the European Parliament (MEP)
**desideroso** *adj* **desideroso di acquisire** acquisitive *adj*
**designare** *vb* nominate sb to a board/ committee
**designato** *pp* **designato di recente** newly-appointed
**destinataria** *nf* addressee *n*
**destinatario** *nm* addressee *n*, consignee *n*, offeree *n*, recipient *n*
**destino** *nm* **f.o.b. destino** ex ship
**detentore** *nm* holder *n* **detentore di polizza** policy holder
**deterioramento** *nm* spoilage *n*
**determinazione** *nf* assessment *n*
**detraibile** *adj* deductible *adj*, tax deductible *adj*
**detrarre** *vb* abate *vb*
**detrazione** *nf* allowance *n*, deduction *n* **detrazione d'imposta** tax allowance
**dettaglio** *nm* resale *n* **commercio al dettaglio** retail trade **mercato al dettaglio** retail market **vendere al dettaglio** (sell) retail *vb*
**diagramma** *nm* **diagramma a colonne** bar chart **diagramma a settori** pie chart
**dicastero** *nm* ministry *n*
**dichiarare** *vb* **dichiarare non assicurabile** (vehicle) write off *vb*
**dichiarato** *pp* **non dichiarato** undeclared *adj*
**dichiarazione** *nf* **dichiarazione doganale** customs declaration
**dicitura** *nf* wording *n*
**difensore** *nm* **difensore civico** ombudsman *n*
**difetto** *nm* defect *n* **assenza di difetti** zero defect **senza defetti** zero defect
**difettoso** *adj* defective *adj*, deficient *adj*
**diffalcare** *vb* abate *vb*
**diffalco** *nm* abatement *n*
**diffamazione** *nf* libel *n*
**differire** *vb* defer *vb*
**differito** *adj* deferred *adj*
**difficoltà** *nf* **difficoltà finanziaria** financial difficulty
**diffondere** *vb* broadcast *vb*
**diffusione** *nf* broadcast *n*
**digitale** *adj* digital *adj*
**dilazionare** *vb* extend a contract *vb*
**dimensione** *nf* size *n*
**dimettersi** *vb* **dimettersi da** resign from office
**dimezzare** *vb* halve *vb*, reduce sth by half *vb*
**diminuire** *vb* cut *vb*, reduce *vb*
**dimissioni** *nfpl* resignation *n* **dare le dimissioni** hand in one's resignation **rassegnare le dimissioni** resign *vb*
**dinamica** *nf* dynamics *npl*
**dinamico** *adj* booming *adj*, dynamic *adj*, high-powered *adj*
**dipartimento** *nm* department *n*
**dipendente** *nm* employee *n*
**direttiva** *nf* regulation *n*
**direttore** *nm* director *n* **direttore di banca** bank manager **direttore esecutivo** chief executive **direttore di filiale** branch manager **direttore finanziario generale** chief financial officer **direttore generale** general manager, chief executive **direttore di medio livello** middle manager **direttore di reparto** head of department **direttore tecnico** technical director

**direttore di zona** area manager, field manager
**direzione** *nf* management *n* **addestramento alla direzione** management training **alta direzione** top management **direzione aziendale** business management **direzione dell'albergo** hotel management **direzione generale** general management **direzione a medio livello** middle management **direzione per obiettivi** management by objectives **direzione di reparto** line management
**dirigente** *nm* boss *n*, executive *n* **dirigenti di primo grado** senior management
**dirigenziale** *adj* **a livello dirigenziale** top-level *adj*
**dirigere** *vb* run *vb*, manage *vb*
**dirigersi** *vb* **dirigersi a** head for *vb*
**diritto** *nm* fee *n*, right *n*, law *n* **certificato di diritto di opzione** warrant **diritti acquisiti** vested rights **diritti di consulenza** consultancy fees, consulting fees (US) **diritti esclusivi** sole rights **diritti di porto** harbour dues, harbour fees **diritti speciali di prelievo** SDRs (special drawing rights) **diritto di autore** copyright **diritto civile** civil law **diritto commerciale** business law **diritto consuetudinario** common law **diritto contrattuale** law of contract **il diritto di fare qualcosa** the right to do sth **diritto internazionale** international law **diritto sull'occupazione** employment law **diritto penale** criminal law **diritto pubblico** public law **il diritto a qualcosa** the right to sth **diritto di rivalsa** right of recourse
**disavanzo** *nm* deficit *n*, budgetary deficit
**discendente** *adj* downward *adj*
**disco** *nm* disk *n* **disco magnetico** magnetic disk
**discrezionale** *adj* arbitrary *adj*
**discriminatorio** *adj* **non discriminatorio** non-discriminatory *adj*
**disdire** *vb* **disdire un appuntamento** cancel an appointment
**disegnare** *vb* design *vb*
**disimballare** *vb* unpack *vb*
**disoccupato** *adj* jobless *adj* **i disoccupati** the jobless **essere disoccupato** be out of work
**disoccupazione** *nf* unemployment *n* **assicurazione contro la disoccupazione** unemployment insurance **disoccupazione di massa** mass unemployment **livello della disoccupazione** level of unemployment **sussidio di disoccupazione** unemployment benefit **tasso di disoccupazione** rate of unemployment
**disonesto** *adj* (dealings) shady* *adj*
**disponibile** *adj* available *adj* **non disponibile** not available
**disporre** *vb* **disporre in tabelle** (data) tabulate *vb*
**disposizione** *nf* (stipulation) provision *n*
**disputa** *nf* **disputa industriale** industrial dispute
**dissipazione** *nf* depletion *n*
**distaccamento** *nm* secondment *n*
**distanza** *nf* **distanza lunga** long-haul
**distinta** *nf* **distinta di accompagnamento** remittance advice
**distribuire** *vb* (document) circulate *vb*
**distributore** *nm* distributor *n* **distributore automatico** vending machine
**distribuzione** *nf* distribution *n* **rete di distribuzione** distribution network
**distruggere** *vb* **distruggere completamente** (vehicle) write off *vb*
**diversificare** *vb* diversify *vb*
**diversificazione** *nf* diversification *n*
**dividendo** *nm* dividend *n* **dividendo extra** bonus **dividendo di fine anno** year-end dividend
**dividere** *vb* split *vb*
**divisa** *nf* currency *n* **divisa estera** foreign currency, foreign exchange
**divisione** *nf* (of company) division *n* **divisione del lavoro** division of labour **divisione in tre parti** three-way split
**documentazione** *nf* record *n*
**documento** *nm* document *n* **documenti** *nmpl* paperwork *n* **nascondere un documento** withhold a document **rifiutare di dare un documento** withhold a document
**dogana** *nf* customs *npl*, customs office *n*
**doganiere** *nm* customs inspector *n*
**dollaro** *nm* dollar *n*, buck* (US)
**doloso** *adj* fraudulent *adj*
**domanda** *nf* demand *n*, letter of application **domanda dei consumatori** consumer demand **domanda determinante** key question **domanda finale** final demand **domanda e offerta** supply and demand **fare domanda di** apply for *vb*
**domandare** *vb* demand *vb*
**doppio** *adj* double *adj*, two-tier *adj*
**dotare** *vb* equip *vb*
**dotazione** *nf* endowment *n* **dotazione di personale** staffing *n*
**dovere** *vb* (debt) owe *vb*

**due** *adj* two *adj* **a due direzioni** two-way **a due livelli** two-tier **a due sensi** two-way **a due vie** two-way
**duplice** *adj* two-tier
**durata** *nf* timescale *n*
**eccedenza** *nf* surplus *n* **eccedenza delle esportazioni** export surplus **eccedenza di finanziamento** financing surplus **eccedenza delle importazioni** import surplus **eccedenza di stanziamento** funds surplus
**eccedere** *vb* exceed *vb*
**eccessivo** *adj* exorbitant *adj*
**eccesso** *nm* **eccesso di capacità produttiva** excess capacity **con eccesso di lavoro** overworked *adj* **eccesso di riserve bancarie** excess reserves
**econometria** *nf* econometrics *n*
**economia** *nf* economy *n* **economia avanzata** advanced economy **economia giovane** young economy **economia globale** global economy **economia liberale** free economy **economia liberista** free economy **economia di mercato** market economy **economia di mercato libero** free market economy **economia mista** mixed economy **economia nazionale** national economy **economia nera** black economy **economia pianificata** planned economy **economia a pianificazione centrale** centrally planned economy **economia progredita** advanced economy **economia sottosviluppata** underdeveloped economy **economia in via di sviluppo** developing economy **economie di scala** economies of scale
**economico** *adj* economical *adj*
**economista** *nmf* economist *n*
**economo** *nm* bursar *n*
**ECU (Unità monetaria europea)** *abbr* ECU (European Currency Unit) *abbr*
**edicolante** *nmf*, newsdealer (US)
**edilizia** *nf* building industry/trade *n*
**editoria** *nf* publishing *n*
**effettivo** *adj* actual *adj*
**effetto** *nm* effect *n* **effetti scontati** bills discounted
**effettuare** *vb* carry out *vb* **effettuare un controllo di** make a check on sth
**efficiente** *adj* businesslike *adj*, efficient *adj*
**efficienza** *nf* efficiency *n*
**EFTA (Associazione europea di libero scambio)** *abbr* EFTA (European Free Trade Association) *abbr*
**EFTS (sistema elettronico di trasferimento fondi)** *abbr* EFT (electronic funds transfer) *abbr*
**elaboratore** *nm* **elaboratore elettronico** computer *n*
**elaborazione** *nf* **elaborazione dati** data processing **elaborazione dati elettronica (EDP)** electronic data processing **elaborazione a distanza** teleprocessing **elaborazione di informazioni** information processing **elaborazione di testi** word processing
**elasticità** *nf* elasticity *n* **elasticità della domanda** elasticity of demand **elasticità della produzione** elasticity of production **elasticità del reddito** income elasticity
**elenco** *nm* list *n* **elenco telefonico** telephone directory
**elettronico** *adj* electronic *adj*
**elezione** *nf* election *n* **elezioni amministrative** local election **elezioni politiche** general election
**elusione** *nf* **elusione fiscale** tax avoidance
**emendamento** *nm* amendment *n*
**emergenza** *nf* emergency *n*
**emettere** *vb* issue *vb* **emettere una fattura** issue an invoice
**emigrazione** *nf* emigration *n*
**emissione** *nf* **emissione azionaria** share issue, stock issue (US) **emissione fiduciaria** fiduciary issue **emissione riservata agli azionisti** rights issue
**energia** *nf* **energia idroelettrica** hydroelectricity *n*
**ente** *nm* (official) authority *n* **ente portuale** harbour authorities **ente statale** government body
**entrata** *nf* **entrata in vigore** entry into force
**entrate** *nfpl* earnings *npl*, revenue *n*
**equilibrio** *nm* equilibrium *n*
**equipaggiare** *vb* equip *vb*
**équipe** *nf* **équipe di ricerca** research team
**equità** *nf* equity *n*
**equivalente** *nmf* opposite number *n*
**equivalere** *vb* **equivalere a** amount to *vb*
**equivoco** *adj* (dealings) shady* *adj*
**equo** *adj* fair *adj*
**eredità** *nf* inheritance *n*
**ereditare** *vb* inherit *vb*
**ergonomia** *nf* ergonomics *n*
**erogare** *vb* disburse *vb*
**errore** *nm* mistake *n* **commettere un errore** make a mistake **errore di calcolo** miscalculation **errore grave** serious fault **errore di lieve entità** minor fault **errore di scrittura** clerical error

**esame** *nm* examination *n* **in esame** on approval
**esaminare** *vb* examine *vb*
**esattezza** *nf* accuracy *n*
**esatto** *adj* accurate *adj*
**esaurimento** *nm* depletion *n*
**esaurire** *vb* (reserves) exhaust *vb*
**esazione** *nf* **esazione di crediti** debt collection
**esborsi** *nmpl* outgoings *npl*
**escludere** *vb* exclude *vb*, foreclose *vb*
**esclusivista** *nm* franchisee *n*
**esclusivo** *adj* (product) up-market
**esecutivo** *nm* executive *n*
**esecutore** *nm* administrator *n*
**esecuzione** *nf* enforcement *n* **esecuzione non autorizzata di copie di software** software piracy
**eseguire** *vb* carry out *vb*
**esentasse** *adj* tax-free *adj*
**esente** *adj* exempt *adj* **esente da imposte** tax-free
**esenzione** *nf* exemption *n*
**esercente** *nmf* trader *n*
**esercenti** *nmpl* trade *n*
**esercizio** *nm* accounting period **costi di esercizio** operating expenditure **esercizio finanziario** financial year, fiscal year, tax year **perdita di esercizio** trading loss
**esibire** *vb* display *vb*, exhibit *vb*
**esigenze** *nfpl* requirement *n* **esigenze dell'industria** needs of industry
**esigere** *vb* demand *vb*
**esito** *nm* outcome *n*
**esonero** *nm* exemption *n*
**espandere** *vb* expand *vb* boom *vb*
**espansione** *nf* expansion *n* **espansione economica** economic expansion **espansione industriale** industrial expansion **espansione urbana incontrollata** urban sprawl **tasso di espansione** rate of expansion
**esperienza** *nf* **fare esperienza di** experience *vb*
**esperto** **1.** *adj* experienced *adj*, expert *adj* **2.** *nm* expert *n*
**esporre** *vb* display *vb*, exhibit *vb*
**esportare** *vb* export *vb*
**esportatore** *nm* exporter *n*
**esportazione** *nf* export *n* **esportazione di capitale** export of capital **esportazione sottocosto** dumping **esportazioni di capitale** capital exports **esportazioni globali** world exports **esportazioni invisibili** invisible exports **esportazioni visibili** visible exports **vendite per esportazione** export sales
**esposizione** *nf* exhibition *n*
**espropriare** *vb* expropriate *vb*
**esproprio** *nm* expropriation *n*
**essenziale** *adj* **non essenziale** non-essential *adj*
**estendere** *vb* extend *vb* **estendere il credito** extend credit
**esterno** *adj* external *adj*
**estero** *adj* foreign *adj*, overseas *adj* **andare all'estero** go abroad
**estinzione** *nf* cancellation *n*, termination *n*
**estorsione** *nf* extortion *n*
**estratto** *nm* abstract *n* **estratti conto trimestrali** quarterly trade accounts **estratto conto** statement of account, bank statement
**esuberante** *adj* redundant *adj* **dichiarare esuberante** make sb redundant
**esuberanza** *nf* **esuberanza di personale** redundancy *n*
**etichetta** *nf* label *n*
**etichettare** *vb* label *vb*
**euro-obbligazione** *nf* eurobond *n*
**eurocapitale** *nm* eurocapital *n*
**eurocrate** *nm* eurocrat *n*
**eurocrazia** *nf* eurocracy *n*
**eurocredito** *nm* eurocredit *n*
**eurodeputato** *nm* Member of the European Parliament (MEP) *n*
**eurodivisa** *nf* eurocurrency *n*
**eurodollaro** *nm* eurodollar *n*
**eurofondi** *nmpl* eurofunds *npl*
**eurofusione** *nf* euromerger *n*
**euromercato** *nm* euromarket *n*
**euromoneta** *nf* eurocurrency *n*, euromoney *n*
**europeo** *adj* European *adj*
**euroscettico** *nm* eurosceptic *n*
**eurovaluta** *nf* eurocurrency *n*, euromoney *n*
**evadere** *vb* evade *vb*
**evasione** *nf* **evasione fiscale** tax evasion *n*
**evitare** *vb* avoid *vb*, evade *vb*
**extraprofitto** *nm* extra profit *n*
**fabbisogno** *nm* requirement *n*
**fabbrica** *nf* factory *n*, works *npl* **consiglio di fabbrica** works committee
**fabbricante** *nm* manufacturer *n*
**fabbricare** *vb* manufacture *vb*
**fabbricato** *adj* **fabbricato in Francia** made in France
**fabbricazione** *nf* manufacture *n*
**faccenda** *nf* **una faccenda urgentissima** a matter of urgency

**facente** *adj* **facente funzione** deputy *n*
**facoltà** *nf* power *n*
**facoltativo** *adj* optional *adj*
**facsimile** *nm* telecopier *n*, telefax *n*
**fallimento** *nm* bankruptcy *n*, failure *n*
**fallire** *vb* be bankrupt *vb*, go out of business *vb*, go to the wall *vb*
**fallito** *adj* bankrupt *adj* **fallito non riabilitato** undischarged bankrupt
**falsificare** *vb* counterfeit *vb*
**falsificazione** *nf* counterfeit *n*, falsification *n*
**falso** *adj* **falso contabile** falsification of accounts
**fare** *vb* **fare concorrenza** compete *vb* **fare da mediatore** mediate *vb* **fare un'offerta** bid *vb* **fare pubblicità** advertise *vb* **far fiasco** go to the wall *vb* **far fronte** tide over *vb*
**FAS (franco lungo bordo)** *abbr* FAS (free alongside ship) *abbr*
**fascicolo** *nm* file *n*
**fatti** *nmpl* **fatti incontrovertibili** the hard facts **fatti noti** known facts
**fattibile** *adj* feasible *adj*, workable *adj*
**fattibilità** *nf* feasibility *n*
**fatto** *adj* **ben fatto** well-made *adj* **fatto dall'uomo** man-made *adj*
**fattore** *nm* factor *n* **fattore limitante** limiting factor **fattore della produzione** factor of production **mercato dei fattori della produzione** factor market **prezzo del fattore della produzione** factor price
**fattura** *nf* invoice *n* **fattura definitiva** final invoice
**fatturare** *vb* (informal) invoice *vb*, bill *vb*
**fatturato** *nm* turnover *n* **fatturato lordo** gross sales **fatturato netto** net, nett sales
**favore** *nm* favour *n* **fare un favore a qualcuno** do sb a favour
**fede** *nf* **in buona fede** bona fide *adj*
**fedeltà** *nf* **fedeltà del consumatore** customer loyalty
**federale** *adj* federal *adj*
**federazione** *nf* federation *n*
**ferie** *nfpl* holidays *npl*, vacation (US) **in ferie** on holiday **ferie pagate** paid holiday
**fermata** *nf* **fermata temporanea** (factory) shutdown *n*
**ferrovia** *nf* railway *n*, railroad (US) **per ferrovia** by rail
**festa** *nf* **festa civile** bank holiday
**fideiussione** *nf* fiduciary bond
**fiduciario** *nm* trustee *n*
**fiera** *nf* **fiera commerciale** trade fair
**filiale** *nf* branch, branch company
**finale** *adj* terminal *adj*
**finanza** *nf* finance *n* **alta finanza** high finance
**finanziamento** *nm* financing *n*, funding *n* **finanziamento in disavanzo** deficit financing
**finanziare** *vb* capitalize *vb*, finance *vb*, fund *vb*
**finanziario** *adj* financial *adj*
**finanziatore** *nm* backer *n*, financier *n*, underwriter *n*
**finanziere** *nm* financier *n*
**fine** *nf* end *n* **fine anno finanziario** fye (fiscal year end) *abbr*
**fiorente** *adj* booming *adj*
**fiorino** *nm* **fiorino olandese** guilder *n*
**firma** *nf* signature *n* **sottoscrivere l'apposizione di una firma come testimone** witness a signature
**firmare** *vb* sign *vb* **firmare un contratto** sign a contract
**firmatario** *nm* signatory *n* **i firmatari del contratto** the signatories to the contract
**fisco** *nm* the Inland Revenue, The Internal Revenue Service (IRS) (US)
**fissare** *vb* fix *vb* **fissare il prezzo** fix the price
**flessibilità** *nf* flexibility *n*
**flessione** *nf* decrease *n*
**fluido** *adj* fluid *adj*
**flusso** *nm* **flusso di cassa** cash flow, funds flow **flusso di cassa attualizzato** discounted cash flow (DCF) **flusso del reddito** flow of income **flusso di tesoreria** funds flow
**flussogramma** *nm* flow chart
**flussoschema** *nm* flow chart
**fluttuare** *vb* fluctuate *vb* (currency) float *vb*
**fluttuazione** *nf* fluctuation *n* **fluttuazione delle vendite** fluctuation in sales
**FOB (franco a bordo)** *abbr* FOB (free on board) *abbr*
**foglio** *nm* ticket *n* **foglio elettronico** spreadsheet *n*
**fondamentale** *adj* basic *adj*
**fondare** *vb* establish *vb* **fondare una società** found a company
**fondatore** *nm* founder *n*
**fondazione** *nf* establishment *n*
**fondere** *vb* amalgamate *vb*
**fondersi** *vb* merge *vb*
**fondo** *nm* fund *n*, bottom *n* **fondi di capitale** capital funds **fondi pubblici** public funds **in fondo** at the bottom **fondo aperto** unit trust **fondo di autoassicurazione** insurance fund **fondo**

comune d'investimento trust fund, unit trust, mutual fund (US) **fondo comune d'investimento mobiliare** investment trust **fondo di emergenza** emergency fund **Fondo europeo di cooperazione monetaria (FECOM)** European Monetary Cooperation Fund (EMCF) **Fondo europeo per lo sviluppo (FES)** European Development Fund (EDF) **Fondo europeo di sviluppo regionale** European Regional Development Fund (ERDF) **fondo fiduciario** trust fund **Fondo monetario internazionale (FMI)** International Monetary Fund (IMF) **Fondo sociale europeo** European Socal Fund (ESF) **istituire un fondo comune d'investimento** set up a trust **ottenere fondi** raise money **prelievo di fondi** withdrawal of funds **toccare il fondo** bottom out

**fonte** *nf* source *n*

**formale** *adj* formal *adj*

**formalità** *nf* **formalità doganali/legali** customs/legal formalities

**formare** *vb* (staff) train *vb* **formare campioni** sample *vb*

**formazione** *nf* training *n* **centro di formazione professionale** training centre **formazione di capitale** capital formation **formazione professionale** vocational training **formazione professionale avanzata** advanced training

**formulazione** *nf* wording *n*

**fornire** *vb* supply *vb*, provide *vb*

**fornitore** *nm* supplier *n*, vendor *n* **fornitore principale** main supplier

**fornitura** *nf* supply *n* **offerta di fornitura** tender *n*

**fortuna** *nf* fortune *n*, destiny *n*, luck *n* **colpo di fortuna** windfall *n* **far fortuna** make a fortune *vb*

**forza** *nf* **forza lavoro** manpower *n*

**fotocopia** *nf* photocopy *n*

**fotocopiare** *vb* photocopy *vb*, xerox *vb*

**fotocopiatrice** *nf* photocopier *n*

**franco** 1. *adj* **franco banchina** ex quay, ex wharf **franco banchina partenza** free on quay **franco bordo** free on board (FOB) **franco bordo nave a destino** ex ship **franco deposito** ex store/warehouse **franco domicilio** franco domicile **franco fabbrica** ex factory/works **franco di nolo** free of freight **franco sottobordo** free alongside ship (FAS) 2. *nm* franc *n* **franco belga** Belgian franc **franco francese** French franc **franco svizzero** Swiss franc

**fraudolento** *adj* fraudulent *adj*

**frazionario** *adj* fractional *adj*

**frazione** *nf* fraction *n*

**frequenza** *nf* frequency *n*

**frode** *nf* false representation *n*, fraud *n*

**frontiera** *nf* frontier *n*

**fruttifero** *adj* interest-bearing *adj*

**fuga** *nf* **fuga di capitali** flight of capital

**funzionamento** *nm* working *n*, functioning *n*

**funzionare** *vb* work *vb*, function *vb*

**funzionario** *nm* executive *n* **funzionario di dogana** customs officer **funzionario statale** civil servant

**funzione** *nf* function *n*, position *n*, task *n* **direzione per funzioni** task management

**fusione** *nf* amalgamation *n*

**fuso** *nm* **fuso orario** time zone

**gamma** *nf* (of products) range *n*

**gara** *nf* **indire una gara d'appalto per** put sth out for tender **vendita con gara di appalto** sale by tender

**garante** *nm* backer *n*, guarantor *n*

**garantire** *vb* warrant *vb*

**garantito** *adj* secure *adj*

**garanzia** *nf* bail *n*, guarantee *n*, pledge *n*, security *n* **garanzia collaterale** collateral, collateral security **garanzia di qualità** quality guarantee **garanzia reale** collateral, collateral security **sotto garanzia** under warranty

**gas** *nm* **gas naturale** natural gas

**gasdotto** *nm* pipeline *n*

**GATT (Accordo generale sulle tariffe e il commercio)** *abbr* GATT (General Agreement on Tariffs and Trade) *abbr*

**generale** *adj* comprehensive *adj*

**generare** *vb* **generare reddito** generate income

**generazione** *nf* **generazione di reddito** income generation

**generosità** *nf* generosity *n*

**geografia** *nf* **geografia economica** economic geography

**gerarchia** *nf* hierarchy *n* **gerarchia dei bisogni** hierarchy of needs **gerarchia dei dati** data hierarchy **gerarchia direttiva** executive hierarchy

**gestione** *nf* administration *n*, management *n* **cattiva gestione** mismanagement **gestione alberghiera** hotel management **gestione dei dati** data handling **gestione finanziaria** financial management **gestione delle informazioni** information management **gestione del personale** personnel

management **gestione della qualità totale** TQM (Total Quality Management) *abbr* **gestione delle risorse umane** human resource management (HRM) **gestione delle transazioni** transaction management **spese di gestione** operating expenditure
**gestire** *vb* handle *vb* **gestire un albergo** run a hotel **gestire un'impresa** operate a business
**giacenze** *nfpl* (goods) stock *n*, inventory (US)
**giacimento** *nm* **giacimento petrolifero** oilfield *n*
**gilda** *nf* guild *n*
**giornale** *nm* journal *n*, newspaper *n* **giornale aziendale** house journal/ magazine **giornale formato normale** broadsheet **giornale radio** news bulletin
**giornalismo** *nm* journalism *n*
**giornata** *nf* **giornata lavorativa** working day *n*, workday (US) **giornata libera** day off work
**giovane** *adj* **più giovane** junior *adj*
**giovare** *vb* **giovare a** benefit *vb*
**girare** *vb* **girare un assegno** (cheque) endorse *vb*
**girata** *nf* endorsement *n*
**giro** *nm* **giro d'affari** turnover *n*
**giudiziale** *adj* judicial *adj*
**giurato** *nm* juror *n*
**giuria** *nf* jury *n*
**giurisdizione** *nf* jurisdiction *n*
**giustificazione** *nf* **giustificazione logica** rationale
**globale** *adj* global *adj*
**globalizzazione** *nf* globalization *n*
**gnomi** *nmpl* **gnomi di Zurigo** the Gnomes of Zurich
**governare** *vb* govern *vb*
**governo** *nm* government *n*
**grafica** *nf* **grafica computerizzata** computer graphics
**gran** *adj* **Gran Bretagna** Britain, British Isles
**grassetto** *nm* bold type
**gratifica** *nf* perk (perquisite) *n*
**grato** *adj* indebted *adj*
**gratuito** *adj* free of charge **a titolo gratuito** free of charge
**grave** *adj* weighty *adj*
**greggio** *adj* raw *adj*
**grossista** *nm* wholesaler *n*
**gruppo** *nm* **gruppo di nazioni** group of countries
**guadagnare** *vb* earn *vb*, gain *vb*, make a profit *vb* **guadagnarsi da vivere** make a living
**guadagnato** *adj* **guadagnato col sudore della fronte** hard-earned **guadagnato con fatica** hard-earned
**guadagno** *nm* earnings *npl* **per guadagno finanziario** for pecuniary gain **guadagno inaspettato** windfall
**guasto 1.** *adj* out of action **2.** *nm* fault *n*
**guerra** *nf* war *n* **guerra commerciale** trade war
**guida** *nf* guide *n* **guida commerciale** trade directory
**holding** *nf* holding company
**igiene** *nf* hygiene *n* **igiene del lavoro** industrial health
**illecito** *adj* illegal *adj*
**illegale** *adj* illegal *adj*
**imballaggio** *nm* packaging *n*
**imballare** *vb* bundle up *vb*, pack *vb*
**imbarcarsi** *vb* go aboard *vb*
**imboscato** *nm* shirker* *n*
**imbroglio** *nm* swindle* *n*
**imbroglione** *nm* shark* *n*, swindler* *n*
**imbucare** *vb* post *vb*
**immagazzinamento** *nm* warehousing *n*
**immagine** *nf* image *n* **immagine aziendale** corporate image **immagine della marca** brand image
**immediato** *adj* prompt *adj*
**immobili** *nmpl* **immobili e impianti** fixtures and fittings
**immobiliare** *nm* property *n* **mercato immobiliare** property market, real estate market (US)
**immobilizzare** *vb* (capital) tie up *vb*
**immobilizzazioni** *nfpl* fixed assets *npl*
**impegnato** *adj* busy *adj*
**impegno** *nm* commitment *n*, obligation *n*, undertaking *n* **far fronte ai propri impegni** meet one's obligations
**imperfetto** *adj* defective *adj*
**impianto** *nm* plant *n*, installation *n*, facility *n* **direttore degli impianti** plant manager **impianti fissi** fixtures and fittings **impianto pilota** pilot plant **leasing di impianti** equipment leasing
**impiegare** *vb* employ *vb* **impiegare personale in soprannumero** overman *vb*
**impiegato, -a** *nm,f* clerk *n*, clerical worker *n* **impiegato di banca** bank clerk **impiegato statale** civil servant
**impiego** *nm* post *n*, job *n* **cessazione di impiego** termination of employment **impiego permanente** permanent employment **impiego precedente** em-

ployment/work history **impiego remunerativo** gainful employment
**implicito** *adj* tacit *adj*
**imponibile** *adj* chargeable *adj*
**imponibilità** *nf* tax liability *n*
**imporre** *vb* (tax) levy *vb* **imporre un calmiere su** put a ceiling on sth **imporre un dazio** impose a tax **imporre un'imposta** impose a tax **imporre restrizioni** impose restrictions
**importante** *adj* weighty *adj*
**importare** *vb* import *vb* **importare di nuovo** reimport *vb*
**importatore** *nm* importer *n*
**importazione** *nf* import *n*, importation *n* **importazioni invisibili** invisible imports
**importuno** *adj* inconvenient *adj*
**imposizione** *nf* imposition *n*, taxation *n* **imposizione dell'onere fiscale** tax liability **stabilire imposizioni** levy taxes
**imposta** *nf* tax *n*, duty *n* **esente da imposte** tax-exempt **imposta addizionale** surtax **imposta sugli affari** turnover tax **imposta sui beni di lusso** luxury tax **imposta di bollo sui trasferimenti di titoli azionari** (shares) transfer duty **imposta sui consumi** excise duty **imposta diretta** direct tax **imposta fondiaria** land tax **imposta sugli immobili** real estate tax, house duty (US) **imposta indiretta** indirect tax **imposta sulle plusvalenza** capital gains tax **imposta sui redditi di capitale** capital gains tax **imposta sul reddito** income tax **imposta sul reddito addizionale** supertax **imposta sul reddito a aliquota fissa** flat-rate income tax **imposta sulle società** corporate taxation, corporation tax **imposta sui sopraprofitti** excess profit(s) tax **imposta sul trasferimento di titoli** transfer tax **imposta valore aggiunto (IVA)** value-added tax, sales tax (US) **imposta sulle vendite al dettaglio** retail sales tax **imposte locali** local taxes, rates **imposte sulle spese** expenditure taxes **al lordo di imposte** before tax **al netto di imposte** after tax **soggetto a imposta** liable for tax
**imprenditore** *nm* entrepreneur *n* **imprenditore edile** builder *n*
**imprenditoriale** *adj* entrepreneurial *adj*
**impresa** *nf* enterprise *n*, firm *n* **impresa di confezionamento**, packing house (US) **impresa familiare** family business **impresa in partecipazione** joint venture **impresa privata** private enterprise **impresa statale** government enterprise **media impresa** medium-sized firm
**imprevisto** *adj* unexpected *adj*
**imputare** *vb* charge sb with sth
**inadeguato** *adj* inadequate *adj*
**inadempiente** *adj* defaulting *adj* **essere inadempiente** default *vb*
**inadempienza** *nf* default *n*
**inadempimento** *nm* non-fulfilment *n* **inadempimento di contratto** breach of contract
**inattività** *nf* slackness *n*, laxity *n*
**inattivo** *adj* idle *adj*
**incanto** *nm* auction *n*
**incaricare** *vb* assign *vb*, appoint sb to a position *vb*
**incarico** *nm* assignment *n*
**incassare** *vb* box sth up **incassare un assegno** cash a cheque
**incassato** *adj* built-in *adj*
**incasso** *nm* takings *npl*
**incentivo** *nm* incentive *n* **incentivo finanziario** financial incentive **salario a incentivo** merit payment
**inchiesta** *nf* inquiry *n* **inchiesta di mercato** market research survey
**incidente** *nm* accident *n*
**incidere** *vb* affect *vb*, bear upon *vb* **incidere su** account for *vb*
**incluso** *adj & pp* **dazi e costi di consegna inclusi** inclusive of tax and delivery costs
**incondizionato** *adj* unconditional *adj*
**incontestabile** *adj* absolute *adj*
**incontrare** *vb* meet *vb*
**incontro** *nm* meeting *n*
**inconveniente** *nm* inconvenience *n*
**incorporare** *vb* amalgamate *vb*
**incorporarsi** *vb* merge *vb*
**incorporato** *adj* built-in *adj*
**incorporazione** *nf* amalgamation *n*, merger *n*
**incrementare** *vb* **incrementare la domanda** boost demand
**incriminare** *vb* charge sb with sth
**indaffarato** *adj* busy *adj*
**indagine** *nf* **indagine sui consumatori** consumer survey **indagine esterna** field investigation **indagine sui nuclei familiari** household survey
**indebitamento** *nm* borrowing *n*
**indebitarsi** *vb* get into debt *vb*
**indebitato** *adj* indebted *adj*
**indebolire** *vb* (market) weaken *vb*
**indennità** *nf* allowance *n*, benefit *n*, indemnity *n* **indennità di disoccupazione** unemployment benefit, unemployment

pay **indennità di licenziamento** severance pay **indennità di percorso** mileage

**indennizzare** *vb* indemnify *vb*

**indennizzo** *nm* compensation *n* **respingere una richiesta d'indennizzo** refuse a claim

**indicare** *vb* indicate *vb*

**indicazione** *nf* indication *n*

**indice** *nm* index *n* **indice azionario** share index **indice delle azioni ordinarie del Financial Times** Thirty-Share Index (UK) **indice del costo della vita** cost of living index **indice di crescita** growth index **indice ponderato** weighted index **indice dei prezzi** price index **indice di rotazione delle attività fisse** fixed asset turnover **indice di rotazione del capitale** capital turnover

**indicizzato** *adj* indexed *adj* **salario minimo indicizzato** index-linked minimum wage

**indipendente** *adj* self-employed *adj*, freelance *adj*

**indiretto** *adj* indirect *adj*

**indirizzare** *vb* address *vb*

**indirizzario** *nm* mailing list *n*

**indirizzo** *nm* address *n* **cambiere indirizzo** change address **senza indirizzo** zero address

**individuazione** *nf* sourcing *n*

**indugio** *nm* **senza indugio** without delay

**industria** *nf* industry *n* **industria aerospaziale** aerospace industry **industria alberghiera** hotel industry/trade **industria assistenziale medica** health care industry **industria automobilistica** automobile industry, motor industry **industria chiave** key industry **industria chimica** chemical industry **industria dell'abbigliamento** (informal) the rag trade **industria dell'acciaio** steel industry **industria dell'edilizia abitativa** housing industry **industria domestica** family industry **industria edile** construction industry **industria farmaceutica** pharmaceutical industry **industria delle materie plastiche** plastics industry **industria mineraria** mining industry **industria nazionale** home industry **industria pesante** heavy industry **industria petrolifera** oil industry, petroleum industry **industria secondaria** secondary industry **industria terziaria** service industry **industria tessile** textile industry

**industriale** *adj* industrial *adj*

**industrializzato** *adj* industrialised *adj* **recentemente industrializzato** newly-industrialised

**inefficiente** *adj* inefficient *adj*

**inerzia** *nf* slackness *n*, laxity *n*

**inflazione** *nf* inflation *n* **inflazione da eccesso di domanda** excess demand inflation **inflazione galoppante** galloping inflation **inflazione nominale** nominal inflation **inflazione da strozzatura** bottleneck inflation **livello dell'inflazione** level of inflation

**inflazionistico** *adj* inflationary *adj* **tasso inflazionistico** rate of inflation

**informare** *vb* inform *vb*

**informarsi** *vb* enquire *vb*

**informatica** *nf* information technology (IT) **rete informatica** computer network

**informato** *adj* **bene informato** well-informed *adj*

**informazione** *nf* information *n* **dare informazioni** give feedback **informazioni di ritorno** feedback *n*

**infortunio** *nm* accident *n* **infortunio sul lavoro** industrial accident

**infrastruttura** *nf* infrastructure *n* **infrastruttura economica** economic infrastructure

**infrazione** *nf* contravention *n*

**infruttifero** *adj* non-interest-bearing *adj*

**ingegneria** *nf* engineering *n* **ingegneria civile** civil engineering **ingegneria elettrica** electrical engineering **ingegneria meccanica** mechanical engineering **ingegneria marittima** marine engineering **ingegneria di precisione** precision engineering

**ingiunzione** *nf* injunction *n* **richiedere l'emissione di un'ingiunzione** take out an injunction

**ingrosso** *adv* wholesale **commercio all'ingrosso** wholesale trade **all'ingrosso** at/by wholesale **mercato all'ingrosso** wholesale market **prezzo all'ingrosso** wholesale price **vendere all'ingrosso** sell sth in bulk, sell sth wholesale

**ininterrotto** *adj* non-stop *adj*

**inizializzare** *vb* (computer) boot *vb*

**iniziativa** *nf* enterprise *n*, undertaking *n*, initiative *n* **iniziativa in collaborazione** collaborative venture **iniziativa privata** private enterprise

**inoltrare** *vb* forward *vb*, turn over *vb*

**inoltro** *nm* forwarding *n*

**inquilino** *nm* tenant *n*

**inscatolare** *vb* box sth up *vb*

**insediare** *vb* instal(l) *vb*

**inserzione** *nf* advertisement *n* **inserzione pubblicitaria** classified advertisement
**insistere** *vb* **insistere su** insist on *vb*
**insoddisfacente** *adj* unsatisfactory *adj*
**insolvente** *adj* insolvent *adj*
**insolvenza** *nf* insolvency *n*
**instabilità** *nf* instability *n*
**installare** *vb* instal(l) *vb*
**installazione** *nf* installation *n*, facility *n*
**insufficiente** *adj* inadequate *adj*
**integrativo** *adj* supplementary *adj*
**integrazione** *nf* **integrazione economica** economic integration **integrazione orizzontale** horizontal integration **integrazione verticale** vertical integration
**intendersi** *vb* **intendersi di** have a working knowledge of sth
**intensificarsi** *vb* escalate *vb*
**intensivo** *adj* intensive *adj*
**interesse** *nm* interest *n* **caricare interessi** charge interest **dare interesse** bear interest **ex interessi** ex interest **fruttare interesse** bear interest **generare interesse** bear interest **interesse composto** compound interest **interesse fisso** fixed interest **interesse lordo** gross interest **interesse nazionale** national interest **interesse netto** net, nett interest **interessi acquisiti** vested interests **interessi maturati** accrued interest **interessi trimestrali** quarterly interest **pagare gli interessi** pay interest **periodo d'interesse** interest period **produrre interesse** bear interest **senza interessi** interest-free **tasso d'interesse** rate of interest
**interfaccia** *nf* interface *n*
**interinale** *adj* interim *adj*
**intermediario** 1. *adj* intermediary *adj* 2. *nm* broker *n*, middleman *n* **intermediario di borsa** floor broker
**intermediazione** *nf* brokerage *n*
**internazionale** *adj* international *adj*
**interno** *adj* inland *adj*
**interruzione** *nf* holdup *n*
**interurbano** *adj* (telephone) long-distance *adj*
**intervallo** *nm* **intervallo fra ordinazione e consegna** lead time **intervallo fra progettazione e produzione** lead time
**intervenire** *vb* intervene *vb*
**intervento** *nm* intervention *n*, action *n* **non intervento** non-intervention **intervento statale** state intervention
**intervista** *nf* interview *n*
**intervistare** *vb* interview *vb*, hold an interview *vb*
**intesa** *nf* understanding *n*
**intestare** *vb* address *vb*, register in sb's name *vb* **intestare un conto** open an account in sb's name **intestare una fattura** make out an invoice to sb
**intestata** *adj* headed *adj* **foglio di carta intestata** letterhead *n*
**intestatario** *nm* nominee *n*
**intestazione** *nf* heading *n*, letterhead *n*
**introdurre** *vb* (product) introduce *vb*
**invendibile** *adj* unmarketable *adj*, unsaleable *adj*
**invenduto** *adj* unsold *adj*
**inventario** *nm* inventory *n*, stocktaking *n* **inventario di fine anno** year-end inventory
**inversione** *nf* **inversione di tendenza** turnabout *n*
**invertire** *vb* reverse *vb*
**investimento** *nm* investment *n* **investimento aziendale** corporate investment **investimento estero** foreign investment **investimento finanziario** financial investment **investimento lordo** gross investment **investimento mobiliare** financial investment **investimento netto** net, nett investment **investimento in valori mobiliari** quoted investment **mancanza di investimenti** lack of investment **tasso di investimento** rate of investment
**investire** *vb* (money) invest *vb*
**investitore** *nm* investor *n*
**inviare** *vb* send *vb*
**invitare** *vb* invite *vb*
**invito** *nm* invitation *n*
**iperinflazione** *nf* hyperinflation *n*
**ipermercato** *nm* hypermarket *n*
**ipoteca** *nf* mortgage *n* **ipoteca legale** legal charge **ipoteca di primo grado** first mortgage **prima ipoteca** first mortgage
**ipotecario** *adj* **contratto ipotecario** mortgage deed **creditore ipotecario** mortgagee **debitore ipotecario** mortgagor **prestito ipotecario** mortgage loan
**ipotesi** *nf* hypothesis *n*
**irrecuperabile** *adj* (loss) irrecoverable *adj*
**irrevocabile** *adj* irrevocable *adj*
**iscritto** *nm* member *n* **iscritto a vita** life member
**iscriversi** *vb* (magazine) subscribe *vb*
**ispettore** *nm* inspector *n* **ispettore di fabbrica** factory inspector

**ispezionare** *vb* inspect *vb*
**ispezione** *nf* inspection *n*
**istituto** *nm* institute *n* **istituto di accettazione bancaria** acceptance house **istituto di credito** bank, credit institution
**istituzione** *nm* institution *n* **istituzione finanziaria** financial institution
**istruire** *vb* (staff) train *vb*
**istrumento** *nm* title deed
**istruzione** *nf* instruction *n* **dare istruzioni a** brief *vb* **istruzioni** *nfpl* briefing *n*, instructions *npl*
**itinerario** *nm* itinerary *n*
**IVA (imposta valore aggiunto)** *abbr nf* VAT (value added tax) *abbr* **essere esenti dall'IVA** be zero-rated for VAT
**kW (chilowatt)** *abbr* kW (kilowatt) *abbr*
**laborioso** *adj* hard-working *adj*
**lagnarsi** *vb* **lagnarsi di** find fault with
**lamentarsi** *vb* complain *vb* **lamentarsi di** complain about sth
**lanciare** *vb* (product) bring out *vb*, launch *vb*
**lanciato** *pp* launched *pp* **essere lanciato sul mercato** hit the market
**lancio** *nm* boost *n*, flotation *n* **lancio di un nuovo prodotto** product launch
**lasciare** *vb* leave *vb* **lasciare in eredità** bequeath *vb*
**lasciarsi** *vb* **lasciarsi sfuggire** overlook *vb*
**lascito** *nm* bequest *n*, legacy *n*
**laurearsi** *vb* graduate *vb*
**laureato, -a** *nm,f* (of university) graduate *n*
**lavarsi** *vb* **lavarsi le mani di** pass the buck* *vb*
**lavorare** *vb* process *vb* **lavorare in orari scomodi** work unsocial hours
**lavoratore, -trice** *nm,f* worker *n* **lavoratore avventizio** casual worker **lavoratore migratore** migrant worker **lavoratore ospite** guest worker **lavoratore specializzato** skilled worker **lavoratore non specializzato** unskilled worker **lavoratore a tempo pieno** full-time worker **lavoratori organizzati in sindacati** organized labour **lavoratori retribuiti a ore** hourly workers
**lavorazione** *nf* manufacture *n* **lavorazione difettosa** faulty workmanship **lavorazione per lotti** (DP) batch processing **linea di lavorazione** production line
**lavoro** *nm* work *n*, labour *n*, labor (US) **ambiente di lavoro** working environment **area di lavoro** working area **a uso intensivo di lavoro** labour-intensive **avere un lavoro** be in work **carico di lavoro** workload **cercare lavoro** look for work **condizioni di lavoro** working conditions **creazione di posti di lavoro** job creation **esperienza di lavoro** work experience **foglio di lavoro** working paper **forza lavoro** workforce **giornata di lavoro** day's work **gruppo di lavoro** working party **lavoro in appalto** contract work **lavoro avventizio** casual work **lavoro a cottimo** piecework **lavoro a distanza** teleworking **lavoro esterno** field work **lavoro di fabbrica** factory work **lavoro impiegatizio** clerical work **lavoro retribuito con paga oraria** hourly-paid work **lavoro d'ufficio** office work, paperwork **lavoro urgente** rush job **legislazione del lavoro** labour law **linguaggio di lavoro** working language **lingua di lavoro** working language **luogo di lavoro** workplace **maniaco del lavoro** workaholic **mercato del lavoro** labour market **offerta di lavoro** job offer **permesso di lavoro** work permit **programma di lavori pubblici** public works programme (GB) **programma di lavoro** work schedule **ripartizione del lavoro** work sharing **studio del lavoro** work study
**lavorodipendente** *nm* workaholic *n*
**leale** *adj* aboveboard *adj*, fair *adj*
**legale** *adj* legal *adj*
**legalmente** *adv* **legalmente vincolante** legally binding
**legato** *nm* bequest *n*
**legge** *nf* law *n*, statute *n* **legge sui diritti d'autore** copyright law **legge finanziaria** Finance Act **legge dei rendimenti decrescenti** law of diminishing returns **leggi sulle successioni** inheritance laws **presentare un progetto di legge** introduce legislation
**legislazione** *nf* legislation *n* **legislazione societaria** company law
**lettera** *nf* **lettera di credito** letter of credit **lettera di credito irrevocabile** irrevocable letter of credit **lettera di presentazione** letter of introduction **lettera raccomandata** registered letter **lettera di richiesta di impiego** letter of application **lettera di sollecito** reminder
**letteralmente** *adv* verbatim *adv*
**libbra** *nf* (weight) pound *n*
**libero** *adj* free *adj*, vacant *adj*, for hire **libera concorrenza** free competition **libero scambio** free trade

**libertà** *nf* **libertà di scelta** freedom of choice
**libraio** *nm* bookseller *n*
**libreria** *nf* bookshop *n*, bookstore (US)
**libretto** *nm* **libretto di assegni** cheque book, checkbook (US)
**libro** *nm* book *n* **libri contabili** the books **libro giornale** (accounting) journal **libro mastro** ledger **libro ordinazioni** order book
**licenza** *nf* leave *n*, licence *n* **dar licenza a** license *vb* **licenza edilizia** building permit **licenza di esportazione** export licence **licenza d'importazione** import licence
**licenziamento** *nm* dismissal *n*, sacking *n*, firing* *n* **indennità di licenziamento** severance pay **licenziamento illecito** wrongful dismissal **licenziamento iniquo** unfair dismissal **preavviso di licenziamento** term of notice
**licenziare** *vb* sack *vb*, fire* *vb*
**licenziatario** *nm* licence holder *n*
**licitare** *vb* bid *vb*
**licitazione** *nf* bid *n*, tendering *n*
**limitare** *vb* restrict *vb* **limitare il tasso d'interese** cap the interest rate
**limitato** *adj* limited *adj*
**limitazione** *nf* restriction *n* **imporre limitazioni a** impose restrictions on
**limite** *nm* limit *n* **limite di credito** credit limit
**linea** *nf* line *n* **essere in linea** (phone) on hold **linea aerea** airline **linea calda** hot line **linea del cambiamento di data** International Date Line **linea diretta** hot line **linea dura** hard-line **linea di navigazione** shipping line **linea di prodotti** product line **mettere in linea** (phone) put sb through (to sb)
**lingotto** *nm* **lingotti d'oro** gold bullion
**lingua** *nf* language *n*
**linguaggio** *nm* language *n* **linguaggio di programmazione** computer language
**liquidare** *vb* liquidate *vb*, sell off *vb*, wind up *vb*
**liquidazione** *nf* settlement *n*, liquidation *n*, golden handshake *n*, winding-up *n* **giorno di liquidazione** (stock exchange) Account Day **liquidazione di un'azienda** closure of a company **mettere in liquidazione** sell up *vb* **mettersi in liquidazione volontaria** go into voluntary liquidation **ordine di liquidazione** winding-up order **procedure di liquidazione** winding-up arrangements **valore di liquidazione** liquidation value
**liquidità** *nf* liquidity *n*
**lira** *nf* (currency) lira *n* **lira sterlina** sterling, pound sterling
**lista** *nf* list *n* **lista d'attesa** waiting list
**listino** *nm* (prices) list *n* **prezzo di listino** list price
**lite** *nf* litigation *n* **comporre una lite** settle a claim
**livellare** *vb* equalize *vb*
**livello** *nm* **ad alto livello** high-level
**locali** *nmpl* premises *npl* **locali adibiti a uffici** office premises **locali aziendali** business premises
**locatario** *nm* leaseholder *n*, lessee *n*, occupant *n*, occupier *n*
**locatore** *nm* landlord *n*, lessor *n*
**locazione** *nf* renting *n*, letting *n* **dare in locazione** lease *vb* **locazione di impianto** plant hire
**logistica** *nf* logistics *npl*
**lordo** *adj* gross *adj*
**lottizzazione** *nf* **lottizzazione fiscale** fiscal zoning
**lotto** *nm* (at auction) lot *n*
**lucrativo** *adj* lucrative *adj*
**lucro** *nm* profit *n*, gain *n* **senza scopo di lucro** non-profitmaking *adj*
**luogo** *nm* place *n* **luogo del convegno** conference venue
**lusso** *nm* luxury *n* **beni di lusso** luxury goods
**macchina** *nf* machine *n* **battere a macchina** type *vb* **macchina affrancatrice** franking machine **macchina distruggi documenti** shredder *n* **macchina da scrivere** typewriter *n* **macchina dello Stato** machinery of government
**macchinario** *nm* machinery *n*
**macroeconomia** *nf* macroeconomics *n*
**madre** *nf* counterfoil *n*
**magazzinaggio** *nm* storage *n*, warehousing *n* **capacità di magazzinaggio** storage capacity
**magazzino** *nm* warehouse *n* **grande magazzino** multiple store **grande magazzino a filiali multiple** chain store **da magazzino** ex stock **magazzino doganale** bonded warehouse, customs warehouse **in magazzino doganale** in bond **magazzino refrigerato** cold storage plant
**maggioranza** *nf* majority *n*
**maggioranza effettiva** *nf* working majority

**maggiore** *adj* greater *adj*, bigger *adj*, better *adj*, major *adj* **nella maggior parte** in the majority
**magnate** *nm* magnate *n*, tycoon *n*
**malattia** *nf* illness *n* **congedo per malattia** sick leave **malattia professionale** occupational disease **sussidio di malattia** sickness benefit
**mallevadore** *nm* guarantor *n*
**malversatore** *nm* embezzler *n*
**manager** *nmf* **manager di zona** area manager
**mancanza** *nf* deficiency *n*, lack *n* **in mancanza di informazioni** in the absence of information
**manchevole** *adj* deficient *adj*
**mancia** *nf* gratuity *n*, tip *n*
**mandare** *vb* send *vb*
**mandatario** *nm* agent *n*
**mandato** *nm* warrant *n*
**manifesto** *nm* (advertising) poster *n*
**mano** *nf* hand *n* **fatto a mano** handmade *adj* **a portata di mano** convenient *adj*, handy *adj* **di prima mano** first-hand **scritto a mano** handwritten *adj*
**manodopera** *nf* labour *n*, manpower *n* **costi della manodopera** labour costs **con eccesso di manodopera** overmanned *adj* **manodopera contrattuale** contract labour **manodopera temporanea** contract labour
**manovale** *nm* labourer *n*, manual worker *n*
**mansione** *nf* task *n*, duty *n* **descrizione delle mansioni** job description **mansioni dirigenziali** executive duties **rotazione delle mansioni** job rotation
**mantenere** *vb* **mantenere scorte** carry stock *vb*
**manto** *nm* bond certificate, share certificate, stock certificate (US)
**manuale** *nm* handbook *n* **manuale d'istruzioni** instruction book
**manutenzione** *nf* maintenance *n* **costi di manutenzione** maintenance costs
**marca** *nf* brand *n* **marca esclusiva** proprietary brand **marca leader** brand leader
**marchio** *nm* **marchio di commercio** trade name **marchio depositato** registered trademark, registered trade name **marchio di fabbrica** brand, brand name, trademark **marchio di garanzia** hallmark **marchio ufficiale di saggio** hallmark
**marco** *nm* **marco tedesco** German Mark
**marginale** *adj* marginal *adj*
**margine** *nm* margin *n* **margine lordo** gross margin **margine di profitto** profit margin **margine di utile** trading margin
**marina** *nf* **marina mercantile** merchant navy, merchant marine (US)
**marittimo** *adj* marine *adj*
**marketing** *nm* **consulente di marketing** marketing consultant **direttore dell'ufficio marketing** marketing director **marketing delle esportazioni** export marketing **marketing di massa** mass marketing **ufficio marketing** marketing department
**massa** *nf* bulk *n*
**massimizzare** *vb* maximise *vb*
**mastro** *nm* **mastro di contabilità di fabbrica** factory ledger
**materia** *nf* **materie prime** raw materials
**materiale** *nm* material *n* **materiali edili** building materials
**maternità** *nf* **congedo per maternità** maternity leave
**matrice** *nf* counterfoil *n*, matrix *n*
**maturare** *vb* mature *vb*
**meccanico** *adj* mechanical *adj*
**meccanismo** *nm* **Meccanismo di regolazione dei cambi** exchange rate mechanism (ERM)
**media** *nf* average *n*, mean *n* **media aritmetica** arithmetical mean **media ponderata** weighted average
**mediano** *adj* median *adj*
**mediatore** *nm* mediator *n* **mediatore di borsa** stockbroker *n*
**mediazione** *nf* mediation *n* **raggiungere un accordo tramite mediazone** mediate *vb*
**medico** *adj* medical *adj*
**medio** *adj* medium *adj* **medio circolante** hard cash **a medio termine** medium term
**membro** *nm* insider *n*, member *n* **membro a vita** life member
**memoria** *nf* (DP) memory *n* **capacità di memoria** memory capacity
**memorizzazione** *nf* **memorizzazione di informazioni** information storage
**meno** *adv* less **addebitare in meno** undercharge *vb* **consegna in meno** short delivery **far pagare meno** undercharge *vb*
**mensile** *adj* monthly *adj*
**mercanteggiare** *vb* bargain *vb*
**mercantile 1.** *adj* mercantile *adj* **2.** *nm* cargo ship, merchant ship
**mercato** *nm* market *n*, mart *n* **analisi di mercato** market analysis **forze di mercato** market forces **informazione riservata sul mercato** market tip **mercato ampio** broad market **mercato aperto** open market **mercato azionario** stock market **mercato dei cambi** foreign ex-

change market **mercato dei capitali** financial market **Mercato Comune** Common Market **mercato dell'oro** gold market **mercato estero** foreign market, overseas market **mercato delle eurovalute** eurocurrency market **mercato fiacco** flat market **mercato finanziario** capital market **mercato globale** global market **mercato instabile** fluid market **mercato interno** domestic market, home market **mercato languido** narrow market **mercato del lavoro** labour market **mercato libero** free market **mercato marginale** fringe market **mercato monetario** money market **mercato nazionale** domestic market **mercato nero** black market **mercato obiettivo** target market **mercato delle operazioni per consegna differita** forward market **mercato al rialzo** bull market, buoyant market, seller's market **mercato al ribasso** bear market, buyer's market **mercato secondario** secondary market **mercato sostenuto** firm market **mercato stabile** firm market **mercato tendente al ribasso** falling market **mercato con tendenza al ribasso** bear market **mercato a termine** futures market, options market, terminal market **mercato dei titoli di stato** gilt-edged market **mercato tranquillo** quiet market **mercato valutario** exchange market **mercato del venditore** seller's market **sfruttare un mercato** tap a market **utilizzare un mercato** tap a market

**merce** *nf* goods *npl* **merce a termine** future commodity **merci in conto deposito** goods on consignment **merci difettose** faulty goods **merci esenti** free goods **merci d'esportazione** export goods **merci d'importazione** import goods **merci in massa** bulk goods **merci nazionali** domestic goods **merci alla rinfusa** bulk goods **merci secche** dry goods **merci soggette a verifica** goods on approval

**meritevole** *adj* **meritevole di credito** creditworthy *adj*

**messaggero** *nm* messenger *n*

**messaggio** *nm* message *n* **messaggio pubblicitario** advertisement *n*

**mestiere** *nm* job *n*, profession *n* **essere del mestiere** (informal) be in the trade **di mestiere** by trade

**metà** *nf* half *n*

**metallo** *nm* metal *n* **metallo prezioso** bullion *n*

**metodico** *adj* businesslike *adj*

**metodo** *nm* system *n*

**metrico** *adj* metric *adj*

**metro** *nm* metre *n*, meter (US) **metro cubo** cubic metre **metro quadro** square metre

**metropoli** *nf* metropolis *n*

**mettere** *vb* **mettere in commercio** market *vb* **mettere in conto** charge *vb* **mettere un embargo** impose an embargo *vb* **mettere a nuovo** refurbish *vb*

**mezzo 1.** *adj* half *adj* **mezz'ora** half-an-hour **mezza paga** half-pay **mezza pensione** half-board **2.** *nm* means *npl*, medium *n* **mezzi finanziari** financial means, financial resources **mezzi pubblicitari** media *npl* **mezzo pubblicitario** advertising medium

**microeconomia** *nf* microeconomics *n*

**microfono** *nm* **microfono spia** (listening device) bug *n*

**microprocessore** *nm* microprocessor *n*

**microscheda** *nf* **microscheda trasparente** microfiche *n*

**miglio** *nm* mile *n* **miglio marino** nautical mile

**migliorare** *vb* improve *vb*, upgrade *vb*

**milionario** *nm* millionaire *n*

**milione** *nm* million *n*

**minerale** *nm* mineral *n*

**miniera** *nf* mine *n* **miniera di carbone** coal mine

**minimizzare** *vb* **minimizzare i danni** minimise losses

**minimizzazione** *nf* **minimizzazione dell'onere fiscale** tax avoidance

**minimo** *adj* minimal *adj*

**ministero** *nm* ministry *n*, government department **Ministero della Sanità** Ministry of Health **Ministero dei Trasporti** Ministry of Transport

**ministro** *nm* minister *n*

**minoranza** *nf* minority *n* **in minoranza** in the minority

**minore** *adj* minor *adj*

**misura** *nf* measure *n* **misure antinflazionistiche** anti-inflationary measures **misure finanziarie** financial measures **misure fiscali** fiscal measures

**misurare** *vb* measure *vb*

**mitigare** *vb* water down *vb*

**mittente** *nm* consigner/or *n*, sender *n*

**mix** *nm* **mix dei prodotti** product mix

**mobilità** *nf* **a mobilità verso l'alto** fast track
**moda** *nf* fashion *n* **fuori moda** out of date
**modello 1.** *adj* standard *adj* **2.** *nm* (person) model *n* **modello funzionante** working model
**moderare** *vb* moderate *vb*
**moderato** *adj* moderate *adj*
**moderazione** *nf* moderation *n*
**modernizzare** *vb* modernize *vb*
**moderno** *adj* modern *adj*
**modo** *nm* mode *n*
**modulo** *nm* module *n* **modulo di domanda** application form **modulo di ordinazione** order form **modulo di sottoscrizione** application form
**molo** *nm* quay *n*
**moltiplicare** *vb* multiply *vb*
**moltiplicarsi** *vb* **moltiplicarsi degli scambi** expansion of trade
**mondiale** *adj* **su scala mondiale** worldwide *adj*
**mondo** *nm* world *n* **mondo commerciale** the commercial world
**moneta** *nf* **moneta calda** hot money **moneta a corso forzoso** fiat money **moneta a corso legale** legal tender **moneta debole** soft currency **moneta divisionaria** fractional money **moneta forte** hard currency **moneta frazionaria** fractional money **moneta d'oro** gold coin
**monetario** *adj* monetary *adj*
**monetarismo** *nm* monetarism *n*
**monopolio** *nm* monopoly *n* **Commissione per i monopoli e le fusioni** Monopolies and Mergers Commission
**montaggio** *nm* **scatola di montaggio** assembly kit *n*
**monte** *nm* **monte premi** jackpot *n*
**mora** *nf* delay *n*
**moroso** *adj* **essere moroso** fall/get into arrears *vb*
**mostra** *nf* exhibition *n* **mostra commerciale** trade fair **mostra mondiale** world fair
**mostrarsi** *vb* **mostrarsi valido** hold up *vb*, withstand scrutiny *vb*
**motto** *nm* **motto pubblicitario** slogan *n*
**movimento** *nm* **movimento libero della merce** free movement of goods
**multilaterale** *adj* multilateral *adj*
**multinazionale 1.** *adj* multinational *adj* **2.** *nf* multinational corporation
**municipio** *nm* town hall
**mutevole** *adj* (prices) volatile *adj*
**mutuante** *nm* lender *n*
**mutuare** *vb* borrow *vb*, lend *vb*
**mutuo 1.** *adj* mutual *adj* **2.** *nm* loan *n* **mutuo edilizio** home loan **mutuo garantito** secured loan
**nastro** *nm* **nastro magnetico** (DP) magnetic tape
**natura** *nf* kind *n*
**nave** *nf* **nave cargo** freighter *n* **nave da carico** freighter *n*, cargo ship **nave mercantile** merchant ship **nave portacontainer** container ship
**navetta** *nf* shuttle *n*
**nazionale** *adj* national *adj*, domestic *adj* **a carattere nazionale** nationwide *adj*
**nazionalità** *nf* nationality *n*
**nazionalizzare** *vb* nationalize *vb*
**nazionalizzazione** *nf* nationalization *n*
**nazione** *nf* nation *n* **nazione commerciale** trading nation **nazione ospitante** host country **nazione progredita** advanced country **nazione in via di sviluppo** developing country **Nazioni Unite (ONU)** United Nations
**necessità** *nf* necessity *n* **accertamento delle necessità** needs assessment
**negligente** *adj* negligent *adj*
**negligenza** *nf* negligence *n* **clausola di negligenza** neglect clause, negligence clause **negligenza nell'esercizio professionale** malpractice **negligenza grave** gross negligence
**negoziabile** *adj* negotiable *adj* **non negoziabile** non-negotiable
**negoziare** *vb* negotiate *vb*
**negoziato** *nm* negotiation *n* **negoziati commerciali** trade talks **negoziati tariffari** tariff negotiations
**negoziatore** *nm* negotiator *n*
**negoziazione** *nf* negotiation *n* **seduta di negoziazione** negotiating session **tramite negoziazione** by negotiation
**negozio** *nm* (shop) shop *n*, store *n* **negozio a catena** chain store **negozio fiduciario** charitable trust, trust agreement
**neretto** *nm* bold type *n*
**netto** *adj* net, nett *adj*
**neutrale** *adj* neutral *adj*
**noleggiare** *vb* hire *vb*
**noleggiatore** *nm* freighter *n*
**nolo** *nm* freight *n*, hire *n* **da nolo** for hire **nolo aereo** air freight
**nome** *nm* **avere un buon nome** enjoy a good reputation **farsi un buon nome** build a reputation **in nome di** in the name

of **di nome** by name **nome e cognome** full name **nome commerciale** trade name
**nomina** *nf* assignment *n*, nomination *n* **nuova nomina** reappointment *n*
**nominale** *adj* nominal *adj*
**nominare** *vb* nominate *vb*, appoint sb to a position
**norma** *nf* provision *n*, stipulation *n*
**normativa** *nf* code of practice **normative commerciali** trading standards
**nota** *nf* **nota di accredito** credit note **nota di copertura** cover note
**notaio** *nm* notary *n*
**notare** *vb* take notice *vb*
**notifica** *nf* notification *n*
**notificare** *vb* notify *vb*
**notizia** *nf* (piece of) news *n* **brutte notizie** bad news **buone notizie** goods news **fare notizia** hit the headlines **notizie** *nfpl* news *n* **notizie finanziarie** financial news **notizie di prima pagina** hard news/information **trattazione delle notizie** news coverage
**notiziario** *nm* news bulletin *n*
**noto** *adj* (well-) known *adj* **fatto noto a tutti** it is common knowledge
**nucleo** *nm* **nucleo familiare** household *n*
**nullo** *adj* null *adj* **nullo e di nessun effetto** null and void
**numero** *nm* number *n* **avente un numero legale** quorate *adj* **numero di casella postale** box number **numero legale** quorum **numero di ordine** order number **numero di riferimento** reference number **numero sbagliato** (phone) wrong number **numero di serie** serial number **numero telefonico** telephone number **numero di telefono** telephone number
**obbligato** *adj* **essere obbligato a** be obliged to do sth
**obbligatorio** *adj* obligatory *adj*
**obbligazione** *nf* bond *n*, debenture *n*, obligation *n* **mercato delle obbligazioni** bond market **obbligazione non garantita** debenture bond **obbligazione municipale** municipal bonds **obbligazione al portatore** bearer bond **obbligazione redimibile** redeemable bond **obbligazione di rischio** junk bond **obbligazione senza garanzia** unsecured bond **obbligazione senza interessi** flat bond **obbligazione solidale** joint obligation **obbligazioni contrattuali** contractual obligations
**obbligazionista** *nm* bondholder *n*
**obiettivo** *nm* objective *n*, target *n* **obiettivo economico** economic objective **obiettivo della produzione** production target **obiettivo delle vendite** sales target **raggiungere uno obiettivo** reach an objective **stabilire un obiettivo** set a target
**obiezione** *nf* objection *n* **sollevare un'obiezione** make/raise an objection
**obsolescenza** *nf* obsolescence *n* **obsolescenza automatica** built-in obsolescence **obsolescenza programmata** planned obsolescence
**obsoleto** *adj* obsolete *adj*
**occasione** *nf* opportunity *n*
**occupare** *vb* (premises) occupy *vb*
**occuparsi** *vb* **occuparsi di** (deal) handle *vb*
**occupato** *adj* busy *adj*
**occupazione** *nf* employment *n*, occupation *n* **livello dell'occupazione** level of employment **occupazione precedente** employment/work history **occupazione remunerativa** gainful employment **occupazione temporanea** temporary employment **piena occupazione** full employment
**offerente** *nm* tenderer *n*
**offerta** *nf* offer *n*, bid *n*, tender *n*, supply *n* **declinare un'offerta** (offer) turn down *vb* **fare un'offerta per un appalto** tender for a contract **offerta d'appalto** bid **offerta in contanti** cash offer **offerta definitiva** final offer **offerta ferma** firm offer **offerta finale** closing bid **offerta di moneta** money supply **offerta più alta** higher bid **offerta proposta per iscritto** offer in writing **offerta provvisoria** tentative offer **offerta pubblica di acquisizione** tender offer **offerta salvo conferma** offer subject to confirmation **offerta non sollecitata** unsolicited offer **offerta speciale** bargain offer **offerta valida fino a...** offer valid until... **presentare un'offerta** lodge a tender **prezzo d'offerta di appalto** tender price **rifiutare un'offerta** turn down an offer **ritirare un'offerta** withdraw an offer
**officina** *nf* workshop *n*
**offrire** *vb* offer *vb*, bid *vb*, supply *vb* **offrire di più di** (auction) outbid *vb*
**oggetto** *nm* re *prep*
**oleodotto** *nm* pipeline *n*
**oligopolio** *nm* oligopoly *n*
**oligopolistico** *adj* **mercato oligopolistico** oligopoly *n*
**omaggio** *nm* giveaway *n*, free gift *n* **in omaggio** complimentary *adj*
**omissione** *nf* oversight *n*

**omologare** *vb* approve *vb*, validate *vb*
**omologazione** *nf* approval *n*, consent *n*
**ondata** *nf* (of mergers, takeovers) wave *n*
**onere** *nm* **oneri fiscali** fiscal charges **oneri fissi** fixed charges, standing charges
**onorario** **1.** *adj* honorary *adj* **2.** *nm* fee *n*
**operaio** *nm* blue-collar worker, manual worker **operaio specializzato** skilled worker **operaio non specializzato** unskilled worker
**operare** *vb* **operare con capitale di prestito** equity trading **operare a piena capacità** work to full capacity
**operativo** *adj* workable *adj*
**operatore** *nm* operator *n* **operatore autorizzato** authorized dealer **operatore di borsa** jobber **operatore di cambio** exchange broker **operatore commerciale** dealer **operatore informatico** computer operator
**operazione** *nf* (of machine) operation *n* **operazione di capitale** equity transaction **operazione commerciale** business transaction, deal, transaction **operazione in compravendita** bargain **operazione per consegna differita** forward transaction **operazione finanziaria** financial operation **operazione a pronti** cash transaction **operazione di scambio** barter transaction **operazioni bancarie elettroniche** electronic banking **operazioni commerciali a termine** futures trading **operazioni di copertura per consegna differita** forward cover **operazioni d'esportazione** export operations **operazioni in valuta estera** foreign exchange dealings, foreign exchange tradings (US)
**operoso** *adj* hard-working
**opporsi** *vb* **opporsi a** object *vb*, withstand *vb*
**opportunità** *nf* opportunity *n* **opportunità di mercato** market opportunity **spiraglio di opportunità** window of opportunity
**opuscolo** *nm* brochure *n*
**opzionale** *adj* optional *adj*
**opzione** *nf* option *n* **opzione di acquisto** option to buy **opzione di annullamento** option to cancel
**ora** *nf* hour *n* **per ogni ora** per hour **ad ora** per hour **ora di punta** rush hour **l'ora zero** zero hour **ore di attività intensa**, busy hours (US) **ore fisse** fixed hours **ore lavorative** working hours **ore d'ufficio** business hours
**orario** *nm* timetable *n* **dopo l'orario di chiusura** after hours **lavorare a orario ridotto** be on short time **orario d'apertura** opening times **orario d'apertura dei negozi** normal trading hours **orario di chiusura** closing time **orario flessibile** flexitime, flextime (US) **orario di sportello** banking hours **orario d'ufficio** normal trading hours, office hours **pagamento orario doppio** double time
**ordinare** *vb* place an order *vb*
**ordinazione** *nf* order *n* **dare un'ordinazione** place an order **ordinazione ripetuta** repeat order **ordinazioni inevase** backlog
**ordine** *nm* **ordine di banca** banker's order **ordine del giorno** agenda **ordine di pagamento** banker's order **ordine urgente** rush order **pagare all'ordine di** pay to the order of... **di prim'ordine** high-class
**organizzare** *vb* organize *vb* **organizzare razionalmente** rationalize *vb*
**organizzazione** *nf* organization *n* **organizzazione funzionale** functional organization **organizzazione per funzioni** functional organization **organizzazione internazionale** international organization
**origine** *nf* origin *n* **dichiarazione di origine** statement of origin **paese d'origine** country of origin
**ormeggio** *nm* mooring *n* **diritti di ormeggio** mooring rights
**oro** *nm* gold *n*
**oscillare** *vb* fluctuate *vb*
**ospitante** *nm* host *n*
**ospitare** *vb* **ospitare un cliente** entertain a client
**ospite** *nm* host *n*
**osservare** *vb* take notice **osservare le regole** observe the rules
**osservazione** *nf* **sotto osservazione** under observation
**ostacolare** *vb* hold up *vb*, delay *vb*
**ostruire** *vb* hold up *vb*, delay *vb*
**ottenere** *vb* obtain *vb*
**p/m (parole al minuto)** *abbr* wpm (words per minute) *abbr*
**pacchetto** *nm* block *n*, packet *n*, package deal **pacchetto azionario** stake *n*, block of shares *n*
**pacco** *nm* package *n*, packet *n*
**padrone** *nm* boss *n*
**paese** *nm* country *n* **paese importatore** importing country **paese d'origine** home country **paese produttore di petrolio** oil state **paese sottosviluppato** underdeveloped country **paese del terzo mondo** third-world country

**paga** *nf* pay *n* **paga oraria** hourly rate **paga settimanale** weekly wages

**pagabile** *adj* **pagabile in anticipo** payable in advance

**pagamento** *nm* payment *n* **mancato pagamento** non-payment **mandato di pagamento** warrant for payment **metodo di pagamento** method of payment **pagamenti scaglionati** staged payments **pagamento in acconto** payment on account **pagamento anticipato** advance payment, prepayment **pagamento di compensazione** clearing payment **pagamento in contanti** cash payment **pagamento in contanti prima della consegna** cash before delivery **pagamento in contanti alla ricevuta della merce** cash on receipt of goods **pagamento contrassegno** cash on delivery (COD) **pagamento eccessivo** overpayment **pagamento forfettario** lump sum settlement **pagamento parziale** part payment **pagamento a pronti** cash payment **pagamento a saldo** full payment **pagamento simbolico** token payment **pagamento a titolo transativo** ex gratia payment **pagamento totale** full payment **pagamento in unica soluzione** lump sum settlement

**pagare** *vb* pay *vb* **far pagare qualcosa** charge for sth **pagare in anticipo** pay in advance **pagare in contanti** pay in cash **pagare il conto** pay a bill **pagare una fattura** pay an invoice, settle an invoice **pagare un onorario** pay a fee **pagare un servizio** pay for a service

**pagato** *adj & pp* paid *adj* **ben pagato** well-paid *adj*

**pagherò** *nm* (informal) IOU *n* **pagherò cambiario** promissory note

**pagina** *nf* page *n* **le Pagine Gialle** the Yellow pages (R) (GB)

**paniere** *nm* **paniere valutario** basket of currencies

**paracadute** *nm* **paracadute d'oro** golden parachute

**pareggiare** *vb* **pareggiare il bilancio** balance the budget

**parere** *nm* advice *n*

**pari** *adj* **sopra la pari** above par, at a premium **sotto la pari** below par

**parità** *nf* parity *n* **parità salariale** equal pay

**parlamento** *nm* **parlamento europeo** European Parliament

**parlare** *vb* **parlare a** (person) address *vb*

**parola** *nf* **dare la propria parola** give one's word **essere di parola** keep one's word **parola chiave** keyword **parola per parola** verbatim

**parte** *nf* part *n* **la maggior parte di** the bulk of **parte di ricambio** spare part

**partecipante** *nm* stakeholder *n*

**partecipare** *vb* **partecipare a** take part in

**partecipazione** *nf* holding *n* **partecipazione di maggioranza/ di minoranza** majority/minority holding **partecipazione operaia** worker participation **partecipazione ai profitti** a share in the profits **partecipazione agli utili** gain sharing **partecipazioni azionarie** equity interests

**partita** *nf* consignment *n* **partita doppia** (bookkeeping) double-entry

**partitario** *nm* **partitario fornitori** bought ledger **partitario vendite** sales ledger

**partner** *nm* **partner commerciale** trading partner

**passare** *vb* hand *vb*

**passeggero** *nm* passenger *n* **passeggero in transito** (transport) transit passenger **treno passeggeri** passenger train

**passibile** *adj* liable *adj*

**passività** *nf* (taxes) liability *n* **passività correnti** current liabilities **passività fisse** fixed liabilities

**passo** *nm* **fare un importante passo avanti** make a breakthrough *vb* **segnare il passo** tick over *vb*

**patria** *nf* home country

**patrimonio** *nm* property *n*, wealth *n* **imposta sul patrimonio** wealth tax **patrimonio nazionale** national wealth

**patrocinatore** *nm* sponsor *n*

**patrocinio** *nm* patronage *n*, sponsorship *n*

**patto** *nm* covenant *n*

**pattuito** *adj* agreed *adj*

**pausa** *nf* **fare una pausa** take a break

**peculato** *nm* embezzlement *n*

**pedaggio** *nm* toll *n*

**peggio** *nf* worst part *n* **avere la peggio** go to the wall

**pegno** *nm* pledge *n* **nota di pegno** warrant *n*

**penalità** *nf* forfeit *n*

**penetrazione** *nf* **penetrazione del mercato** market penetration

**pensionamento** *nm* retirement *n* **pensionamento anticipato** early retirement **piano di pensionamento** pension scheme

**pensione** *nf* pension *n* **andare in pen-**

**sione** retire **andare in pensione anticipatamente** take early retirement **fondo pensioni** pension fund **pensione calcolata in funzione del reddito** earnings-related pension **pensione di vecchiaia** retirement pension

**penuria** *nf* scarcity *n*

**percentuale** *nf* percentage *n* **percentuale di profitto** percentage of profit

**perdere** *vb* waste *vb* **perdere un diritto a** forfeit *vb*

**perdita** *nf* loss *n* **perdita di capitale** capital loss **perdita completa** write-off **perdita finanziaria** financial loss **perdita del lavoro** loss of job **perdita lorda** gross loss **perdita netta** clear loss, net loss **perdita netta di esercizio** net, nett loss **perdita nominale** paper loss **perdita per piccolo furto** pilferage **perdita di reddito** loss of earnings

**perequare** *vb* equalize *vb*

**perequazione** *nf* **perequazione dei carichi tributari** equalization of burdens

**perfetto** *adj* (fig.) watertight *adj*

**perfezionamento** *nm* **mancato perfezionamento** non-completion *n*

**pericolo** *nm* hazard *n* **pericolo naturale** natural hazard **pericolo per la salute** health hazard **segnale di pericolo** warning sign

**pericoloso** *adj* hazardous *adj*

**periferia** *nf* suburbs *npl*

**periferica** *nf* computer terminal *n*

**periferico** *adj* peripheral *adj*

**periodico** *nm* (journal) magazine *n*

**periodo** *nm* **periodo contabile** accounting period **periodo di esenzione fiscale** tax holiday **periodo di grazia** period of grace **periodo di permanenza in carica** term of office **periodo di raffreddamento** cooling-off period

**perito** *nm* expert *n*, technician *n*

**permesso** *nm* permit *n* **permesso di partenza** clearance certificate

**perorare** *vb* advocate *vb*

**persona** *nf* **persona chiave** key person **persona designata** named person **persona giuridica** corporation

**personale 1.** *adj* personal *adj* **2.** *nm* staff *n*, personnel *n* **eccesso di personale** overmanning *n* **gestione del personale** personnel management **personale direttivo** executive personnel **personale esterno** field personnel **personale qualificato** qualified personnel **ufficio del personale** personnel department **valutazione del personale** performance appraisal

**personalizzare** *vb* adapt *vb*, tailor *vb*

**pertinente** *adj* relevant *adj* **non pertinente** not applicable (N/A)

**peso** *nm* weight *n* **eccedenza di peso** excess weight **pesi e misure** weights and measures **peso lordo** gross weight **peso netto** net, nett weight

**petrodollaro** *nm* petrodollar *n*

**pezzo** *nm* (of a machine) part *n*

**pianificare** *vb* plan *vb*

**pianificazione** *nf* planning *n* **pianificazione centrale** central planning **pianificazione economica** economic planning **pianificazione finanziaria** financial planning **pianificazione a lungo termine** long-term planning **pianificazione regionale** regional planning **pianificazione delle strutture** facility planning

**piano** *nm* schedule *n* **piano della campagna** (advertising) plan of campaign **piano economico** economic plan **piano edilizio** housing scheme **piano degli investimenti** capital budget **piano pilota** pilot scheme **piano provvisorio** tentative plan

**picchetto** *nm* picket *n*

**pignoramento** *nm* foreclosure *n*

**pignorare** *vb* foreclose *vb*

**PIL (Prodotto Interno Lordo)** *abbr* GDP (Gross Domestic Product) *abbr*

**pirataggio** *nm* software piracy

**pirateria** *nf* (at sea) piracy *n*

**plenario** *adj* (assembly, session) plenary *adj*

**pluriuso** *adj* multipurpose *adj*

**plusvalenza** *nf* capital gain *n*

**PNL (Prodotto Nazionale Lordo)** *abbr* GNP (Gross National Product) *abbr*

**politica** *nf* politics *n* **Politica Agricola Comunitaria** CAP (Common Agricultural Policy) **politica aziendale** company policy **politica di bilancio** budgetary policy **politica del denaro facile** easy-money policy **politica economica** economic policy **politica finanziaria** financial policy **politica fiscale** fiscal policy **politica monetaria** monetary policy **politica nazionale** domestic policy **politica dei prezzi** pricing policy **politica di reciprocità** fair-trade policy **politica del rischio calcolato** brinkmanship **politica statale** government policy **politica di vendita basata sulla persuasione** soft sell **politica**

**di vendite estremamente aggressiva** hard sell
**politico** *adj* political *adj*
**polizza** *nf* **polizza assicurativa** insurance policy **polizza di assicurazione** insurance policy **polizza di assicurazione contro tutti i danni** comprehensive insurance policy **polizza di carico** bill of lading **polizza di carico per l'estero** export bill of lading **polizza mista** endowment policy
**ponderazione** *nf* weighting *n*
**popolazione** *nf* **popolazione attiva** working population
**portafoglio** *nm* **portafoglio titoli** investment portfolio
**portare** *vb* **portare a termine** accomplish *vb*
**portarinfuse** *nf* bulk carrier *n*
**portata** *nf* **portata lorda** dead weight
**portatile** *adj* portable *adj*
**portatore** *nm* bearer *n*
**portavoce** *nmf* spokesperson *n*
**porto** *nm* harbour *n*, port *n* **porto di arrivo** port of entry **porto assegnato** carriage forward **porto franco** free port **porto pagato** carriage paid
**posizione** *nf* **posizione creditizia** credit rating **posizione finanziaria** credit rating, financial status
**possedere** *vb* own *vb* **possedere pacchetti azionari** have holdings **possedere titoli** have holdings
**possesso** *nm* tenure *n* **possesso immobiliare** leasehold *n* **riprendere possesso di** repossess *vb* **ripresa di possesso** repossession *n*
**possessore** *nm* holder *n*
**possibilità** *nf* **possibilità di manovra** room for manoeuvre
**posta** *nf* **fermo posta** poste restante, general delivery (US) **posta aerea** airmail **posta elettronica** email, electronic mail **posta raccomandata** registered mail
**postdatare** *vb* postdate *vb*
**posticipare** *vb* postpone *vb*
**posto** *nm* post *n*, job *n* **posto vacante** (job) vacancy
**potente** *adj* high-powered *adj*
**potenza** *nf* power *n*
**potenziale** *nm* **potenziale di vendita** sales potential
**potere** *nm* power *n* **potere di acquisto** buying power, purchasing power
**pratica** *nf* practice *n*, experience *n*, file *n*, dossier *n*, practise (US) **pratica spregiudicata** sharp practice **pratiche restrittive** restrictive practices
**praticabilità** *nf* feasibility *n* **studio della praticabilità** feasibility study
**pratico** *adj* businesslike *adj* **essere pratico di** have a working knowledge of sth
**preavviso** *nm* advance notice **con breve preavviso** at short notice **senza preavviso** without warning **termine di preavviso** notice period
**precedere** *vb* forestall *vb*
**prede** *nfpl* **prede di guerra** spoils (of war) *npl*
**preferenza** *nf* **preferenza comunitaria** community preference
**preferenziale** *adj* preferential *adj*
**prefisso** *nm* STD code *n*
**pregiudizio** *nm* **clausola di non pregiudizio** waiver clause
**prelievo** *nm* withdrawal *n*
**premio** *nm* bonus *n*, premium *n* **premio di assicurazione** insurance premium **premio in funzione della performance** performance-related bonus **premio d'ingaggio** golden hello
**prendere** *vb* **prendere in prestito** borrow *vb*
**prenotare** *vb* reserve *vb* **prenotare in anticipo** book in advance **prenotare un biglietto aereo** book a flight **prenotare una camera d'albergo** book a hotel room
**prenotazione** *nf* reservation *n* **fare una prenotazione** make a reservation
**presentare** *vb* (product) introduce *vb*
**presidente** *nm* president *n*
**presiedere** *vb* take the chair **presiedere a una riunione** chair a meeting
**prestare** *vb* lend *vb*
**prestazione** *nf* performance *n*, track record *n* **prestazione economica** economic performance
**prestigio** *nm* kudos *n*
**prestito** *nm* loan *n* **concedere un prestito** lend *vb*, grant a loan **contratto di prestito** loan agreement **prestito bancario** bank loan **prestito compensativo** bridging loan, bridge loan (US) **prestito estero** foreign loan **prestito obbligazionario** debenture loan **prestito personale** personal loan **prestito pubblico** government loan **prestito in valuta forte** hard loan **prestito vincolato** tied loan **richiedere un prestito** request a loan
**presto** *adv* **il più presto possibile** a.s.a.p. (as soon as possible) *abbr*, at your earliest convenience

**prevedere** *vb* forecast *vb*
**preventivare** *vb* estimate *vb*
**preventivo** *nm* estimate *n*
**previdenza** *nf* **previdenza sociale** Social Security (GB)
**previsione** *nf* calculation *n*, forcast *n*, forecasting *n* **previsioni economiche** economic forecast
**prezzo** *nm* price *n* **fare prezzi troppo alti** overcharge *vb* **guerra dei prezzi** price war **livello dei prezzi** level of prices **a metà prezzo** half-price **politica di determinazione dei prezzi** pricing policy **prezzi di borsa** stock exchange prices **prezzi delle case** house prices **prezzi degli immobili** house prices **prezzi più alti** top prices **prezzi al ribasso** falling prices **prezzi di soglia** threshold price **prezzo d'acquisto** purchase price **prezzo di affare** bargain price **a prezzo alto** high-priced **prezzo alto** hard price **prezzo di apertura** opening price **prezzo di chiusura** closing price **prezzo di costo** cost price **prezzo al dettaglio** retail price **prezzo di fabbrica** factory price **prezzo fermo** firm price **prezzo fisso** fixed price **prezzo flessibile** flexible price **prezzo franco** franco price **prezzo limite** limit **prezzo di liquidazione** knockdown price **prezzo massimo** maximum price **prezzo di mercato** market price **prezzo minimo** bottom price, knockdown price **prezzo al minuto** retail price **ad un prezzo nettamente ridotto** at a greatly reduced price **prezzo netto** net, nett price **prezzo nominale** nominal price **prezzo di occasione** bargain price **prezzo reale** real price **prezzo al rivenditore** trade price **prezzo a termine** futures price **prezzo unitario** unit price **prezzo vantaggioso** favourable price **sotto prezzo** at a discount **tener bassi i prezzi** (prices) keep prices down *vb* **tirare sul prezzo** bargain *vb* **vendere a un prezzo inferiore** undersell *vb* **vendere a prezzo inferiore a quello di mercato** undercut *vb*
**primo** *adj* **prima di cambio** first bill of exchange **di primo grado** senior *adj*
**principale 1.** *adj* main *adj*, major *adj* **2.** *nm* boss *n*, employer *n*
**principio** *nm* **principi contabili** accounting conventions
**priorità** *nf* priority *n* **priorità assoluta** top priority
**privatizzare** *vb* denationalize *vb*, privatize *vb*
**privatizzazione** *nf* privatization *n*
**privilegiato** *adj* preferential *adj*
**pro** *nm* **pro e contro** pros and cons **pro capite** per capita **soppesare il pro e il contro** weigh the pros and cons
**procedere** *vb* (research, project) progress *vb*
**processo** *nm* process *n* **processo operativo** process *n*
**procura** *nf* power of attorney **atto di procura** power of attorney
**procurarsi** *vb* **procurarsi il capitale** raise capital
**procuratore** *nm* **procuratore legale** solicitor *n*, lawyer (US)
**prodotto** *nm* produce *n*, product *n* **nuovo prodotto** new product **prodotti chimici** chemical products **prodotti finiti** final products, finished goods, finished stock **prodotti principali** staple commodities **prodotto interno lordo (PIL)** gross domestic product (GDP) **prodotto lordo** gross output **prodotto nazionale lordo (PNL)** gross national product (GNP) **prodotto primario** primary product **prodotto principale** leading product **sostituire con un prodotto migliore** upgrade *vb*
**produrre** *vb* produce *vb*
**produttività** *nf* productivity *n* **incrementi della produttività** productivity gains
**produttivo** *adj* productive *adj*
**produttore** *nm* manufacturer *n*, producer *n*
**produzione** *nf* manufacture *n*, output *n*, production *n* **incrementare la produzione** increase output **linea di produzione** production line **metodo di produzione** production method **produzione a flusso continuo** flow line production, flow production **produzione di massa** mass production **produzione oraria** per hour output **produzione in serie** mass production
**professionale** *adj* vocational *adj* **non professionale** unprofessional *adj*
**professione** *nf* career *n*, profession *n* **le libere professioni** the professions **svolgere contemporaneamente due professioni** moonlight* *vb*
**professionista** *nmf* **professionista freelance** freelancer *n* **professionista indipendente** freelancer *n* **professionista libero** freelancer *n*
**profitto** *nm* profit *n* **margine di profitto** profit margin **profitti e perdite** profit and loss **profitto netto** net profit **profitto**

**nominale** paper profit **registrare un profitto** make a profit **senza profitto** nil profit
**progettare** *vb* design *vb*
**progettato** *adj* planned *adj*, designed *adj* **una macchina progettata bene/male** a machine of good/bad design
**progettista** *nmf* (commercial) designer *n*
**progetto** *nm* design *n*, project *n* **fare progetti** make plans **progetto edilizio** housing project
**programma** *nm* prospectus *n*, schedule *n* (DP) program *n* **programma di aiuti all'estero** foreign aid programme **programma degli investimenti** investment programme, investment program (US) **programma per la ripresa economica europea** European Recovery Plan
**programmare** *vb* budget for *vb*, schedule *vb*
**programmatore** *nm* (DP) programmer *n*
**programmazione** *nf* (DP) programming *n*
**progresso** *nm* headway *n*, progress *n* **fare progressi** make headway
**proibito** *adj* out of bounds *adj*, forbidden *adj*
**promozionale** *adj* promotional *adj*
**promozione** *nf* promotion *n*
**promulgare** *vb* **promulgare leggi** legislate *vb*
**promuovere** *vb* (product) promote *vb*
**pronti** *nmpl* spot cash **mercato a pronti** spot market **prezzo a pronti** spot price **a pronti** for cash **tasso di cambio a pronti** spot rate
**pronto** *adj* ready *adj*, quick *adj* **pronto per la consegna** ready for despatch
**propaganda** *nf* (advertising) publicity *n*
**proponente** *nmf* offeror *n*
**proporre** *vb* (motion, paper) table *vb* **proporre la candidatura di qualcuno ad un comitato** nominate sb to a board/ committe
**proporzionale** *adj* proportional *adj*, pro rata *adj*
**proposta** *nf* **proposta di legge finanziaria** finance bill
**proprietà** *nf* ownership *n*, property *n* **proprietà all'estero** foreign holdings **proprietà immobiliare** real estate **proprietà privata** private property
**proprietario** *nm* owner *n*, proprietor *n* **proprietario d'abitazione** home owner **proprietario di immobile** landlord **proprietario-occupante** owner-occupier **proprietario non residente** absentee landlord **proprietario terriero** landowner
**proroga** *nf* (of contract) extension *n*
**prorogare** *vb* delay *vb*, extend a contract *vb*
**prosperare** *vb* thrive *vb*
**prosperità** *nf* boom *n*, prosperity *n* **periodo di prosperità** upswing *n*
**prospero** *adj* prosperous *adj*
**prospettiva** *nf* **prospettive commerciali** business outlook **prospettive future** future prospects
**prospetto** *nm* prospectus *n*
**protesta** *nf* **raduno di protesta** (strike) sit-in *n*
**protezione** *nf* **protezione antinflazionistica** hedge against inflation
**protezionismo** *nm* protectionism *n*
**protezionista** *adj* protectionist *adj*
**protezionistico** *adj* protectionist *adj*
**prova** *nf* **effettuare prove** carry out trials **mettere a prova** put sth to the test **offerta di prova** trial offer **periodo di prova** trial period **prova preliminare** field test **reggere alla prova** stand the test
**provare** *vb* try out *vb*
**provato** *adj* well-tried *adj*
**proventi** *nmpl* proceeds *npl*
**provvedere** *vb* provide *vb* **provvedere qualcuno di** issue sb with sth
**provvigione** *nf* commission *n* **far pagare la provvigione** charge commission
**provvisorio** *adj* interim *adj*, temporary *adj*
**psicotecnica** *nf* careers advice *n*
**pubblicazione** *nf* **pubblicazione diffamatoria** libel *n*
**pubblicità** *nf* publicity *n* **piccola pubblicità** small ads **pubblicità a mezzo stampa** newspaper advertisement **pubblicità sensazionalistica** hype **pubblicità stravagante** hype
**pubblicitario** *adj* **veicolo pubblicitario** advertising medium
**pubblicizzare** *vb* advertise *vb*
**pubblico** *adj* public *adj* **impresa di pubblici servizi** public utility
**punta** *nf* peak *n* **domanda di punta** peak demand **periodo di punta** peak period
**punto** *nm* point *n* **punto di equilibrio** break-even point **punto franco** entrepôt **punto morto** stalemate **punto di pareggio** break-even point **punto di vendita** market outlet, point of sale **punto di vendita al dettaglio** retail outlet
**qualifica** *nf* qualification *n* **qualifica professionale** professional qualification

**qualifiche necessarie** necessary qualifications
**qualità** *nf* quality *n* **d'altissima qualità** top-of-the-range **controllo della qualità** quality control **di qualità superiore** high-grade **relazione sulla qualità** quality report **standard di qualità** quality standard
**qualitativo** *adj* qualitative *adj*
**quantità** *nf* quantity *n*
**quantitativo 1.** *adj* quantitative *adj* **2.** *nm* quantity *n*
**quanto** *adj* **in quanto** with regard to...
**quartiere** *nm* housing estate, housing tenement (US) **quartiere generale** headquarters
**quasi** *adv* **quasi-contratto** quasi-contract **quasi-rendita** quasi-income
**quattrino** *nm* **far quattrini** make money
**querela** *nf* lawsuit *n*, legal action *n*, writ *n* **emettere una querela** issue a writ
**questionario** *nm* questionnaire *n* **formulazione del questionario** questionnaire design **questionario di ricerca di mercato** market research questionnaire
**quindicinale** *adj* biweekly *adj*
**quorum** *nm* quorum *n* **avente un quorum** quorate *adj* **quorum di creditori** quorum of creditors
**quota** *nf* amount *n*, quota *n* **criterio del riordino per quote** quota buying **quota di mercato** market share **quota di vendite** sales quota
**quotazione** *nf* (price) quotation *n*
**quotidiano** *nm* daily newspaper *n*
**raccolta** *nf* **raccolta dei dati** data capture
**raccolto** *nm* **raccolto per la vendita** cash crop
**raccomandare** *vb* recommend *vb*
**raccomandazione** *nf* recommendation *n*
**racket** *nm* racket *n*
**raffrontare** *vb* **raffrontare idee con** compare notes
**raggio** *nm* **ad ampio raggio** wide-ranging *adj*
**raggiungere** *vb* achieve *vb*
**ragioneria** *nf* accountancy *n*
**ragionevole** *adj* reasonable *adj*
**ragioniere** *nm* accountant *n* **ragioniere capo** chief accountant, head accountant
**rallentamento** *nm* **rallentamento economico** economic slowdown
**rallentare** *vb* slow down *vb*
**rapporto** *nm* ratio *n*, report *n* **rapporti d'affari** business connections **rapporti con la clientela** customer relations **rapporto finanziario** financial report **rapporto di lavoro** working relationship
**rappresentante** *nm* agent *n*, representative *n* **rappresentante di commercio** sales representative **rappresentante sindacale** shop steward **rappresentante di vendite** sales representative **rappresentante di zona** area representative
**rappresentare** *vb* account for *vb*
**rata** *nf* instalment *n*, installment (US)
**rateo** *nm* accrual *n*
**ratifica** *nf* approval *n*, ratification *n*
**ratificare** *vb* approve *vb*, ratify *vb*
**razionalizzare** *vb* rationalize *vb*
**razionalizzazione** *nf* rationalization *n* **misure di razionalizzazione** rationalization measures
**reale** *adj* actual *adj*
**realizzare** *vb* (profit) realize *vb*
**realizzo** *nm* return *n*, proceeds *npl* **realizzo di attività** realization of assets
**realtà** *nf* reality *n* **la realtà nuda e cruda** the hard facts
**reato** *nm* offence *n*, offense (US)
**recapito** *nm* address *n* **recapito personale** home address
**reception** *nf* **presentarsi alla reception dell'albergo** check in a hotel *vb*
**recessione** *nf* **recessione economica** recession *n*
**reciprocamente** *adv* mutually *adv*
**reciprocità** *nf* **reciprocità commerciale** fair trade
**reciproco** *adj* mutual *adj*, reciprocal *adj*
**reclamare** *vb* complain about sth *vb*, make a complaint *vb*
**reclamizzare** *vb* advertise *vb*
**reclamo** *nm* complaint *n* **modulo di reclamo** claim form **procedura di reclamo** claims procedure **reparto reclami** complaints department
**reclutamento** *nm* recruitment *n* **campagna di reclutamento** recruitment campaign **reclutamento del personale** employee recruitment
**reclutare** *vb* recruit *vb*
**recuperabile** *adj* (materials) reclaimable *adj*
**recupero** *nm* **recupero di un documento** document retrieval
**redditività** *nf* profitability *n*
**redditizio** *adj* profitable *adj* **non redditizio** unprofitable *adj*
**reddito** *nm* earnings *npl*, income *n* **reddito annuo** yearly income **reddito di**

**capitale** capital gain, unearned income **reddito del capitale** capital gains **reddito disponibile** disposable income **reddito familiare** family income **reddito dei fattori** factor income **reddito fisso** fixed income **reddito franco da imposta** franked income **reddito imponibile** taxable income **reddito lordo** gross income **reddito minimo** basic income **reddito nazionale** national income **reddito netto** net, nett income **reddito personale** private income **reddito pubblicitario** advertising revenue

**redenzione** *nf* redemption fund *n*

**redigere** *vb* **redigere il bilancio** draw up a budget **redigere un contratto** draw up a contract

**referendum** *nm* referendum *n*

**referenza** *nf* reference *n* **richiedere una referenza** take up a reference

**reflazione** *nf* reflation *n*

**reflazionistico** *adj* reflationary *adj*

**reggere** *vb* hold up *vb*, withstand scrutiny *vb*

**regione** *nf* **regione industriale** industrial region

**registrazione** *nf* record *n*

**registro** *nm* register *n*

**regola** *nf* norm *n* **secondo le regole** according to the regulations

**regolamento** *nm* regulation *n* **regolamenti doganali** customs regulations

**reimportare** *vb* reimport *vb*

**reimportazione** *nf* reimportation *n*

**reinvestire** *vb* (profits) plough back *vb*, plow back (US)

**relazione** *nf* report *n* **presentare una relazione** submit/present a report **redigere una relazione** draw up a report **in relazione a** re **relazione annuale** annual report **relazione annuale di bilancio** annual report **relazione sullo stato dell'economia** economic survey **relazioni industriali** industrial relations, labour relations **relazioni pubbliche** public relations **relazioni umane** human relations

**remunerare** *vb* remunerate *vb* **remunerare eccessivamente** overpay *vb*

**remunerativo** *adj* profitable *adj* **molto remunerativo** moneymaking *adj* **non remunerativo** unprofitable *adj*

**remunerazione** *nf* remuneration *n* **remunerazione eccessiva** overpayment *n*

**rendere** *vb* yield *vb* **non a rendere** non-returnable *adj* **rendere conto di** account for *vb* **rendere esecutivo** (policy) enforce *vb*

**rendiconto** *nm* bank statement *n* **rendiconti finali** final accounts **rendiconto finanziario** financial statement

**rendimento** *nm* **curva di rendimento** yield curve **rendimenti decrescenti** diminishing returns **rendimento del capitale netto** return on equity **rendimento complessivo** earnings yield **rendimento uniforme** flat rate **tasso di rendimento** rate of return

**rendita** *nf* annuity *n*, unearned income **rendita derivante da titoli azionari** yield on shares

**reparto** *nm* department *n* **reparto importazione** import department

**reperimento** *nm* **reperimento dei dati** data capture **reperimento di informazioni** information retrieval

**reputazione** *nf* reputation *n*

**rescindere** *vb* rescind *vb* **rescindere un contratto** cancel a contract

**rescissione** *nf* annulment *n*, termination *n*

**residuale** *adj* residual *adj*

**residuo** **1.** *adj* residual *adj* **2.** *nm* balance *n*

**resistere** *vb* **resistere a** withstand *vb*

**respingere** *vb* negative (US) *vb* **respingere un assegno** (cheque) bounce* **respingere un progetto** kill a project

**responsabile** **1.** *adj* accountable *adj*, liable *adj*, responsible *adj* **considerare qualcuno responsabile di qualcosa** hold sb responsible **2.** *nmf* manager *n*, person in charge *n*

**responsabilità** *nf* accountability *n*, liability *n* **abbiamo la responsabilità di** the onus is on us to... **assumersi la responsabilità** take responsibility for sth **avere la responsabilità** be in charge **condividere le responsabilità** share the responsibilities **piena responsabilità** full responsability **responsabilità collettiva** joint responsibility **responsabilità illimitata** unlimited liability **responsabilità limitata** limited liability

**restituibile** *adj* (deposit) returnable *adj*

**restituzione** *nf* **restituzione di un prestito** repayment of a loan

**resto** *nm* (from purchase) change *n*

**restringere** *vb* (spending) squeeze *vb*

**restrittivo** *adj* restrictive *adj*

**restrizione** *nf* **restrizioni commerciali**

trade restrictions **restrizioni delle importazioni** import restrictions **restrizioni valutarie** exchange restrictions
**rete** *nf* **rete di comunicazione** communication network
**retribuire** *vb* **retribuire inadeguatamente** underpay *vb*
**retribuzione** *nf* salary *n* **retribuzione dei dirigenti** executive compensation **retribuzione per le ferie** holiday pay **retribuzione inadeguata** underpayment
**retroazione** *nf* feedback *n* **retroazione negativa** negative feedback
**retrodatare** *vb* **retrodatare un assegno** backdate a cheque
**rettifica** *nf* adjustment *n*, amendment *n*
**rettificare** *vb* amend *vb*
**revisionare** *vb* revise *vb*
**revisione** *nf* **revisione contabile** audit *n* **revisione contabile esterna** external audit **revisione contabile interna** internal audit
**revisore** *nm* **revisore contabile interno** internal auditor **revisore dei conti** auditor
**revoca** *nf* annulment *n*
**revocare** *vb* (licence) revoke *vb*
**rialzista** *nm* (stock exchange) bull *n*
**rialzo** *nm* (in inflation) rise *n* **mercato al rialzo** bull market
**riassetto** *nm* **riassetto delle spese** cost trimming
**riassicurare** *vb* reinsure *vb*
**riassicurazione** *nf* reinsurance *n*
**riattaccare** *vb* (telephone) hang up *vb*
**ribassamento** *nm* abatement *n*
**ribassare** *vb* (price) knock down *vb*, mark down *vb*
**ribassista** *nm* (stock exchange) bear *n*
**ribasso** *nm* rebate *n*, markdown *n* **mercato al ribasso** buyer's market **al ribasso** downward
**ricambio** *nm* (for machine) spare part
**ricavare** *vb* net, nett *vb*
**ricavo** *nm* proceeds *npl*, revenue *n* **ricavo marginale** marginal revenue
**ricchezza** *nf* wealth *n*
**ricerca** *nf* research *n* **ricerca sui consumatori** consumer research **ricerca esterna** field research **ricerca di mercato** market research **ricerca e sviluppo (R&S)** research and development (R&D)
**ricevere** *vb* receive *vb*
**ricevuta** *nf* receipt *n* **accusare ricevuta di** acknowledge receipt of sth, confirm receipt of sth **emettere una ricevuta** issue a receipt **ricevuta fiscale** fiscal receipt **rilasciare una ricevuta** issue a receipt
**richiamare** *vb* (on phone) call back *vb*
**richiamo** *nm* appeal *n*
**richiedere** *vb* apply for *vb*, call for *vb* **richiedere un prestito** call in a loan **richiedere il risarcimento dei danni** (legal) claim damages
**richiesta** *nf* request *n* **richiesta d'aumento salariale** wage claim **richiesta finale** final demand **richiesta d'informazioni** enquiry **richiesta di informazioni commerciali** credit enquiry **richiesta di pagamento** request for payment
**richiestissimo** *adj* **essere richiestissimi** be in hot demand
**riciclabile** *adj* recyclable *adj*
**riciclare** *vb* recycle *vb*
**ricompensa** *nf* recompense *n*
**ricorrente** *nm* claimant *n*
**ricorrere** *vb* **ricorrere a** (have recourse) resort to *vb* **ricorrere ad un prestito** take out a loan **ricorrere a vie legali** resort to legal proceedings
**ricorso** *nm* appeal *n* **ricorso per rimborso di imposte** tax claim
**ricuperare** *vb* salvage *vb* **ricuperare una somma di denaro da** recover money from sb
**ricupero** *nm* (of debt) recovery *n*
**ridistribuire** *vb* (funds) reallocate *vb*
**ridistribuzione** *nf* (of funds) reallocation
**ridurre** *vb* (stocks) run down *vb* (prices, taxes) lower *vb*, reduce *vb* **ridurre drasticamente i costi** axe* expenditure
**riduzione** *nf* reduction *n* **riduzione dei costi** cost-cutting
**rieleggere** *vb* reappoint *vb*, re-elect *vb*
**rielezione** *nf* re-election *n*
**riferimento** *nm* bench mark *n*, reference *n* **in riferimento a** re, with reference to **in riferimento alla nostra lettera del...** we refer to our letter of...
**rifiutare** *vb* **rifiutare merci** refuse goods **rifiutare pagamento** refuse payment
**rifiuto** *nm* refusal *n* **rifiuti** waste products **rifiuti industriali** industrial waste
**riforma** *nf* amendment *n*, reform *n* **riforma fondiaria** land reform **riforma monetaria** currency reform **riforma tariffaria** tariff reform
**riformare** *vb* amend *vb*
**rifornire** *vb* supply *vb* **rifornire eccessivamente** oversupply *vb*
**riguardare** *vb* (be of importance to) concern *vb*
**riguardo** *nm* **riguardo a** in respect of..., with regard to...

**rilasciare** *vb* (tickets) issue *vb*
**rilassare** *vb* (restrictions) relax *vb*
**rilevamento** *nm* buy-out *n* **rilevamento di un'azienda con leverage** LBO (leveraged buy-out)
**rilevare** *vb* (company) take over *vb* **rilevare il pacchetto di azioni** (business) buy out *vb*
**rimandare** *vb* adjourn *vb*, postpone *vb*
**rimanente** *adj* remaining *adj*
**rimborsabile** *adj* refundable *adj* **non rimborsabile** non-returnable *adj*
**rimborsare** *vb* refund *vb*, reimburse *vb*, repay *vb*
**rimborso** *nm* rebate *n*, refund *n*, reimbursement *n* **concedere un rimborso** grant a rebate **senza rimborso** ex repayment
**rimessa** *nf* remittance *n*
**rimpatrio** *nm* repatriation *n*
**rincrescere** *vb* regret *vb*, be sorry *vb* **ci rincresce informarvi che** we regret to inform you that...
**rinegoziare** *vb* **rinegoziare un debito** reschedule a debt
**ringraziamento** *nm* **ringraziamento pubblico** vote of thanks
**rinnovabile** *adj* renewable *adj*
**rinnovare** *vb* (policy, contract) renew *vb*
**rinomato** *adj* well-known *adj*
**rinominare** *vb* reappoint *vb*
**rinuncia** *nf* waiver *n* **clausola di rinuncia** waiver clause
**rinunciare** *vb* **rinunciare a** resign *vb*, waive *vb*
**rinviare** *vb* hold over (to next period) *vb*, adjourn *vb*, send back *vb* adjourn *vb*, send back *vb*
**rinvio** *nm* adjournment *n*
**riparare** *vb* repair *vb*
**riparazione** *nf* reparation *n*, repair *n* **costi di riparazione** costs of repair
**ripartire** *vb* (funds) reallocate *vb*, allocate *vb*
**ripartizione** *nf* (of funds) reallocation *n*, appropriation *n* **ripartizione dei costi** cost breakdown
**ripercussione** *nf* **ripercussioni finanziarie** financial effects
**riportare** *vb* (to next month) carry over *vb*, bring forward *vb*, carry forward *vb*
**riporto** *nm* **riporto valutario** swap *n*
**riprendere** *vb* **riprendere vigore** (improve) pick up *vb*
**ripresa** *nf* (economy) upturn *n* **ripresa economica** (economic) recovery *n*
**ripudiare** *vb* (contract) repudiate *vb*
**riqualificare** *vb* retrain *vb*
**riqualificazione** *nf* retraining *n* **programma di riqualificazione** retraining programme, retraining program (US)
**risanamento** *nm* **programma di risanamento** recovery scheme
**risanare** *vb* (company) turn round *vb*, turn around (US)
**risarcibile** *adj* refundable *adj*
**risarcimento** *nm* compensation *n*, indemnity *n*, reimbursement *n* **presentare una richiesta di risarcimento** put in a claim **reparto risarcimenti** claims department
**risarcire** *vb* indemnify *vb*
**riscattabile** *adj* redeemable *adj*
**riscattare** *vb* redeem *vb*
**riscatto** *nm* redemption *n*
**rischio** *nm* risk *n* **ad alto rischio** high-risk **analisi del rischio** risk analysis **assumere un rischio** (risk) underwrite *vb* **capitale di rischio** risk capital **gestione del rischio** risk management **perizia del rischio** risk assessment **la polizza copre i seguenti rischi** the policy covers the following risks **rischio di cambio** exchange risk **a rischio dell'acquirente** at the buyer's risk **rischio finanziario** financial exposure, financial risk **rischio professionale** occupational hazard
**risconto** *nm* deferment *n* **risconto passivo** unearned income
**riscontro** *nm* answer *n*, tally *n*
**riscuotere** *vb* (tax) levy *vb* **riscuotere un credito** collect a debt
**riserva** *nf* reservation *n* **riserva valutaria** currency reserve **riserve auree** gold reserves **riserve proporzionali** fractional reserves **riserve valuterie** foreign exchange holdings **tenere in riserva** hold sth in reserve
**riservare** *vb* reserve *vb*
**riservato** *adj* confidential *adj*
**risorsa** *nf* source *n* **risorse** resources *npl* **risorse naturali** natural resources **risorse umane** human resources **sfruttare le risorse** tap resources
**risparmi** *nmpl* savings *npl*
**risparmiatore** *nm* investor *n*
**risparmio** *nm* **risparmio netto** net, nett saving
**rispedire** *vb* send back *vb* **rispedire ad un nuovo indirizzo** (mail) redirect *vb*
**rispettare** *vb* **rispettare le formalità** ob-

serve formalities **rispettare la legge** comply with legislation
**rispondere** *vb* answer *vb* **rispondere a** answer *vb*
**risposta** *nf* answer *n* **in risposta a** in response to... **in risposta alla vostra lettera del...** in reply to your letter of...
**ristagnare** *vb* tick over *vb*
**ristagno** *nm* stagnation *n*
**ristrutturare** *vb* restructure *vb*
**risultare** *vb* (end) turn out *vb* **per quanto mi risulta** to my knowledge **risulta dai dati a nostra disposizione** according to our records
**risultato** *nm* accomplishment *n*, achievement *n*, outcome *n* **risultato netto** net, nett result
**ritardare** *vb* delay *vb*
**ritardo** *nm* delay *n*
**ritirarsi** *vb* **ritirarsi dall'attività** break up *vb*
**ritoccare** *vb* revise *vb*
**riunione** *nf* colloquium *n*, meeting *n* **riunione chiusa** closed session/meeting **riunione di comitato** committee meeting **riunione del consiglio di amministrazione** board meeting **riunione di lavoro** business meeting **tenere una riunione** hold a meeting
**riuscire** *vb* succeed *vb*, be successful *vb* **non riuscire** (attempts, negotiations) fail *vb*
**rivalutare** *vb* revalue *vb*
**rivalutazione** *nf* revaluation *n*
**rivendita** *nf* resale *n*
**rivista** *nf* magazine *n*
**rosso** *adj* **andare in rosso** (banking) overdraw *vb*, overdraw on an account *vb*
**rotazione** *nf* **indice di rotazione** turnover rate, turnover ratio **indice di rotazione del capitale** capital turnover **rotazione delle giacenze** turnover **rotazione dei prodotti finiti** finished turnover
**rottame** *nm* **rottami di ferro** (metal) scrap *n*
**rovina** *nf* (of economy) collapse *n* **mandare in rovina** wreck *vb*
**ruolo** *nm* **essere compreso nel ruolo paga** be on the payroll **ruolo paga** payroll *n*
**saggio** *nm* **saggio base** base rate
**sala** *nf* **sala d'esposizione** exhibition hall **sala riunioni del consiglio di amministrazione** board room
**salariale** *adj* **accordo salariale** wage(s) agreement, wage(s) settlement **aumento salariale** wage rise **categoria salariale** wage zone **conto degli aumenti salariali** wage(s) bill **minimo salariale** minimum wage **pausa salariale** wage restraint **politica salariale** wage policy **richiesta d'aumento salariale** wage(s) claim **trattative salariali** wage negotiations **tregua salariale** wage restraint **zona salariale** wage zone
**salariato** *nm* wage earner *n*
**salario** *nm* salary *n*, wage *n* **aumento di salario** wage rise **blocco dei salari** wage(s) freeze **salario base** basic rate **salario equo** fair wage **salario iniziale** starting wage **salario medio** average wage **salario minimo** minimum wage **salario netto** net, nett wage **salario reale** real wage **scala dei salari** wage scale
**saldare** *vb* (account) settle *vb* **saldare il conto in albergo** check out of a hotel **saldare un debito** pay off a debt
**saldo** *nm* sale *n*, balance *n*, clearance offer *n*, quittance *n* **avere un saldo attivo** be in the black **saldo attivo** trade surplus **saldo attivo della bilancia dei pagamenti** favourable balance of payments **saldo in cassa** balance in hand **saldo di conto bancario** bank balance **saldo a debito** debit balance **saldo demografico** population gap **saldo finale** final balance, final settlement **saldo insoluto** unpaid balance **saldo passivo** debit balance **saldo in sofferenza** unpaid balance
**salire** *vb* escalate *vb*
**salone** *nm* **salone da esposizione** showroom *n*
**salvare** *vb* salvage *vb*
**sanzione** *nf* **sanzione economica** economic sanction **sanzioni commerciali** trade sanctions
**sbaglio** *nm* mistake *n* **faro uno sbaglio** make a mistake **per sbaglio** due to an oversight
**sbocco** *nm* **sbocco di vendita** sales outlet
**sborsare** *vb* disburse *vb*
**sbrigare** *vb* expedite *vb*
**scadente** *adj* (goods) inferior *adj*, shoddy* *adj*
**scadenza** *nf* expiry *n*, termination date, expiration (US) **a scadenza** at term
**scadere** *vb* (business, economy) mature *vb* expire *vb*, fall due *vb*
**scaduto** *adj* overdue *adj*, out of date *adj*
**scafo** *nm* hull *n*
**scaglionare** (payments) space out *vb*, spread out *vb*
**scaglione** *nm* **scaglione fiscale** tax threshold

**scala** *nf* scale *n* **scala mobile** escalator, sliding scale **scala retributiva** salary scale, wage scale **su vasta scala** large-scale
**scambiare** *vb* swap *vb*
**scambio** *nm* **scambi bilaterali** bilateral trade
**scansafatiche** *nm* shirker* *n*
**scaricabarili** *nm* **fare a scaricabarili** pass the buck*
**scaricare** *vb* unload *vb*
**scaricho** *nm* **scarichi industriali** industrial waste
**scarsità** *nf* scarcity *n*, shortage *n*
**scartare** *vb* (goods) reject *vb*
**scarto** *nm* **prodotti di scarto** waste products **scarto inflazionistico** inflationary gap **tasso di scarto** wastage rate
**scheda** *nf* **scheda d'istruzioni** instruction sheet
**schedario** *nm* filing cabinet *n*
**scialacquatore** *adj* spendthrift *adj*
**scioperante** *nm* striker *n*
**scioperare** *vb* strike *vb*
**sciopero** *nm* stoppage *n*, strike *n* **azione di sciopero** strike action **sciopero bianco** go-slow strike, work to rule **sciopero di non collaborazione** slowdown **sciopero dimostrativo** token strike **sciopero generale** general strike **sciopero selvaggio** wildcat strike **sciopero spontaneo** unofficial strike **sciopero ufficiale** official strike
**scontare** *vb* deduct *vb*
**sconto** *nm* discount *n* **sconto di cassa** cash discount **sconto condizionato** no-claims bonus **sconto di quantità** quantity discount **sconto per volume** volume discount
**scontrino** *nm* ticket *n*
**sconveniente** *adj* inconvenient *adj*
**scoperto** *nm* bank overdraft **andare allo scoperto** overdraw, overdraw on an account **essere allo scoperto** be in the red **richiedere uno scoperto di conto** request an overdraft **scoperto di conto** overdraft *n*
**scoprire** *vb* (agreement, policy) thrash out *vb*
**scorretto** *adj* unprofessional *adj*
**scorta** *nf* supply *n*, provision *n* **contrazione delle scorte** stock shrinkage **controllo del livello delle scorte** stock control, inventory control (US) **diminuire la scorte** (stocks) run low **scorta di riserva** reserve stock **scorte** (goods) stock *n*, inventory (US)
**screditare** *vb* (disparage) knock *vb*
**sdoganamento** *nm* customs clearance *n*
**sdoganare** *vb* clear sth through customs *vb*
**sdoganato** *adj & pp* **non sdoganato** (customs) uncleared *adj*
**secco** *adj* ex interest
**secondo** **1.** *adj* second *adj* **avere un secondo lavoro** moonlight* *vb* **di secondo grado** junior *adj* **2.** *prep* in accordance with **secondo le clausole del contratto** under the terms of the contract **secondo le disposizioni del contratto...** it is a requirement of the contract that... **secondo i piani** according to plan
**sede** *nf* branch *n*, residence *n*, seat (of government) *n*, business premises *n* **sede centrale** HO (head office) **sede legale** business address, registered address, registered office **sede sociale** registered office
**segmentazione** *nf* **segmentazione di un mercato** market segmentation
**segnale** *nm* **segnale acustico di linea libera** (phone) dialling tone, dial tone (US) **segnale di occupato** (phone) engaged tone, busy signal (US)
**segretario, -ria** *nm* secretary *n* **segretario dirigenziale** executive secretary **segretario esecutivo** executive secretary **segretario di una società** company secretary
**segreteria** *nf* **segreteria telefonica** Ansaphone (R), answering machine
**segreto** *nm* **segreto commerciale** trade secret
**seguire** *vb* **seguire le istruzioni** follow instructions
**selettivo** *adj* (product) up-market
**selezione** *nf* **selezione casuale** random selection
**semestrale** *adj* biannual *adj*
**semestre** *nm* half-year *n*
**semilavorati** *nmpl* goods in process
**semispecializzato** *adj* semi-skilled *adj*
**sequestrare** *vb* impound *vb*
**serrata** *nf* (of strikers) lockout *n*
**servitù** *nf* **servitù di passaggio** right of way
**servizio** *nm* **servizio di assistenza** after-sales service **servizio compreso** service included **servizio continuo** twenty-four-hour service **servizio del debito pubblico** debt service **servizio a domicilio** home

service **servizio per espresso** express service **servizio giornalistico sulla stampa** newspaper report **servizio ininterrotto** twenty-four-hour service **per servizio pesante** heavy-duty **servizio di un prestito** debt service **servizio pubblico** public service **Servizio sanitario nazionale** National Health Service (GB) **servizi postali** postal services

**settimana** *nf* **settimana lavorativa** working week, workweek (US)

**settore** *nm* sector *n* **settore di attività** line of business **settore primario** primary sector **settore privato** private sector **settore pubblico** government sector, public sector **settore secondario** secondary sector **settore terziario** tertiary sector

**sfitto** *adj* (lodgings, flat) vacant *adj*

**sfratto** *nm* eviction *n*

**sgravio** *nm* **sgravio fiscale** tax cut **sgravio d'imposta** tax allowance

**sicurezza** *nf* security *n* **misura di sicurezza** safety measure **provvedimento di sicurezza** safety measure

**sicuro** *adj* safe *adj*, secure *adj* (product, procedure) well-tried *adj*

**sigillare** *vb* seal *vb*

**sigillo** *nm* seal *n*

**sigla** *nf* abbreviation *n*, initials *npl* **sigla musicale** advertising jingle

**sindacalista** *nmf* union representative

**sindacato** *nm* trade union **iscritti al sindacato** union membership **iscrizione al sindacato** union membership **sindacato industriale** industrial union, syndicate

**sindaco** *nm* **sindaco revisore dei conti** auditor *n*

**sinergia** *nf* synergy *n*

**sintesi** *nf* synthesis *n*

**sintetico** *adj* synthetic *adj*

**sintonia** *nf* **essere in sintonia con qualcuno** be on the same wavelength

**sistema** *nm* establishment *n*, system *n* **conversione nel sistema metrico decimale** metrication **sistema di archiviazione** filing system **sistema del contingentamento** quota system **sistema a due livelli** two-tier system **sistema esperto** expert system **sistema informativo** information systems **sistema monetario aureo** gold standard **Sistema monetario europeo (SME)** European Monetary System (EMS) **sistema monetario standard** gold standard **sistema di partecipazione piramidale** pyramid scheme

**situazione** *nf* **situazione finanziaria** financial situation

**slittamento** *nm* **slittamento salariale** earnings drift

**smercio** *nm* sale *n*

**smontare** *vb* **smontare dal lavoro** (finish work) knock off* *vb*

**sobborgo** *nf* **sobborghi e zone limitrofe** outer suburbs

**soccorso** *nm* **soccorso stradale** breakdown service

**sociale** *adj* corporate *adj*

**società** *nf* company *n*, society *n* **società in accomandita** limited partnership **società affiliata** subsidiary, subsidiary company **società per azioni** joint-stock company, limited company, public company, public limited company **società del benessere** affluent society **società di capitali** joint-stock company **società a carattere familiare** family corporation **società commerciale** trading partnership **società competitiva** competing company **società consociata** subsidiary, subsidiary company **società di controllo** parent company **società cooperativa di consumatori** consumer society **società costituita mediante registrazione** registered company **società di credito edilizio** building society **società creditrice** credit company **società distributrice** distributor *n* **società edilizia** building firm **società estera** foreign company **società fiduciaria** trust company **società finanziaria** finance comapny, financial company, holding company **società fittizia** phoney* company **società garante** underwriter **società di gestione del portafoglio** trust company **società immobiliare** property company **società industriale di prim'ordine** blue-chip company **società d'investimento** investment trust **società d'investimento a capitale variabile** unit trust **società legalmente costituita (US)** corporation **società madre** parent company **società di mutuo soccorso** Friendly Society **società in nome collettivo** general partnership, unlimited company **società offshore** offshore company **società di persone** partnership **società privata a responsabilità limitata** private limited company **società pubblica** public company, public limited company **società**

quotata in borsa quoted company **società registrata** registered company, incorporated company (US) **società regolare**, incorporated company (US) **società a responsabilità illimitata** unlimited company **società a responsabilità limitata** limited company **società semplice** general partnership, partnership **società di trasporti** transport company

**societario** *adj* corporate *adj*

**socio** *nm* member *n*, partner *n*, stockholder *n*, shareholder *n* **socio accomandatario** general partner **socio in affari** business associate **socio non amministratore** silent partner, sleeping partner

**soddisfazione** *nf* **soddisfazione dei consumatori** consumer satisfaction **soddisfazione nel lavoro** job satisfaction

**sofferenza** *nf* **pagamento in sofferenza** unpaid bill

**sollecito** *adj* prompt *adj*

**solvibile** *adj* solvent *adj*

**solvibilità** *nf* solvency *n*

**somma** *nf* amount *n* **somma complessiva** the grand total **somma lorda** gross amount **somma nominale** nominal amount **somma scoperta** outstanding amount

**sommario** *nm* abstract *n*

**somministrare** *vb* administer *vb*

**sopraindicato** *adj* above-mentioned *adj*

**sopravvalutare** *vb* overvalue *vb*

**sopravvenienza** *nf* contingency *n* **sopravvenienza attiva** windfall profit

**sorveglianza** *nf* **comitato di sorveglianza** (figurative) watchdog committee **organo di sorveglianza** (figurative) watchdog

**sospendere** *vb* **sospendere i lavori** adjourn *vb* **sospendere temporaneamente dal lavoro** (workers) lay off *vb*

**sospensione** *nm* (strike) stoppage *n*

**sospensiva** *nf* **essere in sospensiva** fall into abeyance

**sospeso** *adj* **in sospeso** overdue *adj*

**sosta** *nf* **fare una sosta** take a break

**sostegno** *nm* **ottenere il sostegno** win support

**sostenere** *vb* (prices) peg *vb* (expenses) incur *vb* advocate *vb* **il dollaro di Hong Kong sostenuto rispetto al dollaro americano** the HK dollar is pegged to the US dollar **sostenere il morale** boost morale

**sostituire** *vb* replace *vb*

**sostituto** 1. *adj* deputy *adj* 2. *nm* deputy *n*

**sostituzione** *nf* replacement *n*

**sottoassicurato** *adj* underinsured *adj*

**sottocapitalizzato** *adj* undercapitalized *adj*

**sottoccupato** *adj* underemployed *adj*

**sottocosto** *adj* **vendere sottocosto** undersell *vb*

**sottoprodotto** *nm* by-product *n*

**sottoscrittore** *nm* underwriter *n*

**sottoscrivere** *vb* (shares) subscribe *vb* **non completamente sottoscritto** undersubscribed *adj* **sottoscritto in eccesso** oversubscribed *adj* **sottoscrivere una polizza assicurativa** take out insurance

**sottoscrizione** *nf* **domanda di sottoscrizione** (shares) letter of application

**sottovalutare** *vb* undervalue *vb*

**sottrarsi** *vb* **sottrarsi a** evade *vb*

**sovraccaricare** *vb* overload *vb*

**sovrappopolazione** *nf* overpopulation *n*

**sovrapprodurre** *vb* overproduce *vb*

**sovrapproduzione** *nf* overproduction *n*

**sovvenzionare** *vb* subsidize *vb*

**sovvenzione** *nf* **sovvenzione regionale** regional grant **sovvenzione statale** government subsidy, state subsidy **sovvenzioni all esportazioni** export subsidies

**spaccarsi** *vb* split *vb*

**spacciare** *vb* peddle *vb*

**specialista** *nmf* specialist *n* **specialista linguistico** language specialist

**specialità** *nf* speciality *n*

**specializzarsi** *vb* specialize *vb*

**specifica** *nf* specification *n*

**specificare** *vb* itemize *vb*, specify *vb*

**speculare** *vb* speculate *vb* **speculare in borsa** play the market **speculare al rialzo** (stock exchange) bull

**speculatore** *nm* profiteer *n*, speculator *n*

**spedire** *vb* (goods) dispatch *vb*, send *vb*, forward *vb* **spedire con corriere** courier *vb* **spedire per fax** fax *vb*

**spedizione** *nf* dispatch *n*, shipment *n* **bollettino di spedizione** dispatch note **spedizione parziale** part shipment

**spedizioniere** *nm* freighter, freight forwarder, forwarder, forwarding agent, transport agent (US) **spedizioniere marittimo** shipping agent

**spendaccione** *nm* spendthrift *n*

**spendere** *vb* spend *vb*

**sperperare** *vb* squander *vb*

**spesa** *nf* expenditure *n*, expense *n*, spending *n* **franco di spese** free of charge **spesa in conto capitale** capital outlay **spesa del nucleo familiare** household expenditure **spesa statale** state expenditure **spese amministrative** administrative costs **spese di annullamento** cancellation charge **spese di approntamento** handling charges **spese bancarie** bank charges **spese di capitale** capital expenditure **spese da casa** home shopping **spese comuni** overheads **spese di consegna** delivery charges **spese in conto capitale** capital expenditure **spese doganali** customs charges **spese generali di fabbricazione** factory overheads **spese di gestione** operating cost, operating expenses **spese indirette** indirect expenses **spese di missione** travelling expenses, travel expenses (US) **spese occasionali** incidental expenses **spese di rappresentanza** entertainment expenses **spese di spedizione** forwarding charges **spese di trasferta** travelling expenses, travel expenses (US) **spese di trasporto** carriage charge **spese di trasporto incluse** carriage included **spese di viaggio** travelling expenses, travel expenses (US)

**spettatore** *nm* viewer *n*

**spiccioli** *nmpl* (coins) loose/small change *n*

**spiegare** *vb* account for *vb*

**spiegarsi** *vb* make oneself clear *vb*

**spinta** *nf* boost *n*, incentive *n*, spur *n*

**spirale** *nf* **spirale inflazionistica** inflationary spiral

**sponsor** *nm* sponsor *n*

**sponsorizzazione** *nf* sponsorship *n*

**sprecare** *vb* waste *vb* **andare sprecato** go to waste

**spreco** *nm* wastage *n*

**stabile** *adj* stable *adj*

**stabilimento** *nm* factory *n*, works *npl*, workshop *n* **direttore di stabilimento** works manager

**stabilire** *vb* assess *vb*

**stabilità** *nf* **stabilità finanziaria** financial stability

**stabilizzare** *vb* (prices) peg *vb*

**stacanovista** *nm* workaholic *n*

**stagionale** *adj* seasonal *adj*

**stagione** *nf* season *n* **alta stagione** high season **bassa stagione** low season

**stallo** *nm* stalemate *n*

**standard** *adj* standard *adj*

**standardizzare** *vb* standardize *vb*

**standardizzazione** *nf* standardization *n*

**stanza** *nf* **stanza di compensazione** clearing house

**stanziamento** *nm* appropriation *n*, fund *n*, sum set aside *n* **stanziamenti di capitale** capital funds

**stanziare** *vb* allocate *vb*, budget for *vb*

**statistica** *nf* statistics *npl* **statistiche commerciali** trade figures

**stato** *nm* **stato patrimoniale** statement of assets and liabilities **stato assistenziale** welfare state **in buono stato** in good condition **stato d'emergenza** state of emergency **stato fallimentare** bankruptcy **stato d'insolvenza** failure

**statuto** *nm* statute *n*

**stazione** *nf* **stazione degli autobus** bus station

**stazza** *nf* tonnage *n* **polizza di stazza** bill of tonnage **stazza lordo** gross tonnage **stazza netta** net, nett tonnage

**sterlina** *nf* pound sterling *n*, sterling *n* **area della sterlina** sterling area **lira sterlina** pound sterling **saldi in sterline** sterling balance **sterlina verde** green pound

**stima** *nf* appraisal *n*, assessment *n*, estimate *n* **stima dei costi** estimate of costs

**stimare** *vb* assess *vb*, estimate *vb*

**stipendio** *nm* salary *n*, wages *npl*

**stiva** *nf* hold area *n*

**stivaggio** *nm* stowage *n*

**stoccaggio** *nm* (goods) stock *n*, inventory (US)

**stock** *nm* (goods) stock *n*, inventory (US) **in stock** in stock **non in stock** out of stock

**stornare** *vb* (debts) write off *vb*

**strada** *nf* **essere sulla strada giusta** be on the right track **su strada** by road **trasporto su strada** road haulage, road transport

**straordinario** *nm* (working hours) overtime *n*

**strategia** *nf* strategy *n* **strategia economica** economic strategy **strategia delle esportazioni** export strategy **strategia finanziaria** financial strategy **strategia degli investimenti** investment strategy **strategia di sviluppo** growth strategy

**strategico** *adj* strategic *adj*

**stretta** *nf* **stretta creditizia** credit squeeze **stretta di mano** handshake

**stringere** *vb* (spending) squeeze *vb*

**strozzatura** *nf* bottleneck *n*, obstacle *n*

**strumentale** *adj* auxiliary *adj*

**struttura** *nf* facility *n*, framework *n*, structure *n* **struttura finanziaria** financial structure
**subalterno** 1. *adj* junior *adj* 2. *nm* subordinate *n*
**subappaltare** *vb* subcontract *vb*
**subappaltatore** *nm* subcontractor *n*
**subire** *vb* (expenses) incur *vb*
**subordinato** *nm* subordinate *n*
**successo** *nm* **successo strabiliante** jackpot
**succursale** *nf* branch company *n*
**suddetto** *adj* above-mentioned *adj*
**suddivisione** *nf* **suddivisione in zone fiscali** fiscal zoning
**suggerimento** *nm* (suggestion) tip *n*
**summenzionato** *adj* above-mentioned *adj*
**superare** *vb* tide over *vb*
**superiore** *adj* senior *adj*
**supermercato** *nm* supermarket *n*
**superpetroliera** *nf* supertanker *n*
**superpotenza** *nf* **superpotenza economica** economic superpower
**supertassa** *nf* supertax *n*
**supervenduto** *pp* oversold *adj*
**supervisore** *nm* supervisor *n*
**supplementare** *adj* additional *adj*, extra *adj*, supplementary *adj*
**supplemento** *nm* **supplemento di prezzo** additional charge
**surplus** *nm* surplus *n* **surplus della bilancia dei pagamenti** balance of payments surplus
**surriscaldamento** *nm* (of economy) overheating *n*
**sussidio** *nm* benefit *n* **sussidi agricoli** farming subsidies **sussidio di malattia** health benefits **sussidio statale** state subsidy **sussidi statali** welfare benefits
**svalutare** *vb* depreciate *vb*, undervalue *vb*, write down *vb*
**svalutazione** *nf* devaluation *n*
**svantaggio** *nm* inconvenience *n*
**svendere** *vb* sell off *vb*, undersell *vb*
**svendita** *nf* breakup *n*, clearance *n* **svendita per cessazione di esercizio** closing-down sale, closing-out sale (US) **svendita per liquidazione** winding-up sale **prezzo di svendita** knockdown price
**sviluppatore** *nm* **sviluppatore di proprietà immobiliare** property developer
**sviluppo** *nm* **sviluppo alimentato dalle esportazioni** export-led growth **sviluppo economico** economic development, economic expansion **sviluppo zero** zero growth
**svista** *nf* oversight *n* **a causa di una svista** due to an oversight
**tacito** *adj* tacit *adj*
**tagliando** *nm* coupon *n*
**tagliare** *vb* (workforce) trim *vb*
**taglio** *nm* **apportare tagli a** (investment) trim *vb* **taglio delle spese** cost trimming
**tangente** *nf* backhander* *n*, bribe *n*, payola (US)
**tariffa** *nf* tariff *n* **aumentare le tariffe** raise tariffs **riscuotere le tariffe** raise tariffs **tariffa ad aliquota unica** flat-rate tariff **tariffa doganale** (customs) tariff **tariffa forfettaria** flat rate
**tassa** *nf* tax *n* **esente da tasse** free of tax **a netto di tasse** after tax **tassa di licenza** licence fee **tassa di transito** toll
**tassare** *vb* levy a tax *vb* **tassare di** (customs) charge sb with sth
**tassazione** *nf* taxation *n*
**tasso** *nm* rate *n*, percentage *n* **tassazione a tasso zero** zero-rate taxation **tasso annuo di crescita** annual growth rate **tasso di cambio** exchange rate **tasso di cambio flessibile** flexible exchange rate **tasso di cambio fluttuante** floating exchange rate **tasso di crescita** growth rate **tasso decrescente del profitto** falling rate of profit **tasso d'inflazione** rate of inflation **tasso d'interesse** interest rate **tasso di interesse fluttuante** floating interest rate **tasso d'interesse ufficiale di base** base lending rate **tasso minimo di sconto** minimum lending rate **tasso primario d'interesse** fine rate of interest **tasso primario d'interesse ufficiale** prime lending rate **tasso di remunerazione equo** fair rate of return **tasso di sconto** discount rate **tasso ufficiale di sconto** bank rate **tasso variabile** variable rate **tasso zero** zero rate/rating
**tastiera** *nf* keyboard *n* **inserire per mezzo di tastiera** key in *vb*
**tattica** *nf* tactic *n* **tattiche dilazionatorie** delaying tactics **tattiche di vendita** selling tactics
**tecnica** *nf* **tecnica di vendita** sales technique
**tecnico** *nm* technician *n*
**tecnologia** *nf* technology *n* **nuova tecnologia** new technology **tecnologia avanzata** advanced technology, hi-tech **tecnologia dell'informazione** information

technology (IT) **trasferimento di tecnologia** technology transfer
**telecomunicazioni** *nfpl* telecommunications *npl*
**telecopiatrice** *nf* telecopier *n*
**teleelaborazione** *nf* teleprocessing *n*
**telefonare** *vb* call *vb*
**telefonata** *nf* telephone call *n* **registrare abusivamente una telefonata** bug a call **telefonata a carico del destinatario** reverse-charge call, collect call (US) **telefonata con preavviso** person-to-person call
**telefono** *nm* telephone *n* **numero di telefono** telephone number **telefono interno** house telephone
**telematica** *nf* **operazione telematica** teleprocessing
**telespettatore** *nm* viewer *n*
**teletrasmettere** *vb* televise *vb*
**televendite** *nfpl* telesales *npl*
**televisione** *nf* **trasmettere per televisione** televise *vb*
**telex** *nm* telex *n* **inviare un telex** (message) telex *vb* **trasmettere un messaggio a mezzo telex** (message) telex *vb*
**tempestività** *nf* timing *n*
**tempo** *nm* **comportante una considerevole quantità di tempo** time-consuming **gestione del tempo** time management **limite di tempo** time limit **misurazione dei tempi** timing **richiedere tempo** take one's time **con risparmio di tempo** time-saving **spreco di tempo** waste of time **tempo di consegna** delivery time **a tempo parziale** part-time **a tempo pieno** full-time **tempo reale** real time
**temporaneo** *adj* temporary *adj*
**tendenza** *nf* tendency *n*, trend *n* **tendenze del mercato** market tendencies
**tendere** *vb* tend *vb*, aim *vb* **tendere a** tend toward
**tenere** *vb* **tener duro** (wait) hang on *vb* **tenere come garanzia** hold sth as security **tenere responsabile** hold sb liable **tenere una riunione** hold a meeting
**tenore** *nm* **seguire un tenore di vita non conforme alle proprie possibilità** live beyond one's means **tenore di vita** standard of living
**tentativi** *nmpl* trial and error
**tenuta** *nf* **tenuta dei libri** book-keeping *n*
**teoria** *nf* **teoria quantitativa della moneta** quantity theory of money
**teoricamente** *adv* in theory
**terminal** *nm* air terminal *n*
**terminale** *nm* computer terminal *n*
**terminazione** *nf* termination *n*
**termine** *nm* expiry *n*, expiration (US) **a breve termine** short term **a lungo termine** long-range, long-term **a medio termine** medium term **a termine** at term **termini di riferimento** terms of reference **termini di scambio** terms of trade
**territorio** *nm* **territorio estero** overseas territory
**terzo** *nm* third person **terzi** *nmpl* third party *n* **il terzo mondo** the Third World
**tesoriere** *nm* bursar *n* **tesoriere di impresa** company treasurer
**tesoro** *nm* **Ministero del tesoro** the Treasury **il Tesoro** the Treasury
**tessera** *nf* season ticket *n*
**testa** *nf* **alla testa di** at the head of
**testamento** *nm* will *n*
**testare** *vb* **testare il mercato** test-market *vb*
**testimone** *nm* witness *n*
**testimoniare** *vb* witness *vb*
**tetto** *nm* **tetto di spesa** expenditure rate
**timbrare** *vb* **timbrare il cartellino in entrata** clock in *vb* **timbrare il cartellino in uscita** clock out *vb*
**tirata** *nf* long-haul
**tirocinante** *nmf* apprentice *n*, trainee *n* **manager tirocinante** trainee manager
**tirocinio** *nm* apprenticeship *n*
**titolare** *nmf* holder *n*, owner *n*, proprietor *n* **titolare congiunto** joint holder
**titolo** *nm* item *n*, qualification *n*, (shares) bond *n*, claim *n* **mercato dei titoli** market share, market stock **titoli Blue Chip** blue-chip securities **titoli di consolidamento** funding bonds **titoli del debito consolidato** funds **titoli necessari** necessary qualifications **titoli quotati in borsa** listed securities, listed share, listed stock (US) **titoli non quotati in borsa** unlisted securities **titoli di stato** gilt-edged securities, gilts **titolo azionario** share **titolo nominativo** registered bond **titolo al portatore** bearer bond **titolo di prim'ordine** gilt-edged security **titolo di proprietà** title deed **titolo di stato** gilt-edged security, government bond, government security **titolo di studio** academic qualification, educational qualification
**togliere** *vb* **togliere un embargo** lift an embargo **togliere la seduta** close a meeting
**tonnellaggio** *nm* tonnage *n* **tonnellaggio**

**lordo** gross tonnage **tonnellaggio netto** net, nett tonnage
**tonnellata** *nf* ton *n* **tonnellata metrica** metric ton
**topografo** *nm* chartered surveyor *n*
**tornare** *vb* revert *vb*, return *vb*
**totale 1.** *adj* comprehensive *adj*, total *adj* **2.** *nm* total *n* **totale generale** the grand total
**traffico** *nm* **traffico aereo** air traffic **traffico d'armi** arms trade **traffico ferroviario** rail traffic **traffico marittimo** sea traffic **traffico merci** freight traffic **traffico stradale** road traffic
**traguardo** *nm* target *n* **stabilire un traguardo** set a target
**transazione** *nf* transaction *n*
**transito** *nm* transit *n* **banco transiti** (transport) transfer desk **merci in transito** transit goods **sala transiti** (transport) transit lounge **in transito** in transit
**transnazionale** *adj* transnational *adj*
**trarre** *vb* **trarre profitto** benefit *vb*
**trasbordare** *vb* transship *vb*
**trasbordo** *nm* **fare un trasbordo** (transport) transfer *vb* **sala trasbordi** (transport) transfer lounge
**trascrivere** *vb* transcribe *vb*
**trascrizione** *nf* record *n*
**trasferibile** *adj* transferable *adj* **non trasferibile** non-transferable *adj*
**trasferimento** *nm* relocation *n* **prezzo di trasferimento** transfer price **trasferimenti** transfer payments **trasferimento di tecnologie** technology transfer **trasferimento di valuta** currency transfer
**trasferire** *vb* relocate *vb*
**trasgredire** *vb* contravene *vb*
**trasgressione** *nf* offence *n*, offense (US)
**trasmettere** *vb* broadcast *vb*, network *vb*, transcribe *vb*, transmit *vb*
**trasmissione** *nf* broadcast *n*
**trasporto** *nm* freight *n*, transportation *n* **trasporti pubblici** public transport **trasporto aereo** air freight, air transport **trasporto ferroviario** rail transport **trasporto merci** goods transport **trasporto pallettizzato** palletized freight **trasporto stradale** road transport
**tratta** *nf* (financial) draft *n* **tratta a vista** sight draft
**trattare** *vb* handle *vb*
**trattativa** *nf* deal *n* **in fase di trattativa** under negotiation **iniziare le trattative** begin negotiations **intavolare trattative** begin negotiations **trattativa salariale** wage negotiations **trattative di vendita** sales talk
**trattato** *nm* treaty *n* **trattato commerciale** commercial treaty **Trattato di Roma** the Treaty of Rome
**trattenere** *vb* retain *vb* **trattenere soldi** (money) keep back *vb*
**trattenuta** *nf* deduction *n*, retention *n*
**tregua** *nf* **tregua salariale volontaria** voluntary wage restraint
**trend** *nm* trend *n* **creare un trend** set a trend **opporsi ad un trend** buck a trend **trend attuale** current trend **trend dei consumatori** consumer trends **trend dell'economia** economic trend **trend economico** economic trend **trend del mercato** market trend **trend dei prezzi** price trend **trend della spesa** spending patterns
**treno** *nm* **in treno** by rail **treno merci** goods train, freight train (US)
**tribunale** *nm* **in tribunale** in court **tribunale con giurisdizione in materia di espropri** land tribunal **tribunale industriale** industrial tribunal **tribunale penale** criminal court
**tributo** *nm* **esigere tributi** levy taxes **riscuotere tributi** levy taxes
**trimestrale** *adj* quarterly *adj*
**trimestre** *nm* quarter *n*
**truffa** *nf* racket *n*, swindle* *n*
**truffare** *vb* defraud *vb*
**truffatore** *nm* racketeer *n*
**trust** *nm* **istituire un trust** set up a trust
**turismo** *nm* tourism *n*, the tourist trade *n*
**turista** *nm* tourist *n*
**turno** *nm* (working hours) shift *n* **lavoro a turni** shift work **sistema a turni continui** the three-shift system
**ubicazione** *nf* location *n*
**UEO (Unione dell'Europa occidentale)** *abbr nf* WEU (Western European Union) *abbr*
**ufficiale** *adj* official *n* **ufficiale giudiziario** bailiff *n*
**ufficio** *nm* office *n* **attrezzatura di ufficio** office equipment **direzione di ufficio** office management **orario di ufficio** office hours **personale di ufficio** office staff **ufficio centrale** main office **ufficio di collocamento** Job centre **ufficio distaccato** branch office **ufficio doganale** customs **ufficio esportazioni** export department **ufficio importazioni** import department **ufficio del personale** per-

sonnel department **ufficio postale** post office **ufficio regionale** regional office
**ultimo** *adj* last *adj* **ultimo scorso (u.s.)** ultimo *adj*
**umano** *adj* human *adj*
**unanime** *adj* unanimous *adj*
**unificazione** *nf* unification *n*
**unilaterale** *adj* unilateral *adj*
**unione** *nf* **unione doganale** customs union **unione economica** economic union **unione industriale** employer's federation **Unione monetaria ed economica** Economic and Monetary Union
**unità** *nf* **unità centrale (CPU)** (DP) central processing unit (CPU) **unità di conto europea (UCE)** European Unit of Account (EUA) **Unità monetaria europea (UME)** European Monetary Union (EMU) **unità di produzione** unit of production
**urbanistica** *nf* town planning *n*
**urgente** *adj* urgent *adj*
**urgentemente** *adv* urgently *adv*
**uso** *nm* **uso intenso** intensive usage
**usura** *nf* usury *n*
**utente** *nmf* **amichevole per l'utente** user-friendly **utente finale** end user
**utile** 1. *adj* advantageous *adj*, handy *adj* 2. *nm* **dare un utile netto di** net, nett *vb* **utile sul capitale** return on capital **utile sul capitale investito** return on investment **utile contabile** book profit **utile di esercizio** net, nett profit **utile d'esercizio inatteso** windfall profit **utile di gestione** operating income, operating profit **utile netto di esercizio** net, nett earnings **utile sulle vendite** return on sales **utili** earnings **utili non distribuiti** earned surplus
**utilità** *nf* **utilità finale** final utility **utilità marginale** marginal utility
**utilizzare** *vb* make use of sth *vb*, utilize *vb*
**utilizzo** *nm* utilization *n*
**vacanza** *nf* **vacanza pagata** paid holiday
**vaglia** *nm* **vaglia postale** money order
**valere** *vb* be worth *vb*
**validità** *nf* validity *n*
**valido** *adj* valid *adj*
**valore** *nm* value *n* **acquisire valore** gain value **aumentare di valore** gain value **determinazione del valore** valuation **diminuire di valore** lose value **oggetto senza valore** write-off **privo di valore legale** null and void **senza valore commerciale** no commercial value **di valore** valuable **valore contabile** book value **valore equo di mercato** fair market value **valore facciale** nominal value **valore massimo** peak **valore di mercato** market value **valore nominale** face value, nominal value **valore reale** real value **valore straordinario** extraordinary value **valori mobiliari** stocks and shares
**valuta** *nf* currency *n* **valuta chiave** key currency **valuta convertibile** convertible currency **valuta debole** soft currency **valuta estera** foreign currency **valuta forte** hard currency **valuta legale** legal currency **valuta di riserva** reserve currency **valuta verde** green currency
**valutare** *vb* assess *vb*
**valutazione** *nf* appraisal *n*, assessment *n*, valuation *n*
**vantaggio** *nm* advantage *n*, benefit *n* **vantaggio comparato** comparative advantage **vantaggio competitivo** competitive advantage, competitive edge **vantaggio relativo** comparative advantage
**vantaggioso** *adj* advantageous *adj*
**varco** *nm* breakthrough *n*
**variabile** *adj* variable *adj*
**veicolo** *nm* **veicolo industriale** commercial vehicle **veicolo per merci pesanti** heavy goods vehicle
**velocità** *nf* **a due velocità** two-speed
**vendere** *vb* market *vb*, sell *vb* **vendere più di quanto si ha a disposizione** oversell *vb*
**vendita** *nf* sale *n* **ammontare delle vendite** sales figures **gestione delle vendite** sales management **management delle vendite** sales management **previsione delle vendite** sales forecast **in vendita** for sale **vendita di capitale azionario** equity financing **vendita di una casa** house sale **vendita per contanti** cash sale **vendita fittizia** fictitious sale **vendita di liquidazione** clearance sale **vendita con pagamento rateale** hire purchase **vendita piramidale** pyramid selling **vendita porta a porta** door-to-door selling **vendite sul mercato interno** home sales **vendite sul mercato nazionale** home sales **vendite totali** total sales
**venditore** *nm* dealer *n*, salesperson *n*, seller *n*, vendor *n* **capitale del venditore** vendor capital **fare il venditore ambulante** peddle *vb* **venditore congiunto** joint vendor **venditore in partecipazione** joint vendor
**verbale** *nm* **il verbale dell'assemblea** the minutes of the meeting **verbali della conferenza** conference proceedings

**verghe** *nfpl* **verghe auree** gold bullion
**verifica** *nf* tally *n*
**verificare** *vb* check *vb*, examine *vb*
**veritiero** *adj* accurate *adj*
**versamento** *nm* deposit *n* **versamento anticipato** advance payment
**versare** *vb* deposit *vb*
**vertenza** *nf* dispute *n*, grievance *n*
**vertice** *nm* (peak) zenith *n*
**veto** *nm* veto *n* **mettere il veto** veto *vb*
**vettore** *nm* carrier, haulage company, freight company (US) **vettore a contratto** haulage contractor, haulier **vettore per espresso** express carrier **vettore stradale** road haulage company
**viaggiatore** *nm* traveller *n*, traveler (US)
**viaggio** *nm* **perso in viaggio** lost in transit **viaggi all'estero** foreign travel **in viaggio** in transit **viaggio aereo** air travel **viaggio di affari** business trip **viaggio d'affari** business travel, business trip **viaggio d'andata e ritorno** round trip **viaggio di dovere** tour of duty **viaggio in gruppo** group travel **viaggio tutto compreso** package tour
**vice** *adj* deputy *adj*
**vicedirettore** *nm* deputy director *n*, assistant manager *n*
**video** *nm* video *n* **attrezzature video** video facilities **impianti video** video facilities **mezzi video** video facilities
**videotelefono** *nm* visual telephone *n*
**vietato** *adj* out of bounds, forbidden
**vigore** *nm* effect *n*
**vincolante** *adj* binding *adj*
**vincolo** *nm* obligation *n*, commitment *n* **soggetto a vincolo doganale** in bond
**violare** *vb* contravene *vb*
**visita** *nf* visit *n*
**visitare** *vb* visit *vb*
**visitatore** *nm* visitor *n*
**visto** *nm* (customs) visa *n* **visto d'ingresso** entry visa
**visualizzatore** *nm* visual display unit (VDU) *n*
**vita** *nf* life *n* **periodo di vita lavorativa** working life
**vitalità** *nf* viability *n*
**vivace** *adj* (competition) keen *adj*
**vizio** *nm* defect *n* **vizio occulto** hidden defect
**vocazionale** *adj* vocational *adj*
**voce** *nf* item *n* **voce contabile** ledger entry
**volo** *nm* (in plane) flight *n* **volo charter** charter flight
**volubile** *adj* (prices) volatile *adj*
**volume** *nm* bulk *n* **avere un volume d'affari di** turn over *vb*
**votare** *vb* vote *vb*
**voto** *nm* vote *n* **dare il voto** vote *vb* **diritto di voto** voting right **voto di sfiducia** vote of no confidence
**yen** *nm* (currency) yen *n* **obbligazione in yen** yen bond
**zecca** *nf* mint *n*
**zenit** *nm* zenith *n*
**zero** *nm* nil *n*, zero *n* **sotto zero** below zero
**zona** *nf* zone *n* **suddividere in zone** zone *vb* **suddivisione in zone** zoning **zona di esclusione** exclusion zone **zona del franco** franco zone **zona industriale** trading estate **zona postale** postal zone

# English–Italian

**abandon** *vb* abbandonare *vb*, desistere da *vb*
**abandoned** *adj* **abandoned goods** beni abbandonati *nmpl*
**abate** *vb* ribassare *vb*, diffalcare *vb*, detrarre *vb*
**abatement** *n* ribassamento *nm*, diffalco *nm*
**abbreviate** *vb* abbreviare *vb*
**abbreviated** abbreviato *adj*
**abbreviation** *n* abbreviazione *nf*
**abeyance** *n* **to fall into abeyance** essere in sospensiva
**ability** *n* abilità *nf*, capacità *nf* **ability to pay** capacità di pagare, capacità contributiva
**aboard** *adv* **to go aboard** imbarcarsi *vb*
**abolish** *vb* abolire *vb*
**abolition** *n* abolizione *nf*
**above-mentioned** *adj* summenzionato *adj*, suddetto *adj*, sopraindicato *adj*
**aboveboard** *adj/adv* leale *adj*, lealmente *adv*
**abroad** *adv* **to go abroad** andare all'estero *vb*
**absence** *n* **in the absence of information** in mancanza di informazioni
**absent** *adj* assente *adj*
**absentee** *adj* assente *nm* **absentee landlord** proprietario non residente *nm*
**absenteeism** *n* assenteismo *nm*
**absolute** *adj* assoluto *adj*, incontestabile *adj*
**absorb** *vb* **to absorb surplus stock** assorbire le rimanenze
**abstract** *n* estratto *nm*, sommario *nm*
**abundance** *n* abbondanza *nf*
**abuse** **1.** *n* (misuse) abuso *nm* **abuse of power/trust** abuso di autorità/di fiducia **2.** *vb* abusare di *vb*, prevaricare da *vb*
**accelerate** *vb* accelerare *vb*
**acceleration** *n* accelerazione *nf*
**accept** *vb* **accept delivery** ricevere in consegna
**acceptance** *n* **consumer acceptance** accettazione del consumatore *nf* **acceptance house** istituto di accettazione bancaria *nm* **market acceptance** accettazione da parte del mercato *nf*
**access** **1.** *n* accesso *nm* **2.** *vb* accedere a *vb*
**accessibility** *n* accessibilità *nf*
**accident** *n* incidente *nm*, infortunio *nm* **industrial accident** infortunio sul lavoro
**accidental** *adj* **accidental damage** danno accidentale
**accommodation** *n* alloggio *nm*, comodo *nm* **accommodation allowance** assegno integrativo d'alloggio **accommodation bill** cambiale di comodo **to come to an accommodation** raggiungere un compromesso
**accomplish** *vb* portare a termine *vb*
**accomplishment** *n* compimento *nm*, risultato *nm*
**accordance** *n* **in accordance with** in conformità con *prep*, secondo *prep*
**according to** *prep* **according to plan** secondo i piani **according to the minister** secondo il ministro
**account** *n* (at shop, bank) conto *nm* **bank account** conto bancario **Account Day** (stock exchange) giorno di liquidazione **expense account** conto spese **payment on account** pagamento in acconto **profit and loss account** conto profitti e perdite **savings account** conto di risparmio **accounts receivable** conto debitori diversi **statement of account** estratto conto **to open an account** aprire un conto **to overdraw on an account** andare allo scoperto, andare in rosso **to settle an account** saldare un conto **to take sth into account** prendere in considerazione, tenere in conto **trading account** conto merci, conto esercizio commerciale
**account for** *vb* rendere conto di *vb*, rappresentare *vb*, spiegare *vb*, incidere su *vb*
**accountability** *n* responsabilità *nf*

**accountable** *adj* responsabile *adj*, tenuto a rendere conto *adj*
**accountancy** *n* ragioneria *nf*
**accountant** *n* ragioniere *nm*, contabile *nmf* **chartered accountant** commercialista *nmf*
**accounting** *n* **accounting conventions** principi contabili *nmpl* **financial accounting** contabilità finanziaria *nf* **management accounting** contabilità gestionale *nf* **accounting period** periodo contabile *nm*, esercizio *nm*
**accredit** *vb* accreditare *vb*
**accrual** *n* accumulazione *nf*, attribuzione *nf*, rateo *nm* **rate of accrual** saggio di accumulazione
**accrued** *adj* **accrued interest** interessi maturati *nmpl*
**accumulate** *vb* accumulare *vb*, accumularsi *vb*
**accumulated** *adj* accumulato *adj*, arretrato *adj*
**accuracy** *n* esattezza *nf*
**accurate** *adj* esatto *adj*, veritiero *adj*
**achieve** *vb* raggiungere *vb*, conseguire *vb*
**achievement** *n* risultato *nm*, conseguimento *nm*
**acknowledge** *vb* **to acknowledge receipt of sth** accusare ricevuta di
**acknowledgement** *n* **acknowledgement of debt** riconoscimento di un debito
**acquaintance** *n* **business acquaintance** contatto nel mondo degli affari *nm* **to make the acquaintance of sb** fare la conoscenza di *vb*
**acquire** *vb* acquisire *vb*, acquistare *vb*
**acquisition** *n* acquisizione *nf*, acquisto *nm*
**acquisitive** *adj* desideroso di acquisire *adj*, acquisitivo *adj*
**action** *n* **industrial action** azione industriale *nf* **legal action** querela *nf* **out of action** guasto *nm*
**actual** *adj* effettivo *adj*, reale *adj*
**actuality** *n* realtà *nf*
**actuary** *n* attuario *nm*
**acumen** *n* **business acumen** acume in affari *nm*
**additional** *adj* supplementare *adj* **additional charge** supplemento di prezzo *nm*
**address 1.** *n* indirizzo *nm* **home address** recapito personale *nm* **registered address** sede legale *nf* **to change address** cambiare indirizzo **2.** *vb* indirizzare *vb*, parlare a *vb*
**addressee** *n* destinatario *nm*, destinataria *nf*
**adjourn** *vb* rimandare *vb*, rinviare *vb* sospendere i lavori *vb*
**adjournment** *n* rinvio *nm*
**adjust** *vb* **to adjust a claim** stabilire l'entità del danno **to adjust the figures** rettificare i conti, conguagliare i conti
**adjustment** *n* rettifica *nf*, adeguamento *nm*, conguaglio *nm*
**administer** *vb* amministrare *vb*, somministrare *vb*
**administration** *n* amministrazione *nf*, gestione *nf*
**administrative** *adj* **administrative costs** spese amministrative *nfpl*
**administrator** *n* amministratore *nm*, curatore *nm*, esecutore *nm*
**advance 1.** *adj* **advance notice** preavviso *nm* **advance payment** pagamento anticipato *nm*, versamento anticipato *nm* **2.** *n* (on salary) anticipo *nm*, prestito *nm*, rialzo *nm* **cash advance** anticipo in contanti **payable in advance** pagabile in anticipo **3.** *vb* (salary) anticipare *vb*
**advanced** *adj* **advanced country** nazione progredita *nf* **advanced technology** tecnologia avanzata *nf*
**advantage** *n* vantaggio *nm*, beneficio *nm* **comparative advantage** vantaggio comparato *nm*, vantaggio relativo *nm* **competitive advantage** vantaggio competitivo *nm*
**advantageous** *adj* vantaggioso *adj*, utile *adj*
**adverse** *adj* **adverse balance of trade** bilancia commerciale passiva *nf*, deficit della bilancia commerciale *nm*
**advertise** *vb* fare pubblicità *vb*, pubblicizzare *vb*, reclamizzare *vb*
**advertisement** *n* annuncio pubblicitario *nm*, messaggio pubblicitario *nm*, inserzione *nf*
**advertising** *n* **advertising agency** agenzia di pubblicità *nf* **advertising budget** budget pubblicitario *nm* **advertising campaign** campagna pubblicitaria *nf* **advertising medium** mezzo pubblicitario *nm* **advertising revenue** reddito pubblicitario *nm*
**advice** *n* consiglio *nm*, consigli *nmpl*, parere *nm*
**advise** *vb* **to advise sb about sth** consigliare qualcosa a qualcuno
**adviser/advisor** *n* consulente *nm*, consigliere *nm*
**advisory** *adj* consultivo *adj*

**advocate** *vb* difendere *vb*, sostenere *vb*, perorare *vb*

**aerospace** *adj* **aerospace industry** industria aerospaziale *nf*

**affidavit** *n* affidavit *nm*, deposizione giurata *nf*

**affiliated** *adj* **affiliated company** azienda affiliata *nf*

**affluent** *adj* **affluent society** società del benessere *nf*

**afford** *vb* **I can't afford (to buy a new printer)** Non posso permettermi (di comprare una stampante nuova) **we cannot afford (to take) the risk** non possiamo permetterci di rischiare

**after-sales service** *n* assistenza alla clientela *nf*, servizio di assistenza post-vendita *nm*

**agency** *n* agenzia *nf* **advertising agency** agenzia di pubblicità **employment agency** agenzia di collocamento **travel agency** agenzia di viaggi

**agenda** *n* ordine del giorno *nm*

**agent** *n* agente *nm*, rappresentante *nm*, mandatario *nm*

**AGM (Annual General Meeting)** *abbr* assemblea generale degli azionisti *nf*

**agrarian** *adj* agricolo *adj*

**agree** *vb* concordare *vb*, convenire *vb*, mettersi d'accordo *vb*

**agreed** *adj* concordato *adj*, convenuto *adj*, pattuito *adj*

**agreement** *n* accordo *nm*, consenso *nm* **by mutual agreement** per mutuo consenso **verbal agreement** accordo verbale **wage agreement** accordo salariale

**agribusiness** *n* agribusiness *nm*

**agriculture** *n* agricoltura *nf*

**agronomist** *n* agronomo *nm*

**aid** *n* **financial aid** assistenza finanziaria *nf*

**air** *n* **by air** in aereo **air-conditioned** ad aria condizionata **air freight** nolo aereo *nm*, trasporto aereo *nm* **air traffic controller** controllore di volo *nm*

**airline** *n* linea aerea *nf*

**airmail** *n* posta aerea *nf*

**airport** *n* aeroporto *nm*

**allocate** *vb* stanziare *vb*, ripartire *vb*, distribuire *vb*

**allowance** *n* indennità *nf*, detrazione *nf*, abbuono *nm* **family allowance** assegni familiari *nmpl*

**amalgamate** *vb* incorporare *vb*, fondere *vb*

**amalgamation** *n* fusione *nf*, incorporazione *nf*

**amend** *vb* rettificare *vb*, riformare *vb*

**amendment** *n* emendamento *nm*, rettifica *nf*, riforma *nf*

**amends** *npl* **to make amends** fare ammenda *vb*

**amenities** *npl* impianti *nmpl*, conforts *nmpl*, strutture *nfpl*

**amortization** *n* ammortamento *nm*

**amortize** *vb* ammortizzare *vb*, ammortare *vb*

**amount** *n* ammontare *nm*, somma *nf*, quota *nf*

**amount to** *vb* costituire *vb*, equivalere a *vb*

**analysis** *n* analisi *nf* **cost-benefit analysis** analisi dei costi e dei benefici **systems analysis** analisi dei sistemi

**analyze** *vb* analizzare *vb*

**annual** *adj* **annual general meeting (AGM)** assemblea generale degli azionisti *nf*, assemblea ordinaria *nf* **annual report** relazione annuale di bilancio *nf*

**annuity** *n* rendita *nf*, assegno annuale *nm*

**annulment** *n* annullamento *nm*, revoca *nf*, rescissione *nf*

**Ansaphone (R)** *n* segreteria telefonica *nf*

**answer 1.** *n* risposta *nf*, riscontro *nm* **2.** *vb* rispondere a *vb*

**answering** *n* **answering machine** segreteria telefonica *nf*

**anti-inflationary** *adj* **anti-inflationary measures** misure antinflazionistiche *nfpl*

**antitrust** *adj* **antitrust laws** leggi antitrust *nfpl*

**appeal 1.** *n* richiamo *nm*, ricorso *nm*, appello *nm* **2.** *vb* fare appello a *vb*, ricorrere a *vb*

**application** *n* **application form** modulo di domanda *nm*, modulo di sottoscrizione *nm* **letter of application** lettera di richiesta di impiego *nf*

**apply for** *vb* fare domanda di *vb*, richiedere *vb*

**appoint** *vb* **to appoint sb to a position** incaricare *vb*, nominare *vb*

**appointment** *n* (to meet) appuntamento *nm* (to a position) nomina *nf* **to make an appointment** fissare *vb*, prendere un appuntamento *vb*

**appraisal** *n* valutazione *nf*, stima *nf*

**appreciate** *vb* (rise in value) aumentare di prezzo *vb*

**appreciation** *n* (in value) aumento di valore *nm*

**apprentice** *n* apprendista *nmf*, tirocinante *nmf*
**apprenticeship** *n* apprendistato *nm*, tirocinio *nm*
**appropriation** *n* stanziamento *nm*, ripartizione *nf*, appropriazione *nf*
**approval** *n* approvazione *nf*, benestare *nm*, omologazione *nf*, ratifica *nf* **on approval** salvo vista e verifica, in esame
**approve** *vb* approvare *vb*, ratificare *vb*, omologare *vb*
**approximate** *adj* approssimativo *adj*
**approximately** *adv* approssimativamente *adv*, circa *adv*
**arbitrage** *n* arbitraggio *nm*
**arbitrary** *adj* arbitrario *adj*, discrezionale *adj*
**arbitrate** *vb* arbitrare *vb*, sottoporre ad arbitrato *vb*
**arbitration** *n* arbitrato *nm*, arbitraggio *nm*
**arbitrator** *n* arbitro *nm*
**area** *n* **area manager** direttore di zona *nm*, manager di zona *nm*
**arithmetic** *n* aritmetica *nf*
**arithmetical** *adj* **arithmetical mean** media aritmetica *nf*, media *nf*
**arms** *npl* **arms trade** traffico d'armi *nm*
**arrangement** *n* (agreement) accordo *nm*, concordato *nm*
**arrears** *npl* arretrati *nmpl* **in arrears** in arretrato **to fall/get into arrears** essere moroso *vb*, essere in arretrato *vb*
**articulated** *adj* **articulated lorry** auto articulato *nm*
**asap (as soon as possible)** *abbr* il più presto possibile
**asking** *adj* **asking price** prezzo di domanda *nm*
**assembly** *n* **assembly line** catena di montaggio *nf*
**assess** *vb* stimare *vb*, valutare *vb*, stabilire *vb*, accertare *vb*
**assessment** *n* determinazione *nf*, accertamento *nm*, valutazione *nf*, stima *nf*
**asset** *n* attività *nf*, attivo *nm*, bene *nm* **capital assets** capitale fisso
**assign** *vb* assegnare *vb*, incaricare *vb*, cedere *vb*
**assignee** *n* assegnatario *nm*, cessionario *nm*, avente causa *nm*
**assignment** *n* incarico *nm*, compito *nm*, nomina *nf*, cessione *nf*
**assistant** *adj* **assistant manager** vicemanager *nm*, vicedirettore *nm*
**associate** 1. *adj* **associate director** condirettore *nm* 2. *n* collaboratore in affari *nm*
**attestation** *n* attestazione *nf*, attestato *nm*, autenticazione *nf*
**attorney** *n* procuratore legale *nm*, avvocato *nm* **power of attorney** procura *nf*, atto di procura *nm*
**auction** 1. *n* asta *nf*, incanto *nm* 2. *vb* vendere all'asta *vb*
**auctioneer** *n* banditore *nm*
**audit** *n* revisione contabile *nf*, controllo dei conti *nm*
**auditor** *n* revisore dei conti *nm*, sindaco revisore dei conti *nm*
**authority** *n* (official) autorità *nf*, potere *nm*, ente *nm*
**authorize** *vb* autorizzare *vb*
**authorized** *adj* **authorized dealer** operatore autorizzato *nm*
**automatic** *adj* automatico *adj* **automatic cash dispenser** cassa automatica *nf*
**automation** *n* automazione *nf*
**automobile** *n* **automobile industry** industria automobilistica *nf*
**autonomous** *adj* autonomo *adj*
**auxiliary** *adj* ausiliare *adj*, strumentale *adj*, accessorio *adj*
**average** 1. *adj* **average unit** unità media *nf* 2. *n* media *nf*, avaria *nf*
**avoid** *vb* evitare *vb*
**avoidance** *n* **tax avoidance** minimizzazione dell'onere fiscale *nf*, elusione fiscale *nf*
**axe, ax** (US) *vb* **to axe expenditure** ridurre drasticamente i costi *vb*
**back** *vb* **to back a venture** appoggiare un'impresa rischiosa *vb*
**back pay** *n* arretrati di paga *nmpl*
**backdate** *vb* **to backdate a cheque** retrodatare un assegno *vb*
**backer** *n* avallante *nm*, finanziatore *nm*, garante *nm*
**backhander*** *n* tangente *nf*, bustarella *nf*
**backing** *n* appoggio *nm*, copertura *nf*
**backlog** *n* arretrato *nm*, ordinazioni inevase *nfpl*
**bad** *adj* **bad cheque** assegno scoperto *nm* **bad debt** credito inesigibile *nm*
**bail** *n* cauzione *nf*, garanzia *nf*
**bailiff** *n* ufficiale giudiziario *nm*
**balance** 1. *n* (financial) saldo *nm*, residuo *nm* **bank balance** saldo di conto bancario **final balance** saldo finale **balance in hand** saldo in cassa **balance of payments** bilancia dei pagamenti *nf* **balance of payments deficit** deficit della

bilancia dei pagamenti *nm* **balance of payments surplus** surplus della bilancia dei pagamenti *nm* **balance of trade** bilancia commerciale *nf* **balance sheet** bilancio patrimoniale *nm* **trade balance** bilancia commerciale *nf* **2.** *vb* **to balance the books** fare il bilancio dei libri contabili *vb* **to balance the budget** pareggiare il bilancio *vb*

**bank 1.** *n* banca *nf*, istituto di credito *nm* **bank account** conto bancario *nm* **bank balance** saldo di conto bancario *nm* **bank card** carta di credito *nf* **bank charges** commissioni bancarie *nfpl*, spese bancarie *nfpl* **bank clerk** impiegato,a di banca *nm,f* **bank draft** assegno circolare *nm* **bank holiday** bank holiday *nf*, festa civile *nf* **bank loan** prestito bancario *nm* **bank manager** direttore di banca *nm* **bank overdraft** scoperto *nm*, credito allo scoperto *nm* **bank rate** tasso ufficiale di sconto *nm* **bank statement** rendiconto *nm*, estratto conto *nm* **2.** *vb* **to bank a cheque** versare un assegno *vb*

**banker** *n* banca *nf*, banchiere *nm* **banker's order** ordine di banca *nm*, ordine di pagamento *nm*

**banking** *n* **banking circles** il mondo bancario *nm*, le banche *nfpl* **banking hours** orario di sportello *nm*

**banknote** *n* banconota *nf*

**bankrupt** *adj* fallito *adj* **to be bankrupt** fallire *vb*

**bankruptcy** *n* fallimento *nm*

**bar code** *n* barcode *nm*

**bargain 1.** *n* affare *nm*, operazione in compravendita *nf* **it's a bargain** è un buon affare, è un'occasione **bargain offer** offerta speciale *nf* **bargain price** prezzo di affare *nm*, prezzo di occasione *nm* **2.** *vb* contrattare *vb*, mercanteggiare *vb*, tirare sul prezzo *vb*

**barrier** *n* **trade barrier** barriera commerciale *nf*, barriera al libero scambio *nf*

**barrister, lawyer** (US) *n* avvocato *nm*, avvocatessa *nf*

**barter 1.** *n* baratto *nm* **barter agreement** accordo di scambio *nm* **barter transaction** operazione di scambio *nf* **2.** *vb* barattare *vb*

**base** *adj* **base lending rate** tasso d'interesse ufficiale di base *nm*

**basic** *adj* basilare *adj*, fondamentale *adj* **basic commodity** bene economico basilare *nm* **basic income** reddito minimo *nm* **basic rate** salario base *nm* **basic training** addestramento di base *nm*, training di base *nm*

**basis** *n* **basis of assessment** criterio basilare di accertamento *nm*

**basket** *n* **basket of currencies** paniere valutario *nm*

**batch** *n* (of goods) lotto *nm*, partita *nf* **batch processing** (DP) lavorazione per lotti *nf*

**bear 1.** *n* (stock exchange) ribassista *nm* **bear market** mercato al ribasso *nm*, mercato con tendenza al ribasso *nm* **2.** *vb* **to bear interest** dare interesse *vb*, produrre interesse *vb*

**bearer** *n* portatore *nm* **bearer bond** obbligazione al portatore *nf*, titolo al portatore *nm* **bearer cheque** assegno al portatore *nm* **bearer share** azione al portatore *nf*

**bench** *n* **bench mark** punto di riferimento *nm* **bench mark price** prezzo di riferimento *nm*

**benefactor** *n* benefattore *nm*

**benefit 1.** *n* (social security) indennità *nf*, vantaggio *nm*, beneficio *nm*, sussidio *nm* **2.** *vb* beneficiare *vb*, trarre profitto *vb* giovare a *vb*

**bequeath** *vb* lasciare in eredità *vb*

**bequest** *n* lascito *nm*, legato *nm*

**best** *adj* **best-before date** da consumarsi entro *vb* **best seller** best seller *nm*

**biannual** *adj* semestrale *adj*

**bid 1.** *n* offerta *nf*, licitazione *nf*, offerta d'appalto *nf* **2.** *vb* (auction) offrire *vb*, fare un'offerta *vb*, licitare *vb*

**biennial** *adj* biennale *adj*

**bilateral** *adj* **bilateral trade** commercio bilaterale *nm*, scambi bilaterali *nmpl*

**bill 1.** *n* (invoice) conto *nm*, fattura *nf* **bill of exchange** cambiale *nf*, tratta *nf* **bill of lading** polizza di carico *nf* **bill of sale** atto di cessione *nm*, atto di vendita *nm* **bills discounted** effetti scontati *nmpl* **to pay a bill** pagare il conto *vb* **2.** *vb* (invoice) fatturare *vb*

**bimonthly** *adj* bimensile *adj*, bimestrale *adj*

**binding** *adj* vincolante *adj* **legally binding** legalmente vincolante *adj*

**biweekly** *adj* quindicinale *adj*, bimensile *adj*

**black** *adj* **black economy** economia nera *nf* **black market** borsa nera *nf* **to be in the black** essere in credito *vb*, avere un saldo attivo *vb*

**blank** *adj* **blank cheque** assegno in bianco *nm*
**block** 1. *n* blocco *nm*, lotto *nm*, pacchetto *nm* 2. *vb* bloccare *vb*
**blockade** 1. *n* blocco *nm*, assedio *nm* 2. *vb* bloccare *vb*, assediare *vb*
**blocked** *adj* **blocked account** conti bloccati *nmpl*
**blue** *adj* **blue-chip company** società industriale di prim'ordine *nf*, società Blue Chip *nf* **blue-collar worker** operaio *nm*, colletto blu *nm* **blue-chip securities** titoli Blue Chip *nmpl*
**board** *n* **Board of Trade** Ministero (britannico) del commercio estero *nm* **board meeting** riunione del consiglio di amministrazione *nf* **board of directors** consiglio di amministrazione *nm* **board room** sala riunioni del consiglio di amministrazione *nf*
**bona fide** *adj* in buona fede *adv*
**bond** *n* obbligazione *nf*, titolo *nm* **bond certificate** certificato obbligazionario *nm*, manto *nm* **government bond** titolo di stato *nm* **in bond** in magazzino doganale, soggetto a vincolo doganale
**bonded** *adj* **bonded warehouse** magazzino doganale *nm*, deposito franco *nm*
**bondholder** *n* obbligazionista *nm*
**bonus** *n* premio *nm*, gratifica *nf*, dividendo extra *nm*
**book** 1. *n* **cheque book** libretto di assegni *nm* **book profit** utile contabile *nm* **the books** libri contabili *nmpl* **book value** valore contabile *nm* 2. *vb* **to book a hotel room** prenotare una camera d'albergo *vb* **to book in advance** prenotare in anticipo *vb*
**book-keeper** *n* contabile *nm*
**book-keeping** *n* contabilità *nf*, tenuta dei libri *nf*
**booking** *n* (reservation) prenotazione *nf*
**bookseller** *n* libraio *nm*
**bookshop, bookstore** (US) *n* libreria *nf*
**boom** 1. *n* **economic boom** boom economico *nm* **boom in demand** boom della domanda *nm* 2. *vb* espandere *vb*
**booming** *adj* fiorente *adj*, dinamico *adj*
**boost** 1. *n* spinta *nf*, lancio *nm* 2. *vb* **to boost demand** incrementare la domanda *vb* **to boost morale** sostenere il morale *vb* **to boost production** aumentare la produzione *vb* **to boost sales** aumentare le vendite *vb*, incrementare le vendite *vb*
**boot** *vb* **to boot a computer** dar il via alle attività del sistema operativo *vb*, inizializzare *vb*, lanciare *vb*
**booth** *n* (voting) cabina *nf*
**borrow** *vb* prendere in prestito *vb*, mutuare *vb*
**borrowing** *n* indebitamento *nm*, credito passivo *nm*
**boss** *n* capo *nm*, principale *nm*, padrone *nm*, dirigente *nm*
**bottleneck** *n* strozzatura *nf* **bottleneck inflation** inflazione da strozzatura *nf*
**bottom** 1. *adj* **bottom price** prezzo minimo *nm* 2. *n* **at the bottom** (letter) in calce *adv*, in fondo *adv* 3. *vb* **to bottom out** toccare il fondo *vb*
**bought** *adj* **bought ledger** libro mastro dei torniton *nm*
**bounce*** *vb* (cheque) respingere un assegno *vb*
**bound** *n* **out of bounds** proibito *adj*, vietato *adj*
**box** 1. *n* **box number** numero di casella postale *nm* **box office** botteghino (ticket office) *nm*, box-office (proceeds of a film) *nm* **PO box** casella postale *nf* 2. *vb* **to box sth up** inscatolare *vb*, incassare *vb*
**boycott** 1. *n* boicottaggio *nm* 2. *vb* boicottare *vb*
**bracket** *n* **tax bracket** categoria fiscale *nf*
**branch** *n* filiale *nf* **branch company** filiale *nf*, succursale *nf* **branch manager** direttore di filiale *nm* **branch office** ufficio distaccato *nm*
**brand** *n* marca *nf*, marchio di fabbrica *nm* **brand image** immagine della marca *nf* **brand leader** marca leader *nf*, brand leader *nm*
**breach** *n* **breach of contract** inadempimento di un contratto *nm*
**break** 1. *n* **to take a break** fare una sosta *vb*, fare una pausa *vb* 2. *vb* **to break an agreement** violare un accordo *vb*, venir meno ad un accordo *vb*
**break even** *vb* chiudere un bilancio in pareggio *vb*
**break up** *vb* cessare l'attività *vb*, ritirarsi dall'attività *vb*
**break-even** *adj* **break-even point** punto di equilibrio *nm*, punto di pareggio *nm*
**breakdown** *n* (of figures) analisi stratificata delle cifre *nf* **breakdown service** soccorso stradale *nm*
**breakthrough** *n* conquista *nf*, varco *nm* **to make a breakthrough** fare un importante passo avanti *vb*

**breakup** *n* svendita *nf*, realizzo *nm*, demolizione *nf*
**bribe** 1. *n* tangente *nf* 2. *vb* corrompere *vb*, comprare *vb*
**bribery** *n* corruzione *nf*
**bridging** *adj* **bridging loan, bridge loan** (US) prestito compensativo *nm*
**brief** 1. *n* informazioni *nfpl*, brevi istruzioni *nfpl* 2. *vb* dare istruzioni a *vb*
**briefing** *n* informazioni *nfpl*, istruzioni *nfpl*, briefing *nm*
**bring down** *vb* (prices) abbassare *vb*
**bring forward** *vb* riportare *vb*
**bring out** *vb* (product) lanciare *vb*
**brinkmanship** *n* politica del rischio calcolato *nf*
**Britain** *n* Gran Bretagna *nf*
**British** *adj* britannico *adj* **British Isles** le Isole Britanniche *nfpl*, Gran Bretagna *nf*
**broad** *adj* **broad market** mercato ampio *nm*
**broadcast** 1. *n* diffusione *nf*, trasmissione *nf* 2. *vb* diffondere *vb*, trasmettere *vb*
**broadsheet** *n* giornale formato normale *nm*
**brochure** *n* opuscolo *nm*, brochure *nf*
**broker** *n* intermediario *nm*, broker *nm*
**brokerage** *n* intermediazione *nf*, brokeraggio *nm* **brokerage firm** agenzia di compravendita *nf*, agenzia d'intermediazione *nf*
**buck*** *n* (US familiar: dollar) dollaro *nm* **to pass the buck*** lavarsi le mani di *vb*, fare a scaricabarile *vb*
**budget** *n* budget *nm*, bilancio preventivo *nm* **to draw up a budget** redigere il bilancio *vb*
**budget for** *vb* programmare *vb*, stanziare *vb*
**budgetary** *adj* **budgetary deficit** disavanzo *nm*, deficit di bilancio *nm* **budgetary policy** politica di bilancio *nf*
**bug** 1. *n* (listening device) microfono spia *nm*, (computer) baco *nm* 2. *vb* **to bug a call** registrare abusivamente una telefonata *vb*
**build** *vb* **to build a reputation** farsi un buon nome *vb*
**builder** *n* costruttore *nm*, imprenditore edile *nm*
**building** *adj* **building contractor** appaltatore edile *nm* **building firm** società edilizia *nf* **building industry/trade** edilizia *nf* **building permit** licenza edilizia *nf* **building site** cantiere edilizio *nm*, area fabbricabile *nf* **building society** società di credito edilizio *nf*
**built-in** *adj* incorporato *adj*, incassato *adj*, automatico *adj*
**built-up** *adj* **built-up area** zona urbana *nf*, zona abitata *nf*
**bulk** *n* massa *nf*, volume *nm* **the bulk of** la maggior parte di *nf* **to buy in bulk** acquistare all'ingrosso *vb*
**bull** 1. *n* (stock exchange) rialzista *nm* **bull market** mercato al rialzo *nm* 2. *vb* (stock exchange) speculare al rialzo *vb*
**bulletin** *n* bollettino *nm*, comunicato *nm* **bulletin board** bacheca *nf*
**bullion** *n* metallo prezioso *nm*
**bump up** *vb* (prices) aumentare i prezzi *vb*
**bundle** *n* balla *nf*
**bundle up** *vb* imballare *vb*
**buoyant** *adj* **buoyant market** mercato al rialzo *nm*
**bureau** *n* **bureau de change** agenzia di cambiavalute *nf* **Federal Bureau (US)** Federal Bureau *nm*
**bureaucracy** *n* burocrazia *nf*
**bureaucrat** *n* burocrate *nm*
**bureaucratic** *adj* burocratico *adj*
**bursar** *n* economo *nm*, tesoriere *nm*
**bus** *n* autobus *nm* **bus station** autostazione *nf*, stazione degli autobus *nf*
**business** 1. *adj* **business address** recapito *nm*, sede legale *nf* **business associate** socio in affari *nm* **business consultant** consulente *nmf* **business expenses** spese generali *nfpl* **business hours** ore d'ufficio *nfpl* **business premises** locali aziendali *nmpl* **business studies** studi di amministrazione aziendale *nmpl* **business suit** completo *nm* **business transaction** operazione commerciale *nf* **business trip** viaggio di affari *nm* 2. *n* affari *nmpl* **to go out of business** fallire *vb* **big business** i grossi affari *nmpl*, l'alta finanza *nf*, business ad alto livello *nm* **family business** impresa familiare *nf* **to set up in business** avviare un'azienda *vb*
**businesslike** *adj* efficiente *adj*, pratico *adj*, metodico *adj*
**busy** *adj* impegnato *adj*, indaffarato *adj*, occupato *adj* **busy signal (US)** segnale di occupato *nm*
**buy** 1. *n* **a good buy** un buon affare *nm* 2. *vb* **to buy sth at a high price** comprare a prezzo alto *vb* **to buy sth on credit** comprare a credito *vb* **to buy sth second hand** acquistare di seconda mano *vb* **to**

**buy sth wholesale** acquistare all'ingrosso *vb*
**buy out** *vb* rilevare il pacchetto di azioni *vb*
**buy-out** *n* acquisto in blocco *nm*, rilevamento *nm*
**buyer** *n* compratore *nm*, addetto agli acquisti *nm* **buyer's market** mercato al ribasso *nm*
**buying** *n* **buying and selling** compravendita *nf* **buying power** potere di acquisto *nm* **buying price** prezzo di acquisto *nm* **buying rate** cambio di acquisto *nm*, corso di acquisto *nm*
**by-product** *n* sottoprodotto *nm*
**bypass** *vb* aggirare *vb*
**byte** *n* byte *nm*
**c.i.f. (cost, insurance and freight)** *abbr* c.i.f. (costo, assicurazione e nolo) *abbr*
**CAD (computer-aided or assisted design)** *abbr* CAD (Design assistito da calcolatore) *abbr*
**calculate** *vb* calcolare *vb*
**calculation** *n* calcolo *nm*, previsione *nf*
**calculator** *n* calcolatrice *nf*
**call 1.** *n* **call money** denaro a richiesta *nm* **person-to-person call** telefonata con preavviso *nf* **reverse-charge call, collect call** (US) telefonata a carico del destinatario *nf* **2.** *vb* **to call a meeting** convocare una riunione *vb*, convocare un'assemblea *vb* **to call it a deal** Affare fatto! *nm*
**call back** *vb* (on phone) richiamare *vb*
**call for** *vb* avere bisogno di *vb*, richiedere *vb*
**call in** *vb* (demand the repayment of a loan) richiedere un prestito *vb*
**campaign** *n* **advertising campaign** campagna pubblicitaria *nf* **publicity campaign** campagna pubblicitaria *nf* **sales campaign** campagna di vendita *nf* **to run a campaign** fare una campagna *vb*
**cancel** *vb* **cancel a contract** rescindere un contratto *vb* **cancel an appointment** disdire un appuntamento *vb*
**cancellation** *n* cancellazione *nf*, estinzione *nf*, annullamento *nm* **cancellation charge** spese di annullamento *nfpl*, costo di rescissione *nm*
**candidate** *n* (for job) candidato,-a *nm,f*
**cap** *vb* **to cap the interest rate** limitare il tasso d'interese *vb*
**CAP (Common Agricultural Policy)** *abbr* Politica Agricola Comunitaria *nf*
**capacity** *n* **earning capacity** capacità di reddito *nf* **industrial capacity** capacità industriale *nf* **in my capacity as chairman** in veste di presidente *prep* **manufacturing capacity** capacità industriale *nf* **storage capacity** capacità di magazzinaggio *nf* **to expand capacity** ampliare la capacità *vb* **to work to full capacity** operare a piena capacità *vb*
**capital 1.** *adj* **capital assets** capitale fisso *nm* **capital budget** piano degli investimenti *nm*, budget degli investimenti di capitale *nm* **capital cost** costo di capitale *nm* **capital expenditure** spese in conto capitale *nfpl*, spese di capitale *nfpl* **capital exports** esportazioni di capitale *nfpl* **capital funds** fondi di capitale *nmpl*, stanziamenti di capitale *nmpl* **capital gains** plusvalenza *nf*, reddito del capitale *nm* **capital gains tax** imposta sui redditi di capitale *nf*, imposta sulle plusvalenze *nf* **capital goods** beni capitali *nmpl*, beni indiretti *nmpl*, beni strumentali *nmpl* **capital loss** perdita di capitale *nf* **capital market** mercato finanziario *nm* **capital turnover** indice di rotazione del capitale *nm* **2.** *n* capitale *nm* **fixed capital** capitale fisso *nm*, capitale investito *nm* **initial capital** capitale d'impianto *nm* **invested capital** capitale investito *nm* **to raise capital** procurarsi il capitale *vb* **venture capital** capitale di rischio *nm* **working capital** capitale netto di esercizio *nm*
**capitalism** *n* capitalismo *nm*
**capitalist** *n* capitalista *nm*
**capitalize** *vb* capitalizzare *vb*, finanziare *vb*
**card** *n* **bank card** carta di credito *nf* **business card** biglietto di visita *nm* **chargecard** carta di addebito *nf* **cheque card** carta assegni *nf* **credit card** carta di credito *nf* **identity card** carta d'identità *nf* **smart card** carta intelligente *nf*, smart card *nf*
**career** *n* carriera *nf*, professione *nf* **careers advice** psicotecnica *nf*
**cargo** *n* carico *nm* **bulk cargo** carico alla rinfusa *nm*, carico a massa *nm* **cargo ship** nave da carico *nf*, mercantile *nm*
**carriage** *n* **carriage charge** spese di trasporto *nfpl* **carriage costs** costi di trasporto *nmpl* **carriage forward** porto assegnato *nm* **carriage included** spese di trasporto incluse *nfpl* **carriage paid** porto pagato *nm*
**carrier** *n* vettore *nm* **bulk carrier**

portarinfuse *nf* **express carrier** vettore per espresso *nm*

**carry** *vb* (stock) mantenere scorte *vb*

**carry forward** *vb* riportare *vb*

**carry out** *vb* eseguire *vb*, condurre *vb*, effettuare *vb*

**carry over** *vb* (to next month) riportare *vb*, prorogare *vb*

**carrying** *adj* **carrying cost** costo di utilizzazione *nm*

**cartel** *n* cartello *nm*, consorzio *nm*

**cash** 1. *adj* **cash crop** raccolto per la vendita *nm* **cash desk** cassa *nf* **cash discount** sconto di cassa *nm* **cash flow** cash flow *nm*, flusso di cassa *nm* **cash machine/dispenser** cassa automatica *nf* **cash offer** offerta in contanti *nf* **cash payment** pagamento in contanti *nm*, pagamento a pronti *nm* **cash sale** vendita per contanti *nf* **cash transaction** operazione a pronti *nf* 2. *n* contante *nm*, contanti *nmpl*, denaro liquido *nm* **cash and carry** cash and carry *nm* **cash before delivery** pagamento in contanti prima della consegna *nm* **for cash** in contanti *adv*, a pronti *adv* **cash on delivery (COD)** pagamento contrassegno *nm* **cash on receipt of goods** pagamento in contanti alla ricevuta della merce *nm* **to pay in cash** pagare in contanti *vb* **cash with order** contanti all'ordinazione *nmpl* 3. *vb* **to cash a cheque** incassare un assegno *vb*

**cash up** *vb* chiudere la cassa *vb*

**cashier** *n* cassiere, -a *nm,f*

**cater for** *vb* soddisfare *vb*, tenere conto di *vb*

**caution** *n* **caution money** cauzione *nf*

**ceiling** *n* (on prices) calmiere *nm* **to put a ceiling on sth** imporre un calmiere su *vb*

**central** *adj* **central bank** banca centrale *nf* **central planned economy** economia a pianificazione centrale *nf* **central planning** pianificazione centrale *nf* **central processing unit (CPU)** (DP) unità centrale di elaborazione (CPU) *nf*

**centralization** *n* accentramento *nm*, centralizzazione *nf*

**centralize** *vb* centralizzare *vb*, accentrare *vb*

**centre** *n* **business centre** centro commerciale *nm* **Jobcentre** ufficio di collocamento *nm*

**certificate** 1. *n* certificato *nm*, attestato *nm* **clearance certificate** permesso di partenza *nm* **marriage certificate** certificato di matrimonio *nm* **certificate of employment** certificato di lavoro *nm* **certificate of origin** certificato di origine *nm* **certificate of ownership** atto *nm*, certificato di nazionalità *nm* **share certificate, stock certificate** (US) certificato azionario *nm*, manto *nm* 2. *vb* certificare *vb*, attestare *vb*

**certified** *adj* **certified cheque** assegno bancario a copertura garantita *nm*

**certify** *vb* certificare *vb*, attestare *vb*, autenticare *vb*

**chain** *n* **chain of shops** catena di negozi *nf* **retail chain** catena di negozi al dettaglio *nf* **chain store** grande magazzino appartenente ad una catena *nm*

**chair** *vb* **to chair a meeting** presiedere a una riunione *vb*

**chamber** *n* **Chamber of Commerce** camera di commercio *nf*

**chancellor** *n* **chancellor of the exchequer (GB)** Cancelliere dello Scacchiere *nm*

**change** *n* (from purchase) cambio *nm*, spiccioli *nmpl*, resto *nm* **bureau de change** agenzia di cambiavalute *nf* **loose/small change** (coins) spiccioli *nmpl*

**charge** 1. *adj* **charge account** conto di credito *nm* 2. *n* **bank charges** spese bancarie *nfpl*, competenze bancarie *nfpl* **delivery charges** spese di consegna *nfpl* **handling charges** spese di approntamento *nfpl* **legal charge** ipoteca legale *nf* **to be in charge** avere la responsabilità *vb*, comandare *vb* 3. *vb* **to charge commission** addebitare la provvigione *vb* **to charge for sth** far pagare qualcosa *vb* **to charge a price** addebitare *vb*, mettere in conto *vb* **to charge sth to an account** addebitare una somma su un conto *vb* **to take charge of sth** assumere la responsabilità *vb*, prendersi cura di *vb* **to charge sb with sth** accusare *vb*, imputare *vb*, incriminare *vb*, tassare di *vb*

**chargeable** *adj* imponibile *adj*, da addebitarsi

**charitable** *adj* **charitable trust** charitable trust *nm*, negozio fiduciario *nm*

**charity** *n* beneficenza *nf*

**chart** *n* **bar chart** diagramma a colonne *nm* **flow chart** flussoschema *nm*, flussogramma *nm* **pie chart** diagramma a settori *nm*

**charter** *n* **charter flight** volo charter *nm*

**chartered** *adj* **chartered accountant** (GB) commercialista *nmf* **chartered bank**

chartered bank *nf* **chartered surveyor** topografo *nm*

**chattels** *npl* beni mobili *nmpl*

**check 1.** *n* **customs check** controllo doganale *nm* **to make a check on sth** effettuare un controllo di *vb* **2.** *vb* controllare *vb*, verificare *vb*

**check in** *vb* (at airport) fare il check-in *vb* (in hotel) presentarsi alla reception dell'albergo *vb*

**check out** *vb* (from hotel) saldare il conto in albergo *vb*

**checkbook (US)** *n* libretto di assegni *nm*

**chemical** *adj* **chemical industry** industria chimica *nf* **chemical products** prodotti chimici *nmpl*

**cheque, check** (US) *n* assegno *nm* **return a cheque to drawer** restituire un assegno all'emittente *vb* **blank cheque** assegno in bianco *nm* **cheque book** libretto di assegni *nm* **crossed cheque** assegno sbarrato *nm* **dud cheque** assegno scoperto *nm*, assegno a vuoto *nm* **a cheque for the amount of £100** assegno per la somma di 100 sterline *nm* **to bounce a cheque** restituire un assegno all'emittente *vb* **to cash a cheque** incassare un assegno *vb* **to make out a cheque** scrivere un assegno *vb* **to pay by cheque** pagare con assegno *vb* **to sign a cheque** firmare un assegno *vb* **to stop a cheque** bloccare un assegno *vb*, mettere un fermo ad un assegno *vb* **traveller's cheque, traveler's cheque** (US) assegno turistico *nm*

**chief** *adj* **chief accountant** ragioniere capo *nm* **chief cashier** cassiere capo *nm* **chief executive** direttore esecutivo *nm*, direttore generale *nm* **chief financial officer** direttore finanziario generale *nm*

**circular** *n* (letter) circolare *nf*

**circulate** *vb* (document) circolare *vb*, far circolare *vb*, distribuire *vb*

**circulation** *n* **in circulation** in circolazione *adv*

**circumstance** *n* circostanza *nf* **circumstances beyond our control** circostanze al di fuori del nostro controllo **due to unforeseen circumstances** a causa di circostanze impreviste **under no circumstances** in nessun caso

**civil** *adj* **civil engineering** ingegneria civile *nf* **civil servant** impiegato statale *nm*, funzionario statale *nm* **civil service** amministrazione pubblica *nf*

**claim 1.** *n* **claim form** modulo di reclamo *nm* **claims department** reparto risarcimenti *nm* **claims procedure** procedura di reclamo *nf* **to put in a claim** presentare una richiesta di risarcimento *vb* **to settle a claim** comporre una lite *vb* **wage claim** richiesta d'aumento salariale *nf* **2.** *vb* (demand) **to claim for damages** pretendere il risarcimento dei danni *vb*

**claimant** *n* ricorrente *nm*, attore *nm*

**class** *n* **business class** (plane) classe business *nf* **first class** (plane) prima classe *nf*

**classified** *adj* **classified advertisement** annuncio economico *nm*, inserzione pubblicitaria *nf* **classified information** dati riservati *nmpl*

**clause** *n* (in contract) clausola *nf*, comma *nm* **escape clause** clausola di storno *nf* **option clause** clausola di opzione *nf*

**clear 1.** *adj* **clear loss** perdita netta *nf* **to make oneself clear** spiegarsi *vb* **2.** *vb* **to clear a cheque** compensare un assegno *vb* **to clear sth through customs** sdoganare *vb*

**clearance** *n* **clearance offer** saldo *nm* **clearance sale** liquidazione *nf*, vendita di liquidazione *nf*

**clearing** *adj* **clearing bank** banca affiliata alla stanza di compensazione *nf* **clearing house** stanza di compensazione *nf* **clearing payment** pagamento di compensazione *nm*

**clerical** *adj* **clerical error** errore di scrittura *nm* **clerical work** lavoro impiegatizio *nm*

**clerk** *n* impiegato, -a *nm,f*

**client** *n* cliente *nm*

**clientele** *n* clientela *nf*

**clinch** *vb* **clinch a deal** concludere un affare *vb*

**clock in** *vb* timbrare il cartellino in entrata *vb*

**clock out** *vb* timbrare il cartellino in uscita *vb*

**close** *vb* **to close a business** chiudere un'azienda *vb* **to close a deal** concludere un affare *vb* **to close a meeting** togliere la seduta *vb* **to close an account** chiudere un conto *vb*

**closed** *adj* chiuso *adj* **closed session/meeting** riunione chiusa *nf* **closed shop** closed shop *nm*

**closing** *adj* **closing bid** offerta finale *nf* **closing price** prezzo di chiusura *nm* **closing time** orario di chiusura *nm*

**closure** *n* **closure of a company** chiusura

di un'azienda *nf*, liquidazione di un'azienda *nf*

**COD (cash on delivery), (collect on delivery)** (US) *abbr* contrassegno *nm*

**code** *n* **bar code** bar code *nm* **professional code of practice** normativa *nf* **post code, zip code** (US) CAP - codice di avviamento postale *abbr* **telephone code** prefisso *nm* **tax code** codice fiscale *nm*

**collaborate** *vb* collaborare *vb*

**collaborative** *adj* **collaborative venture** iniziativa in collaborazione *nf*

**collapse** *n* (of company) fallimento *nm* (of economy) rovina *nf* (on stock market) crollo (del mercato finanziario) *nm*

**collateral** 1. *adj* **collateral security** garanzia reale *nf*, garanzia collaterale *nf* 2. *n* garanzia reale *nf*, garanzia collaterale *nf*

**colleague** *n* collega *nm*, collega *nf*

**collect** *vb* **to collect a debt** riscuotere un credito *vb*

**collecting** *adj* **collecting agency** agenzia di riscossione *nf*

**collection** *n* **debt collection** esazione di crediti *nf*

**collective** 1. *adj* **collective agreement** contratto collettivo di lavoro *nm* **collective bargaining** contrattazione collettiva *nf* 2. *n* collettivo *nm* **workers' collective** collettivo operaio *nm*

**colloquium** *n* riunione *nf*

**comment** *n* commento *nm*

**commerce** *n* commercio *nm*

**commercial** *adj* commerciale *adj* **commercial bank** banca di credito ordinario *nf*, banca commerciale *nf* **commercial traveller, commercial traveler** (US) commesso viaggiatore *nm* **commercial vehicle** veicolo industriale *nm*

**commission** *n* commissione *nf*, provvigione *nf* **commission agent** commissionario *nm* **commission broker** commissionario di borsa valori *nm* **commission fee** competenza di commissione *nf* **to charge commission** addebitare *vb*, far pagare la provvigione *vb*

**commit** *vb* commettere *vb*, affidare *vb*

**commitment** *n* impegno *nm*

**committee** *n* comitato *nm*, commissione *nf* **advisory committee** comitato consultivo *nm* **committee meeting** riunione di comitato *nf*

**common** *adj* **Common Agricultural Policy (CAP)** politica agricola comunitaria *nf* **Common Market** Mercato Comune *nm* **common law** diritto consuetudinario *nm*

**communication** *n* comunicazione *nf* **communication network** rete di comunicazione *nf*

**company** *n* società *nf*, azienda *nf*, compagnia *nf* **holding company** holding *nf*, società finanziaria *nf* **incorporated company (US)** società regolare *nf*, società registrata *nf* **joint-stock company** società per azioni *nf*, società di capitali *nf* **company law** legislazione societaria *nf* **limited company** società a responsabilità limitata *nf* **parent company** società madre *nf*, casa madre *nf* **company policy** politica aziendale *nf* **private limited company** società privata a responsabilità limitata *nf* **public limited company** società pubblica *nf*, società per azioni *nf* **registered company** società registrata *nf* **company secretary** segretario di una società *nm* **sister company** consorella *nf* **subsidiary company** società consociata *nf*, società affiliata *nf*

**comparative** *adj* comparato *adj*

**compatible** *adj* compatibile *adj*

**compensate for** *vb* compensare *vb*

**compensation** *n* risarcimento *nm*, compenso *nm*, indennizzo *nm*, compensazione *nf* **to claim compensation** chiedere il risarcimento dei danni *vb* **to pay compensation** risarcire i danni *vb*

**compete** *vb* competere *vb*, concorrere *vb*, fare concorrenza *vb* **to compete with a rival** fare concorrenza a *vb*

**competing** *adj* **competing company** società competitiva *nf*, concorrente *nf*

**competition** *n* concorrenza *nf* **cut-throat competition** concorrenza spietata *nf* **market competition** concorrenza del mercato *nf* **unfair competition** concorrenza sleale *nf*

**competitive** *adj* competitivo *adj*, concorrenziale *adj*

**competitiveness** *n* competitività *nf*

**competitor** *n* concorrente *nm*

**complain** *vb* **to complain about sth** lamentarsi di *vb*, reclamare *vb*

**complaint** *n* reclamo *nm* **to make a complaint** reclamare *vb* **complaints department** reparto reclami *nm*

**complete** *vb* completare *vb*, compilare *vb*

**complex** 1. *adj* complesso *adj* 2. *n* **housing complex** complesso urbano *nm*

**complimentary** *adj* in omaggio *adv*

**comply** *vb* **to comply with legislation** rispettare la legge *vb* **to comply with the rules** attenersi alle regole *vb*

**compound** *adj* **compound interest** interesse composto *nm*

**comprehensive** *adj* generale *adj*, totale *adj*, completo *adj* **comprehensive insurance policy** polizza di assicurazione contro tutti i rischi *nf*

**compromise** *n* compromesso *nm* **to reach a compromise** venire a un compromesso *vb*

**computer 1.** *n* computer *nm*, elaboratore elettronico *nm* **computer-aided design (CAD)** CAD - disegno assistito da computer **computer-aided learning (CAL)** CAL - computer aided learning **computer-aided manufacture (CAM)** CAM - produzione assistita dal calcolatore **computer centre, center** (US) centro di calcolo *nm*, centro informatico *nm* **computer file** file di computer *nm* **computer language** linguaggio di programmazione *nf* **laptop computer** laptop computer *nm* **computer literate** abile nell'uso dei computer *adj* **mainframe computer** mainframe *nm* **computer operator** operatore informatico *nm* **personal computer (PC)** PC *nm*, personal *nm*, personal computer *nm* **portable computer** computer portatile *nm* **computer program** programma *nm* **computer programmer** programmatore *nm* **computer terminal** terminale *nm*

**concern 1.** *n* **going concern** azienda in attività *nf*, azienda avviata *nf* **2.** *vb* (be of importance to) riguardare *vb*, concernere *vb*

**concur** *vb* concordare *vb*, condividere *vb*

**condition** *n* **living conditions** condizioni di vita *nfpl* **conditions of purchase** condizioni di acquisto *nfpl* **conditions of sale** condizioni di vendita *nfpl* **working conditions** condizioni di lavoro *nfpl*

**conference** *n* conferenza *nf* **conference proceedings** verbali della conferenza *nmpl* **to arrange a conference** organizzare una conferenza *vb* **conference venue** luogo del convegno *nm*

**confidence** *n* **in strictest confidence** in via strettamente confidenziale

**confidential** *adj* riservato *adj*

**confirm** *vb* **to confirm receipt of sth** accusare ricevuta di *vb*

**confirmation** *n* conferma *nf*

**conglomerate** *n* conglomerato di aziende *nm*, conglomerata *nf*

**congress** *n* congresso *nm*

**connect** *vb* **could you connect me to...** (telephone) potrebbe mettermi in comunicazione con

**connection** *n* **business connections** rapporti d'affari *nmpl*

**consent 1.** *n* consenso *nm*, benestare *nm*, omologazione *nf* **2.** *vb* acconsentire a *vb*

**consequence** *n* conseguenza *nf*

**consideration** *n* (for contract) considerazione *nf*

**consignee** *n* destinatario *nm*, consegnatario *nm*

**consigner/or** *n* mittente *nmf*

**consignment** *n* spedizione *nf*, partita *nf*

**consolidate** *vb* consolidare *vb*

**consolidated** *adj* **consolidated figures** cifre consolidate *nfpl*

**consortium** *n* consorzio *nm*

**construction** *n* **construction industry** industria edile *nf*

**consul** *n* console *nm*

**consulate** *n* consolato *nm*

**consult** *vb* consultare *vb* **to consult with sb** consultare con qualcuno *vb*

**consultancy, consulting** (US) *n* **consultancy firm** consulenza *nf* **consultancy fees** diritti di consulenza *nmpl* **consultancy work** attività di consulenza *nf*

**consultant** *n* consulente *nm*

**consumer 1.** *adj* **consumer credit** credito al consumo *nm* **consumer demand** domanda dei consumatori *nf* **consumer habits** abitudini del consumatore *nfpl* **consumer research** ricerca sui consumatori *nf* **consumer satisfaction** soddisfazione dei consumatori *nf* **consumer survey** indagine sui consumatori *nf* **consumer trends** trend dei consumatori *nmpl* **2.** *n* consumatore *nm*

**consumerism** *n* consumerismo *nm*

**contact 1.** *n* **business contacts** contatti di affari *nmpl* **to get in contact with sb** mettersi in contatto con *vb* **2.** *vb* contattare *vb*

**container** *n* contenitore *nm*, container *nm* **container depot** deposito per container *nm* **container ship** nave portacontainer *nf* **container terminal** terminal container *nm*

**contract 1.** *adj* **contract labour** manodopera temporanea *nf*, manodopera contrattuale *nf* **contract**

**work** lavoro in appalto *nm* **2.** *n* contratto *nm* **breach of contract** inadempimento di contratto *nm* **draft contract** contratto preliminare *nm* **law of contract** diritto contrattuale *nm* **the terms of the contract** clausole del contratto *nfpl*, condizioni del contratto *nfpl* **the signatories to the contract** i firmatari del contratto *nmpl* **to cancel a contract** rescindere un contratto *vb* **to draw up a contract** redigere un contratto *vb* **to sign a contract** firmare un contratto *vb* **to tender for a contract** concorrere ad un appalto *vb*, fare un'offerta per un appalto *vb* **under the terms of the contract** secondo le clausole del contratto

**contracting** *adj* **the contracting parties** le parti contraenti *nfpl*, le parti in causa *nfpl*

**contractor** *n* appaltatore *nm* **building contractor** appaltatore edile *nm* **haulage contractor** vettore a contratto *nm*

**contractual** *adj* **contractual obligations** obbligazioni contrattuali *nfpl*

**contravene** *vb* contravvenire a *vb*, violare *vb*, trasgredire *vb*

**contravention** *n* contravvenzione *nf*, infrazione *nf*

**contribute** *vb* contribuire *vb*

**contribution** *n* **social security contributions** contributi previdenziali *nmpl*

**control** *n* **financial control** controllo finanziario *nm* **production control** controllo della produzione *nm* **quality control** controllo della qualità *nm* **stock control** controllo del livello delle scorte *nm*

**convene** *vb* **to convene a meeting** convocare un'assemblea *vb*

**convenience** *n* **at your earliest convenience** al più presto possibile

**convenient** *adj* conveniente *adj*, a portata di mano

**convertible** *adj* **convertible currency** valuta convertibile *nf*

**copier** *n* (photocopier) fotocopiatrice *nf*

**copy 1.** *n* copia *nf* **2.** *vb* (photocopy) fotocopiare *vb*

**copyright** *n* diritto di autore *nm*, copyright *nm* **copyright law** legge sui diritti d'autore *nf*

**corporate** *adj* sociale *adj*, societario *adj*, aziendale *adj* **corporate image** immagine aziendale *nf* **corporate investment** investimento aziendale *nm*

**corporation** *n* persona giuridica *nf*, società legalmente costituita (US) *nf* **corporation tax** imposta sulle società *nf*

**correspondence** *n* corrispondenza *nf*

**corruption** *n* corruzione *nf*

**cosignatory** *n* cofirmatario *nm*

**cost 1.** *n* costo *nm* **cost breakdown** ripartizione dei costi *nf* **cost centre** centro di costi *nm* **cost-cutting** riduzione dei costi *nf* **cost of living** carovita *nm* **operating cost** costi di esercizio *nmpl*, spese di gestione *nfpl* **cost price** prezzo di costo *nm* **running cost** costi correnti *nmpl* **2.** *vb* **to cost a job** stabilire i costi di commessa *vb*

**counterfeit 1.** *n* falsificazione *nf*, contraffazione *nf* **2.** *vb* falsificare *vb*, contraffare *vb*

**counterfoil** *n* matrice *nf*, madre *nf*

**countersign** *vb* controfirmare *vb*

**country** *n* **developing country** nazione in via di sviluppo *nf* **third-world country** paese del terzo mondo *nm*

**coupon** *n* buono *nm*, tagliando *nm*, coupon *nm*

**courier 1.** *n* corriere *nm*, accompagnatore turistico *nm* **by courier service** tramite servizio di corrieri **2.** *vb* spedire con corriere *vb*

**court** *n* **Court of Appeal, Court of Appeals** (US) Corte d'Appello *nf* **criminal court** tribunale penale *nm* **in court** in tribunale

**covenant** *n* convenzione *nf*, patto *nm*

**covenantee** *n* creditore *nm*

**covenantor** *n* debitore *nm*

**cover** *n* **insurance cover** copertura assicurativa *nf* **cover note** nota di copertura *nf*

**credit 1.** *adj* **credit agency** agenzia di informazioni commerciali *nf* **credit card** carta di credito *nf* **credit company** società creditrice *nf* **credit control** controllo del credito *nm* **credit enquiry** richiesta di informazioni commerciali *nf* **credit note** nota di accredito *nf* **credit rating** posizione finanziaria *nf*, posizione creditizia *nf* **credit terms** condizioni di credito *nfpl* **2.** *n* credito *nm*, accredito *nm*, avere *nm* **to buy sth on credit** comprare a credito *vb* **in credit** in credito **letter of credit** lettera di credito *nf* **long credit** credito a lunga scadenza *nm* **3.** *vb* **to credit sth to an account** accreditare un conto di una somma *vb*

**creditor** *n* creditore *nm*

**creditworthiness** *n* capacità di credito *nf*

**creditworthy** *adj* meritevole di credito *adj*

**crossed** *adj* **crossed cheque** assegno sbarrato *nm*

**currency** *n* valuta *nf*, divisa *nf* **convertible currency** valuta convertibile *nf* **foreign currency** valuta estera *nf*, divisa estera *nf* **hard currency** valuta forte *nf*, moneta forte *nf* **legal currency** valuta legale *nf* **paper currency** cartamoneta *nf* **soft currency** moneta debole *nf*, valuta debole *nf* **currency transfer** trasferimento di valuta *nf*

**current** *adj* **current account** conto corrente *nm*

**curriculum vitae (CV), résumé** (US) *n* curriculum vitae *nm*, curricolo *nm*

**customer** *n* cliente *nm* **customer loyalty** fedeltà del consumatore *nf* **regular customer** cliente abituale *nm*, cliente regolare *nm* **customer relations** rapporti con la clientela *nmpl*

**customs** *npl* dogana *nf*, ufficio doganale *nm* **customs charges** spese doganali *nfpl* **customs clearance** sdoganamento *nm* **customs declaration** dichiarazione doganale *nf* **customs office** dogana *nf* **customs officer** funzionario di dogana *nm* **customs regulations** regolamenti doganali *nmpl* **to clear sth through customs** sdoganare *vb* **customs union** unione doganale *nf* **customs warehouse** magazzino doganale *nm*, deposito franco *nm*

**cut** **1.** *n* **tax cut** sgravio fiscale *nm* **2.** *vb* (reduce) diminuire *vb*, ridurre *vb*, calare *vb*

**damage** **1.** *n* danno *nm*, avaria *nf* **to cause extensive damage** causare danni ingenti *vb* **to claim damages** (legal) richiedere il risarcimento dei danni *vb* **damage to goods in transit** danni alle merci in transito *nmpl* **damage to property** danni a proprietà *nm pl* **2.** *vb* danneggiare *vb*

**data** *npl* dati *nmpl* **data bank** banca dati *nf* **data capture** raccolta dei dati *nf*, reperimento dei dati *nm* **data processing** elaborazione dati *nf*

**database** database *nf*, base dati *nf*

**date** *n* **delivery date** data di consegna *nf* **out of date** (product) scaduto *adj*, (fashion) fuori moda *adv* **up to date** aggiornato *adj*, d'attualità

**deal** *n* trattativa *nf*, operazione commerciale *nf* **it's a deal!** affare fatto!

**dealer** *n* operatore commerciale *nm*, venditore *nm* **foreign exchange dealer** cambiavalute *nm*, cambiavalute *nf*

**dealing, trading** (US) *n* contrattazione *nf* **foreign exchange dealings** operazioni in valuta estera *nfpl* **insider dealing** insider dealing *nm*, insider trading *nm*

**debenture** *n* obbligazione *nf* **debenture bond** obbligazione non garantita *nf* **debenture capital, debenture stock** (US) capitale obbligazionario *nm* **debenture loan** prestito obbligazionario *nm*

**debit** **1.** *n* addebito *nm* **debit balance** saldo a debito *nm*, saldo passivo *nm* **2.** *vb* (account) addebitare *vb*

**debiting** *n* **direct debiting** addebitamento diretto *nm*

**debt** *n* debito *nm* **corporate debt** debito aziendale *nm* **to get into debt** indebitarsi *vb* **to pay off a debt** saldare un debito *vb* **to reschedule a debt** rinegoziare un debito *vb* **debt service** servizio del debito pubblico *nm*, servizio di un prestito *nm*

**debtor** *n* debitore *nm*

**decline** *n* declino *nm*

**decrease** **1.** *n* calo *nm*, flessione *nf* **2.** *vb* decrescere *vb*

**deduct** *vb* dedurre *vb*, scontare *vb*

**deductible** *adj* detraibile *adj*

**deduction** *n* detrazione *nf*, trattenuta *nf*

**deed** *n* (law) atto scritto *nm* **deed of sale** atto di compravendita *nm* **deed of transfer** atto di cessione *nm*

**default** **1.** *n* inadempienza *nf* **2.** *vb* essere inadempiente *vb*

**defect** *n* difetto *nm*, vizio *nm*

**defective** *adj* difettoso *adj*, imperfetto *adj*

**defer** *vb* (postpone) differire *vb*, posticipare *vb*

**deferment** *n* risconto *nm*, proroga *nf*

**deferred** *adj* (tax) differito *adj*

**deficiency** *n* mancanza *nf*

**deficient** *adj* manchevole *adj*, difettoso *adj*

**deficit** *n* deficit *nm*, disavanzo *nm* **deficit financing** finanziamento in disavanzo *nm*

**deflation** *n* deflazione *nf*

**deflationary** *adj* deflazionistico *adj*, deflatorio *adj*

**defraud** *vb* defraudare *vb*, truffare *vb*

**del credere** *adj* **del credere agent** agente del credere *nm*

**delay** **1.** *n* ritardo *nm*, mora *nf* **without delay** senza indugio *adv* **2.** *vb* ritardare *vb*, prorogare *vb*

**delegate** **1.** *n* delegato *nm*, delegata *nf* **2.** *vb* delegare *vb*

**delegation** *n* delega *nf*

**deliver** *vb* (goods) consegnare *vb*
**delivery** 1. *adj* **delivery date** data di consegna *nf* **delivery time** tempo di consegna *nm* 2. *n* consegna *nf* **cash on delivery** pagamento contrassegno *nm* **free delivery** consegna franco spese *nf*, consegna gratuita *nf* **general delivery (US)** fermo posta *nm* **recorded delivery** consegna registrata con ricevuta di ritorno *nf*
**demand** 1. *n* domanda *nf* **supply and demand** domanda e offerta *nf* 2. *vb* domandare *vb*, esigere *vb*
**demography** *n* demografia *nf*
**demote** *vb* (employee) degradare *vb*
**denationalize** *vb* privatizzare *vb*
**department** *n* dipartimento *nm*, reparto *nm* **government department** ministero *nm* **personnel department** ufficio del personale *nm* **department store** grande magazzino *nm*
**depletion** *n* esaurimento *nm*, dissipazione *nf*
**deposit** *n* deposito *nm*, versamento *nm* depositare *vb*, versare *vb* **deposit account** deposito a risparmio *nm*
**depository** *n* depositario *nm*
**depreciate** *vb* deprezzare *vb*, svalutare *vb*
**depreciation** *n* deprezzamento *nm*, ammortamento *nm*
**depression** *n* depressione *nf*
**deputy** 1. *adj* vice *adj*, sostituto *adj* **deputy director** vicedirettore *nm* 2. *n* facente funzione *adj*, sostituto *nm*
**design** 1. *n* design *nm*, progetto *nm* **a machine of good/bad design** una macchina progettata bene/male *nf* 2. *vb* progettare *vb*, disegnare *vb*
**designer** *n* designer *nmf*, progettista *nmf*
**devaluation** *n* svalutazione *nf*
**developer** *n* developer *nm*, sviluppatore *nm*
**digital** *adj* digitale *adj*
**diminishing** *adj* **diminishing returns** rendimenti decrescenti *nmpl*
**director** *n* amministratore *nm*, direttore *nm* **board of directors** consiglio di amministrazione *nm* **managing director** amministratore delegato *nm*
**disburse** *vb* sborsare *vb*, erogare *vb*
**discount** *n* sconto *nm* **at a discount** sotto prezzo *adv* **discount rate** tasso di sconto *nm*
**discounted** *adj* **discounted cash flow (DCF)** flusso di cassa attualizzato *nm*, cash flow attualizzato *nm*
**disk** *n* disco *nm* **disk drive** disk drive *nm* **floppy disk** floppy disk *nm* **hard disk** hard disk *nm* **magnetic disk** disco magnetico *nm*
**dismiss** *vb* (employee) licenziare *vb*
**dispatch** 1. *n* **date of dispatch** data di spedizione *nf* 2. *vb* (goods) spedire *vb*
**dispatcher** *n* addetto all'ufficio spedizioni *nm*
**display** 1. *n* (of goods) esposizione *nf* 2. *vb* esporre *vb*, esibire *vb*
**disposable** *adj* (not for reuse) disponibile *adj* **disposable income** reddito disponibile *nm*
**dispute** *n* vertenza *nf* **industrial dispute** conflitto industriale *nm*
**distribution** *n* distribuzione *nf*
**distributor** *n* distributore *nm*, società distributrice *nf*
**diversification** *n* diversificazione *nf*
**diversify** *vb* diversificare *vb*
**dividend** *n* dividendo *nm*
**division** *n* (of company) divisione *nf* **division of labour** divisione del lavoro *nf*
**dock** 1. *n* (for berthing) bacino *nm*, dock *nm* 2. *vb* (ship) mettere in bacino *vb* (ship) attraccare *vb*, entrare in bacino *vb*
**dockyard** *n* cantiere navale *nm*, darsena *nf*
**document** *n* documento *nm* **document retrieval** recupero di un documento *nm*
**domestic** *adj* **domestic policy** politica nazionale *nf*
**door** *n* **door-to-door selling** vendita porta a porta *nf*
**double** *adj* **double-entry** (bookkeeping) partita doppia *nf*
**Dow-Jones average (US)** *n* indici Dow-Jones (US) *nmpl*
**down** *adj* **down payment** acconto *nm*
**downturn** *n* (economic) contrazione *nf*
**downward** 1. *adj* discendente *adj* 2. *adv* al ribasso *adv*
**draft** *n* (financial) tratta *nf*
**draw** *vb* (cheque) emettere un assegno *vb*
**dry** *adj* **dry goods** merci secche *nfpl*
**dumping** *n* esportazione sottocosto *nf*, dumping *nm*
**durable** *adj* **durable goods** beni non deperibili *nmpl*
**duty** *n* (customs) dazio *nm* **duty-free** (goods) esente da dazio *adj*
**dynamic** *adj* dinamico *adj*
**dynamics** *npl* dinamica *nf*
**early** *adj* **early retirement** pensionamento anticipato *nm*
**earn** *vb* guadagnare *vb* **earned income**

reddito di lavoro *nm*, reddito guadagnato *nm* **earned surplus** utili non distribuiti *nmpl*, capitale di risparmio *nm*

**earnest** *adj* **earnest money** caparra *nf*, anticipo *nm*

**earning 1.** *adj* **earning capacity** capacità di reddito *nf* **earning power** capacità di reddito *nf* **2.** *n* **earnings** utili *nmpl*, entrate *nfpl*, reddito *nm* **earnings drift** slittamento salariale *nm* **loss of earnings** perdita di reddito *nf* **earnings-related pension** pensione calcolata in funzione del reddito *nf* **earnings yield** rendimento complessivo *nm*

**easy** *adj* **easy-money policy** politica del denaro facile *nf*

**EC (European Community)** *abbr* CE (Comunità Europea) *abbr*

**econometrics** *n* econometria *nf*

**economic** *adj* **economic adviser** consigliere economico *nm* **economic analysis** analisi economica *nf* **economic crisis** crisi economica *nf* **economic cycle** ciclo economico *nm* **economic decline** declino economico *nm* **economic development** sviluppo economico *nm* **Economic and Monetary Union** Unione monetaria ed economica *nf* **economic expansion** espansione economica *nf*, sviluppo economico *nm* **economic forecast** previsioni economiche *nfpl* **economic geography** geografia economica *nf* **economic growth** crescita economica *nf* **economic infrastructure** infrastruttura economica *nf* **economic integration** integrazione economica *nf* **economic objective** obiettivo economico *nm* **economic performance** prestazione economica *nf*, performance economica *nf* **economic planning** pianificazione economica *nf* **economic policy** politica economica *nf* **economic sanction** sanzione economica *nf* **economic slowdown** rallentamento economico *nm* **economic strategy** strategia economica *nf* **economic superpower** superpotenza economica *nf* **economic survey** relazione sullo stato dell'economia *nf* **economic trend** trend dell'economia *nm* **economic union** unione economica *nf*

**economical** *adj* economico *adj*

**economics** economia *nf*

**economist** *n* economista *nmf*

**economy** *n* economia *nf* **advanced economy** economia avanzata *nf*, economia progredita *nf* **developing economy** economia in via di sviluppo *nf* **free market economy** economia di mercato libero *nf* **global economy** economia globale *nf* **economies of scale** economie di scala *nfpl* **national economy** economia nazionale *nf* **planned economy** economia pianificata *nf* **underdeveloped economy** economia sottosviluppata *nf*

**ECSC (European Coal and Steel Community)** *abbr* CECA (Comunità europea del carbone e dell'acciaio) *abbr*

**ECU (European Currency Unit)** *abbr* ECU (Unità monetaria europea) *abbr*

**edge** *n* **competitive edge** vantaggio competitivo *nm*

**effect** *n* effetto *nm*, vigore *nm* **financial effects** ripercussioni finanziarie *nfpl*

**efficiency** *n* efficienza *nf*

**efficient** *adj* efficiente *adj*

**EFT (electronic funds transfer)** *abbr* EFTS (sistema elettronico di trasferimento fondi) *abbr*

**EFTA (European Free Trade Association)** *abbr* EFTA (Associazione europea di libero scambio) *abbr*

**elasticity** *n* elasticità *nf* **income elasticity** elasticità del reddito *nf* **elasticity of demand** elasticità della domanda *nf* **elasticity of production** elasticità della produzione *nf*

**election** *n* elezione *nf* **general election** elezioni politiche *nfpl* **local election** elezioni amministrative *nfpl*

**electronic** *adj* elettronico *adj* **electronic banking** operazioni bancarie elettroniche *nfpl* **electronic data processing** elaborazione dati elettronica (EDP) *nf* **electronic mail** posta elettronica *nf*

**elimination** *n* **elimination of tariffs** abolizione delle tariffe *nfpl*

**email** *n* posta elettronica *nf*

**embargo** *n* embargo *nm* **to impose an embargo** mettere un embargo *vb* **to lift an embargo** togliere un embargo *vb* **trade embargo** embargo *nm*

**embassy** *n* ambasciata *nf*

**embezzle** *vb* appropriarsi indebitamente di *vb*

**embezzlement** *n* peculato *nm*, appropriazione indebita *nf*

**embezzler** *n* malversatore *nm*

**emergency** *n* emergenza *nf* **emergency fund** fondo di emergenza *nf*

**emigration** *n* emigrazione *nf*

**employ** *vb* impiegare *vb*, occupare *vb*

**employee** *n* dipendente *nm* **employee recruitment** reclutamento del personale *nm* **employee training** addestramento del personale *nm*
**employer** *n* datore di lavoro *nm*, principale *nm* **employer's federation** unione industriale *nf*, associazione dei datori di lavoro *nf* **employers' liability insurance** assicurazione contro la responsabilità civile del datore di lavoro *nf*
**employment** *n* impiego *nm*, occupazione *nf* **employment agency** agenzia di collocamento *nf* **employment contract** contratto di lavoro *nm* **full employment** piena occupazione *nf* **employment law** diritto sull'occupazione *nm*
**encashment** *n* incasso *nm*
**enclose** *vb* allegare *vb*, accludere *vb*
**enclosure** *n* allegato *nm*
**end** *n* **end consumer** consumatore finale *nm* **end user** utente finale *nm*, utente finale *nf*
**endorse** *vb* (cheque) girare (un assegno) *vb*
**endorsement** *n* girata *nf*
**endowment** *n* dotazione *nf* **endowment insurance** assicurazione mista *nf*, assicurazione per il caso di sopravvivenza *nf* **endowment policy** polizza mista *nf*
**enforce** *vb* (policy) rendere esecutivo *vb*, applicare *vb*
**enforcement** *n* esecuzione *nf*, applicazione *nf*
**engagement** *n* (meeting) impegno *nm*
**engineering** *n* ingegneria *nf* **civil engineering** ingegneria civile *nf* **electrical engineering** ingegneria elettrica *nf* **mechanical engineering** ingegneria meccanica *nf* **precision engineering** ingegneria di precisione *nf*
**enhance** *vb* (value) aumentare *vb*, accrescere *vb*
**enlarge** *vb* ampliare *vb*
**enquire** *vb* informarsi *vb*
**enquiry** *n* richiesta d'informazioni *nf*
**enterprise** *n* (project) impresa *nf*, iniziativa *nf* **private enterprise** impresa privata *nf*, iniziativa privata *nf*
**entertain** *vb* **to entertain a client** ospitare un cliente *vb*
**entrepôt** *n* punto franco *nm*, deposito franco *nm*
**entrepreneur** *n* imprenditore *nm*
**entrepreneurial** *adj* imprenditoriale *adj*
**entry** *n* **entry for free goods** bolla di merce esente *nf* **entry into force** entrata in vigore *nf* **port of entry** porto di arrivo *nm* **entry visa** visto d'ingresso *nm*
**equalization** *n* **equalization of burdens** perequazione dei carichi tributari *nf*
**equalize** *vb* livellare *vb*, perequare *vb*
**equilibrium** *n* equilibrio *nm*
**equip** *vb* dotare *vb*, equipaggiare *vb*
**equipment** *n* attrezzatura *nf*, impianto *nm* **equipment leasing** leasing di impianti *nm*
**equity** *n* capitale netto *nm*, equità *nf* **equity capital** capitale netto *nm* **equity financing** equity financing *nm*, vendita di capitale azionario *nf* **equity interests** partecipazioni azionarie *nfpl* **equity share** azione ordinaria *nf* **equity trading** operare con capitale di prestito *nm* **equity transaction** operazione di capitale *nf*
**ergonomics** *n* ergonomia *nf*
**escalate** *vb* aggravarsi *vb*, intensificarsi *vb*, aumentare *vb*, salire *vb*
**escalation** *n* (prices) aumento *nm*, escalation *nf*
**escalator** *n* scala mobile *nf*
**escudo** *n* escudo *nm*
**establish** *vb* (company) fondare *vb*, (decide) decidere *vb*
**establishment** *n* sistema *nm*, costituzione *nf*, fondazione *nf*
**estate** *n* **estate agency, real estate agency** (US) agenzia immobiliare *nf* **estate agent, real estate agent** (US) agente immobiliare *nm*
**estimate** **1.** *n* preventivo *nm*, stima *nf* **estimate of costs** stima dei costi *nf* **2.** *vb* preventivare *vb*, stimare *vb*
**eurobond** *n* euro-obbligazione *nf*
**eurocapital** *n* eurocapitale *nm*
**eurocheque** *n* eurocheque *nm*
**eurocracy** *n* eurocrazia *nf*
**eurocrat** *n* eurocrate *nm*
**eurocredit** *n* eurocredito *nm*
**eurocurrency** *n* eurovaluta *nf*, euromoneta *nf*, eurodivisa *nf* **eurocurrency market** mercato delle eurovalute *nm*
**eurodollar** *n* eurodollaro *nm*
**eurofunds** *npl* eurofondi *nmpl*
**euromarket** *n* euromercato *nm*
**euromerger** *n* eurofusione *nf*
**euromoney** *n* euromoneta *nf*, eurovaluta *nf*
**European** *adj* europeo *adj* **Council of Europe** Consiglío europeo **European Advisory Committee** European Advisory Committee **European Commission** Commissione delle comunità europee

**European Community (EC)** Comunità Europea (CE) **European Court of Justice (ECJ)** Corte di giustizia europea **European Development Fund (EDF)** Fondo europeo per lo sviluppo (FES) **European Investment Bank (EIB)** Banca europea degli investimenti (BEI) **European Monetary Agreement (EMA)** Accordo monetario europeo (AME) **European Monetary Cooperation Fund (EMCF)** Fondo europeo di cooperazione monetaria (FECOM) **European Monetary System (EMS)** Sistema monetario europeo (SME) **European Monetary Union (EMU)** Unità monetaria europea (UME) **European Parliament** parlamento europeo **European Recovery Plan** programma per la ripresa economica europea **European Regional Development Fund (ERDF)** Fondo europeo di sviluppo regionale **European Social Fund (ESF)** Fondo sociale europeo **European Unit of Account (EUA)** unità di conto europea (UCE)

**eurosceptic** *n* euroscettico *nm*

**evade** *vb* evadere *vb*, evitare *vb*, sottrarsi a *vb*

**evasion** *n* **tax evasion** evasione fiscale *nf*

**eviction** *n* sfratto *nm*

**ex** *prep* **ex factory/works** franco fabbrica **ex gratia payment** pagamento a titolo transativo *nm* **ex interest** ex interessi, secco **ex quay** franco banchina **ex repayment** senza rimborso *adv* **ex ship** franco bordo nave a destino, f.o.b. destino **ex stock** da magazzino **ex store/warehouse** franco deposito **ex wharf** franco banchina

**examination** *n* esame *nm*

**examine** *vb* esaminare *vb*, verificare *vb*

**exceed** *vb* eccedere *vb*

**excess** *adj* **excess capacity** eccesso di capacità produttiva *nm*, sovracapitalizzazione *nf* **excess demand inflation** inflazione da eccesso di domanda *nf* **excess profit(s) tax** imposta sui sopraprofitti *nf* **excess reserves** eccesso di riserve bancarie *nm*

**exchange** 1. *adj* **exchange broker** operatore di cambio *nm* **exchange cheque** assegno incrociato *nm*, assegno di comodo *nm* **exchange clearing agreement** accordo di compensazione di cambio *nm* **exchange control** controllo dei cambi *nm* **exchange market** mercato valutario *nm* **exchange rate** cambio *nm*, corso del cambio *nm*, tasso di cambio *nm* **exchange rate mechanism (ERM)** Meccanismo di regolazione dei cambi **exchange restrictions** restrizioni valutarie *nfpl* **exchange risk** rischio di cambio *nm* 2. *n* **foreign exchange** cambio estero *nm*, divisa estera *nf* **Stock Exchange** borsa valori *nf*

**excise** *adj* **excise duty** imposta sui consumi *nf* **the Board of Customs and Excise** organo statale britannico che gestisce il servizio doganale *nm*

**exclude** *vb* escludere *vb*

**exclusion** *n* **exclusion clause** clausola d'esclusione *nf* **exclusion zone** zona di esclusione *nf*

**executive** 1. *adj* **executive committee** comitato esecutivo *nm* **executive compensation** retribuzione dei dirigenti *nf* **executive duties** mansioni dirigenziali *nfpl* **executive hierarchy** gerarchia direttiva *nf* **executive personnel** personale direttivo *nm* 2. *n* funzionario *nm*, dirigente *nm*, esecutivo *nm*

**exempt** *adj* esente *adj* **tax-exempt** esente da imposte *adj*

**exemption** *n* esenzione *nf*, esonero *nm*

**exhaust** *vb* (reserves) esaurire *vb*

**exhibit** *vb* esporre *vb*, esibire *vb*

**exhibition** *n* mostra *nf*, esposizione *nf*

**exorbitant** *adj* eccessivo *adj*

**expand** *vb* espandere *vb*

**expansion** *n* espansione *nf* **expansion of capital** aumento del capitale *nm* **expansion of trade** moltiplicarsi degli scambi *nm*

**expectation** *n* aspettativa *nf* **consumer expectations** aspettative dei consumatori *nfpl*

**expedite** *vb* accelerare *vb*, sbrigare *vb*

**expenditure** *n* spesa *nf* **expenditure rate** tetto di spesa *nm* **state expenditure** spesa statale *nf* **expenditure taxes** imposte sulle spese *nfpl*

**expense** 1. *adj* **expense account** conto spese *nm* **expense control** controllo delle spese *nm* 2. *n* spesa *nf* **entertainment expenses** spese di rappresentanza *nfpl* **travelling expenses, travel expenses** (US) spese di trasferta *nfpl*

**experience** 1. *n* esperienza *nf* **experience curve** curva di esperienza *nf* 2. *vb* fare esperienza di *vb*, subire *vb*

**experienced** *adj* esperto *adj*, competente *adj*

**expert** 1. *adj* esperto *adj*, competente *adj* 2. *n* esperto *nm*, perito *nm*
**expertise** *n* competenza *nf*
**expiration** *n* (contract) scadenza *nf*
**expire** *vb* scadere *vb*
**expiry, expiration** (US) *n* scadenza *nf*, termine *nm* **expiry date** data di scadenza *nf*
**export** 1. *adj* d'esportazione *adj* **export bill of lading** polizza di carico per l'estero *nf* **export credit** credito all'esportazione *nm* **export credit insurance** assicurazione-credito nel commercio estero *nf* **export department** ufficio esportazioni *nm* **export-led growth** sviluppo alimentato dalle esportazioni *nm* **export licence** licenza di esportazione *nf* **export marketing** marketing delle esportazioni *nm* **export operations** operazioni d'esportazione *nfpl* **export strategy** strategia delle esportazioni *nf* **export subsidies** sovvenzioni alle esportazioni *nfpl* **export surplus** eccedenza delle esportazioni *nf* **export tax** dazio d'esportazione *nm* **export trade** commercio di esportazione *nm* 2. *n* esportazione *nf*, bene d'esportazione *nm* **export of capital** esportazione di capitale *nf* 3. *vb* esportare *vb*
**exporter** *n* esportatore *nm*
**express** *adj* **express agency** agenzia di spedizioni per espresso *nf* **express delivery** consegna per espresso *nf* **express service** servizio per espresso *nm*
**expropriate** *vb* espropriare *vb*
**expropriation** *n* esproprio *nm*
**extend** *vb* **to extend a contract** dilazionare *vb*, prorogare *vb* **to extend credit** estendere il credito *vb* **to extend the range** ampliare la gamma *vb*
**extension** *n* (of contract) ampliamento *nm*, proroga *nf*
**extent** *n* **extent of cover** ammontare della copertura *nm*
**external** *adj* esterno *adj* **external audit** revisione contabile esterna *nf*
**extortion** *n* estorsione *nf*
**extra** *adj* addizionale *adj*, supplementare *adj* **extra cost** costo aggiuntivo *nm* **extra profit** extraprofitto *nm*
**extraordinary** *adj* **extraordinary meeting** assemblea straordinaria *nf* **extraordinary value** valore straordinario *nm*
**facility** *n* impianto *nm*, installazione *nf*, struttura *nf* **facility planning** pianificazione delle strutture *nf*
**facsimile (fax)** *n* fax *nm*
**factor** 1. *adj* **factor income** reddito dei fattori *nm* **factor market** mercato dei fattori della produzione *nm* **factor price** prezzo del fattore della produzione *nm* 2. *n* (buyer of debts) factor *nm*, fattore *nm*, commissionario *nm* **limiting factor** fattore limitante *nm* **factor of production** fattore della produzione *nm* 3. *vb* (debts) cedere i debiti dell'impresa ad un factor *vb*
**factoring** *n* (of debts) factoring *nm*, trasferimento dei credito *nm*
**factory** *n* fabbrica *nf*, stabilimento *nm* **factory board** consiglio di fabbrica *nm* **factory costs** costi di fabbricazione *nmpl* **factory inspector** ispettore di fabbrica *nm* **factory ledger** mastro di contabilità di fabbrica *nm* **factory overheads** spese generali di fabbricazione *nfpl* **factory price** prezzo di fabbrica *nm*
**fail** *vb* (attempts, negotiations) non riuscire *vb*
**failure** *n* fallimento *nm*, stato d'insolvenza *nm*
**fair** *adj* equo *adj*, leale *adj* **fair competition** concorrenza leale *nf* **fair market value** valore equo di mercato *nm* **fair rate of return** tasso di remunerazione equo *nm* **fair-trade agreement** accordo di prezzo imposto *nm*, accordo di mantenimento dei prezzi *nm* **fair-trade policy** politica di reciprocità *nf* **fair-trade practice** correttezza commerciale *nf* **fair trading** correttezza commerciale *nf* **fair wage** salario equo *nm*
**fall due** *vb* scadere *vb*
**falling** *adj* **falling prices** prezzi al ribasso *nmpl* **falling rate of profit** tasso decrescente del profitto *nm*
**false** *adj* **false representation** frode *nf*
**falsification** *n* falsificazione *nf* **falsification of accounts** falso contabile *nm*
**family** *n* **family allowance** assegno familiare *nm* **family branding** family branding *nm* **family corporation** società a carattere familiare *nf* **family income** reddito familiare *nm* **family industry** industria domestica *nf*
**farm out** *vb* dare in appalto *vb*
**farming** *n* agricoltura *nf* **farming of taxes** concessione del diritto di esazione delle imposte *nf* **farming subsidies** sussidi agricoli *nmpl*
**FAS (free alongside ship)** *abbr* FAS (franco lungo bordo) *abbr*

**fast** *adj* **fast-selling goods** articoli di rapida vendita *nmpl* **fast track** a mobilità verso l'alto

**fault** *n* guasto *nm*, colpa *nf* **minor fault** guasto *nm*, errore di lieve entità *nm* **serious fault** guasto *nm*, errore grave *nm* **to find fault with** lagnarsi di *vb*, criticare *vb*

**faulty** *adj* **faulty goods** merci difettose *nfpl* **faulty workmanship** lavorazione difettosa *nf*

**favour** *n* favore *nm* **to do sb a favour** fare un favore a qualcuno *vb*

**favourable** *adj* **favourable balance of payments** saldo attivo della bilancia dei pagamenti *nm* **favourable balance of trade** bilancia commerciale attiva *nf* **favourable exchange** cambio favorevole *nm* **favourable price** prezzo vantaggioso *nm* **favourable terms** condizioni vantaggiose *nfpl*

**fax** **1.** *n* fax *nm* **2.** *vb* spedire per fax *vb*

**feasibility** *n* fattibilità *nf*, praticabilità *nf* **feasibility study** studio della praticabilità *nm*

**feasible** *adj* fattibile *adj*

**federal** *adj* federale *adj*

**federation** *n* federazione *nf*

**fee** *n* onorario *nm*, diritto *nm* **to charge a fee** addebitare un onorario/ una tassa/ un compenso *vb* **to pay a fee** pagare un onorario *vb*

**feedback** *n* retroazione *nf*, feedback *nm*, informazioni di ritorno *nfpl* **to give feedback** dare informazioni *vb*, dare feedback *vb*

**fiat** *n* **fiat money** moneta a corso forzoso *nf*

**fictitious** *adj* **fictitious assets** attività fittizie *nfpl* **fictitious purchase** acquisto fittizio *nm* **fictitious sale** vendita fittizia *nf*

**fidelity** *n* **fidelity bond** contratto di assicurazione di fedeltà *nm* **fidelity insurance** assicurazione di fedeltà *nf*, assicurazione contro l'infedeltà *nf*

**fiduciary** *adj* **fiduciary bond** fideiussione *nf* **fiduciary issue** emissione fiduciaria *nf*

**field** *n* **field investigation** indagine esterna *nf* **field manager** direttore di zona *nm* **field personnel** personale esterno *nm* **field research** ricerca esterna *nf* **field test** prova preliminare *nf* **field work** lavoro esterno *nm*

**FIFO (first in first out)** *abbr* FIFO (First In First Out) *abbr*

**file** **1.** *n* fascicolo *nm*, archivio *nm*, file *nm* **2.** *vb* archiviare *vb*

**filing** *n* **filing cabinet** schedario *nm*, casellario *nm* **filing system** sistema di archiviazione *nm*

**final** *adj* **final accounts** rendiconti finali *nmpl* **final demand** richiesta finale *nf*, domanda finale *nf* **final entry** trasferimento di una scrittura contabile dal libro di prima nota al mastro *nm* **final invoice** fattura definitiva *nf* **final offer** offerta definitiva *nf* **final products** prodotti finiti *nmpl* **final settlement** saldo finale *nm* **final utility** utilità finale *nf*

**finance** **1.** *adj* **finance bill** cambiale finanziaria *nf*, cambiale di credito *nf*, proposta di legge finanziaria *nf* **finance company** società finanziaria *nf* **Finance Act** legge finanziaria *nf* **2.** *n* finanza *nf* **3.** *vb* finanziare *vb*

**financial** *adj* finanziario *adj* **financial accounting** contabilità finanziaria *nf* **financial assets** attivi finanziari *nmpl* **financial balance** bilancio finanziario *nm* **financial company** società finanziaria *nf* **financial consultancy** consulenza finanziaria *nf* **financial consultant** consulente finanziario *nm* **financial control** controllo finanziario *nm* **financial crisis** crisi finanziaria *nf* **financial difficulty** difficoltà finanziaria *nf* **financial exposure** rischio finanziario *nm* **financial incentive** incentivo finanziario *nm* **financial institution** istituzione finanziaria *nf* **financial investment** investimento finanziario *nm*, investimento mobiliare *nm* **financial loan** credito finanziario *nm* **financial management** gestione finanziaria *nf* **financial market** mercato dei capitali *nm* **financial measures** misure finanziarie *nfpl* **financial operation** operazione finanziaria *nf* **financial planning** pianificazione finanziaria *nf* **financial policy** politica finanziaria *nf* **financial report** rapporto finanziario *nm* **financial resources** mezzi finanziari *nmpl* **financial risk** rischio finanziario *nm* **financial situation** situazione finanziaria *nf* **financial stability** stabilità finanziaria *nf* **financial statement** rendiconto finanziario *nm* **financial strategy** strategia finanziaria *nf* **financial structure** struttura finanziaria *nf* **financial year** esercizio finanziario *nm*, anno contabile *nm*

**financier** *n* finanziere *nm*, finanziatore *nm*

**financing** *n* finanziamento *nm* **financing surplus** eccedenza di finanziamento *nf*

**fine** *adj* **fine rate of interest** tasso primario d'interesse *nm*

**finished** *adj* **finished goods** prodotti finiti *nmpl* **finished stock** prodotti finiti *nmpl* **finished turnover** rotazione dei prodotti finiti *nf*

**fire*** *vb* licenziare *vb*

**firm** *adj* **firm offer** offerta ferma *nf* **firm price** prezzo fermo *nm*

**first** *adj* **first bill of exchange** prima di cambio *nf*, prima copia di cambiale *nf* **first class** prima classe *nf*, prim'ordine *nm* **first-class paper** carta di prim'ordine *nf* **first customer** primo cliente *nm* **first-hand** di prima mano **first mortgage** ipoteca di primo grado *nf*, prima ipoteca *nf* **first-rate** di prim'ordine

**fiscal** *adj* **fiscal agent** agente finanziario *nm* **fiscal balance** bilancio fiscale *nm*, bilancio finanziario *nm* **fiscal charges** oneri fiscali *nmpl* **fiscal measures** misure fiscali *nfpl* **fiscal policy** politica fiscale *nf* **fiscal receipt** ricevuta fiscale *nf* **fiscal year** anno finanziario *nm* **fiscal year end (fye)** fine anno finanziario *nf* **fiscal zoning** lottizzazione fiscale *nf*, suddivisione in zone fiscali *nf*

**fix** *vb* **fixed assets** attività fisse *nfpl*, immobilizzazioni *nfpl* **fixed asset turnover** indice di rotazione delle attività fisse *nm* **fixed budget** budget rigido *nm*, budget fisso *nm* **fixed charges** oneri fissi *nmpl* **fixed costs** costi fissi *nmpl* **fixed credit** credito fisso *nm* **fixed income** reddito fisso *nm* **fixed interest** interesse fisso *nm* **fixed liabilities** passività fisse *nfpl* **fixed price** prezzo fisso *nm* **to fix the price** fissare il prezzo *vb*

**fixture** *n* **fixtures and fittings** impianti fissi *nmpl*, immobili e impianti *nmpl*

**flat** *adj* **flat bond** obbligazione senza interessi *nf* **flat market** mercato fiacco *nm* **flat rate** rendimento uniforme *nm*, tariffa forfettaria *nf*, aliquota fissa *nf* **flat-rate income tax** imposta sul reddito a aliquota fissa *nf* **flat-rate tariff** tariffa ad aliquota unica *nf*

**flexibility** *n* flessibilità *nf*

**flexible** *adj* **flexible budget** budget flessibile *nm* **flexible exchange rate** tasso di cambio flessibile *nm* **flexible price** prezzo flessibile *nm*

**flexitime, flextime** (US) *n* flexitime *nm*, orario flessibile *nm*

**flight** *n* (aviation) volo *nm* **flight of capital** fuga di capitali *nf* **to book a flight** prenotare un biglietto aereo *vb*

**float** *vb* (currency) fluttuare *vb*, (company) lanciare *vb*

**floating** *adj* **floating assets** attività correnti *nfpl* **floating exchange rate** tasso di cambio fluttuante *nm* **floating rate interest** tasso di interesse fluttuante *nm*

**floor** *n* **floor broker** intermediario di borsa *nm* **shopfloor** base operaia *nf*

**flotation** *n* lancio *nm*

**flow** *n* **cash flow** cash flow *nm*, flusso di cassa *nm* **flow chart** flussoschema *nm*, flussogramma *nm* **flow line production** produzione a flusso continuo *nf* **flow of income** flusso del reddito *nm* **flow production** produzione a flusso continuo *nf*

**fluctuate** *vb* fluttuare *vb*, oscillare *vb*

**fluctuation** *n* fluttuazione *nf* **fluctuation in sales** fluttuazione delle vendite *nf*

**fluid** *adj* fluido *adj* **fluid market** mercato instabile *nm*

**FOB (free on board)** *abbr* FOB (franco a bordo) *abbr*

**for** *prep* **for sale** in vendita

**forced** *adj* **forced currency** carta-moneta inconvertibile *nf*

**forecast** **1.** *n* previsione *nf* **2.** *vb* prevedere *vb*

**forecasting** *n* previsione *nf*

**foreclose** *vb* pignorare *vb*, escludere *vb*

**foreclosure** *n* pignoramento *nm*

**foreign** *adj* estero *adj* **foreign aid** aiuto all'estero *nm* **foreign aid programme** programma di aiuti all'estero *nm* **foreign bank** banca estera *nf* **foreign company** società estera *nf* **foreign competition** concorrenza estera *nf* **foreign currency** valuta estera *nf* **foreign exchange** cambio estero *nm* **foreign exchange dealer** cambiavalute *nm* **foreign exchange market** mercato dei cambi *nm* **foreign currency holdings** proprietà all'estero *nfpl* **foreign investment** investimento estero *nm* **foreign loan** prestito estero *nm* **foreign travel** viaggi all'estero *nmpl*

**foreman** *n* capo reparto *nm*

**forestall** *vb* precedere *vb*, accaparrare *vb*

**forestalling** *adj* **forestalling policy** politica di accaparramento *nf*

**forfeit** **1.** *n* ammenda *nf*, penalità *nf*,

confisca *nf* (shares) confisca di azioni *nf* 2. *vb* perdere un diritto a *vb*
**forfeiture** *n* confisca *nf*
**forgery** *n* contraffazione *nf*
**form** *n* (document) modulo *nm*
**formal** *adj* formale *adj* **formal agreement** accordo formale *nm* **formal contract** contratto formale *nm*
**formality** *n* **customs formalities** formalità doganali/legali *nfpl* **to observe formalities** rispettare le formalità *vb*
**formation** *n* (of company) costituzione *nf* **capital formation** formazione di capitale *nf*
**forward** 1. *adj* **forward contract** contratto di cambio per consegna differita *nm* **forward cover** operazioni di copertura per consegna differita *nfpl* **forward market** mercato delle operazioni per consegna differita *nm* **forward transaction** operazione per consegna differita *nf* 2. *vb* inoltrare *vb*, spedire *vb*
**forwarder** *n* spedizioniere *nm*
**forwarding** *n* inoltro *nm*, spedizione *nf* **forwarding agency** agenzia di spedizioni *nf* **forwarding agent** spedizioniere *nm* **forwarding charges** spese di spedizione *nfpl* **forwarding note** bollettino di spedizione *nm*
**found** *vb* **to found a company** fondare una società *vb*
**founder** *n* fondatore *nm*
**fraction** *n* frazione *nf*
**fractional** *adj* frazionario *adj* **fractional money** moneta divisionaria *nf*, moneta frazionaria *nf* **fractional shares** riserve proporzionali *nfpl*
**franc** *n* **Belgian franc** franco belga *nm* **French franc** franco francese *nm* **Swiss franc** franco svizzero *nm*
**franchise** 1. *adj* **franchise outlet** affiliante *nm* 2. *n* franchise *nm*, affiliazione commerciale *nf* 3. *vb* concedere il franchising di *vb*
**franchisee** *n* esclusivista *nm*, affiliato *nm*
**franchising** *n* franchising *nm*
**franchisor** *n* affiliante *nm*
**franco** *adj* **franco domicile** franco domicilio **franco price** prezzo franco *nm* **franco zone** zona del franco *nf*
**frank** *vb* affrancare *vb*
**franked** *adj* **franked income** reddito franco da imposta *nm*
**franking** *n* **franking machine** macchina affrancatrice *nf*
**fraud** *n* frode *nf*
**fraudulent** *adj* fraudolento *adj*, doloso *adj*
**free** *adj* **free agent** agente generale *nm* **free alongside ship (FAS)** franco sottobordo **free on board (FOB)** franco bordo **free of charge** gratuito *adj*, a titolo gratuito, franco di spese *adj* **free competition** libera concorrenza *nf* **free delivery** consegna franco spese *nf* **duty free** esente da dazio *adj* **free economy** economia liberale *nf*, economia liberista *nf* **free entry** bolla di merce esente *nf* **free of freight** franco di nolo *adj* **free goods** merci esenti *nfpl* **free market** mercato libero *nm* **free market economy** economia di mercato libero *nf* **free movement of goods** movimento libero della merce *nm* **free port** porto franco *nm* **free on quay** franco banchina partenza **free of tax** esente da tasse *adj* **free trade** libero scambio *nm* **free trade area** area di libero scambio *nf*
**freedom** *n* **freedom of choice** libertà di scelta *nf*
**Freefone (R) (GB)** *n* Freefone (R) (GB) telefonata a carico del destinatario *nf*, Numero Verde *nm*
**freelance** 1. *adj* freelance *adj*, indipendente *adj* 2. *n* freelance *nmf*, professionista freelance *nmf*
**freelancer** *n* professionista indipendente *nmf*, professionista libero *nmf*
**Freepost (R) (GB)** *n* Freepost (GB) - affrancatura a carico del destinatario *nf*
**freeze** 1. *n* (on prices, wages) blocco *nm*, congelamento *nm* 2. *vb* (prices, wages) congelare *vb*, bloccare *vb*
**freight** *n* nolo *nm*, trasporto *nm* **freight forwarder** spedizioniere *nm* **freight traffic** traffico merci *nm*
**freighter** *n* noleggiatore *nm*, spedizioniere *nm*, nave da carico *nf*, nave cargo *nf*
**frequency** *n* frequenza *nf*
**friendly** *adj* **Friendly Society** *n* società di mutuo soccorso *nf*
**fringe** *adj* **fringe benefits** benefici aggiuntivi *nmpl*, benefici accessori *nmpl* **fringe market** mercato marginale *nm*
**frontier** *n* frontiera *nf*
**fronting** *n* fronting *nm*
**frozen** *adj* **frozen assets** attività congelate *nfpl*, attività di non immediato realizzo *nfpl* **frozen credits** crediti congelati *nmpl*
**FT Index (Financial Times Index)** *n* Indice azionario del Financial Times *nm*
**full** *adj* **full cost** costo pieno *nm* **full liability** piena responsabilità *nf* **full**

**payment** pagamento a saldo *nm*, pagamento totale *nm*

**full-time** *adj, adv* a tempo pieno *adj, adv*, full-time *adj, adv*

**function** *n* funzione *nf*

**functional** *adj* **functional analysis** analisi funzionale *nf* **functional organization** organizzazione funzionale *nf*, organizzazione per funzioni *nf*

**fund** 1. *n* fondo *nm*, stanziamento *nm* **funds** *npl* fondi *nmpl*, titoli del debito consolidato *nmpl* **funds flow** flusso di cassa *nm*, flusso di tesoreria *nm* **funds surplus** eccedenza di stanziamento *nf* 2. *vb* finanziare *vb*

**funded** *adj* **funded debt** debito fondato *nm*

**funding** *n* consolidamento *nm*, finanziamento *nm* **funding bonds** titoli di consolidamento *nmpl*

**furlough (US)** 1. *n* congedo *nm* 2. *vb* concedere il congedo a *vb*

**future** *adj* **future commodity** merce a termine *nf* **future delivery** consegna futura *nf* **future goods** beni a termine *nmpl*

**futures** 1. *adj* **futures contract** contratto a termine *nm* **futures exchange** borsa dei contratti a termine *nf* **futures market** mercato a termine *nm* **futures marketing** contrattazione a termine *nf* **futures price** prezzo a termine *nm*, corso a termine *nm* **futures trading** operazioni commerciali a termine *nfpl* 2. *npl* contratti a termine *nmpl*

**fye (fiscal year end)** *abbr* fine anno finanziario *nf*

**gain** 1. *n* **capital gain** reddito di capitale *nm*, plusvalenza *nf* **capital gains tax** imposta sui redditi di capitale *nf* **gain in value** aumento del valore *nm* **gain sharing** partecipazione agli utili *nf* 2. *vb* guadagnare *vb*

**gainful** *adj* **gainful employment** impiego remunerativo *nm*, occupazione remunerativa *nf*

**galloping** *adj* **galloping inflation** inflazione galoppante *nf*

**Gallup** *n* **Gallup poll (R)** sondaggio d'opinioni Gallup *nm*

**gap** *n* **population gap** saldo demografico *nm* **trade gap** deficit della bilancia commerciale *nm*

**gas** *n* **natural gas** gas naturale *nm*

**GATT (General Agreement on Tariffs and Trade)** *abbr* GATT (Accordo generale sulle tariffe e il commercio) *abbr*

**gazump** *vb* gazump (vendere al maggior offerente non mantenendo l'impegno) *vb*

**GDP (Gross Domestic Product)** *abbr* PIL (Prodotto Interno Lordo) *abbr*

**general** *adj* **general accounting** contabilità generale *nf* **general agencies (US)** agenzie di assicurazioni generali *nfpl* **general agent** agente generale *nm* **general average** avaria generale *nf* **general election** elezioni politiche *nfpl* **general management** direzione generale *nf* **general manager** direttore generale *nm* **general partner** socio accomandatario *nm* **general partnership** società in nome collettivo *nf*, società semplice *nf* **general strike** sciopero generale *nm*

**generate** *vb* **to generate income** generare reddito *vb*

**generation** *n* **income generation** generazione di reddito *nf*

**generosity** *n* generosità *nf*

**gentleman** *n* **gentleman's agreement** accordo tra gentiluomini *nm*

**gilt-edged** *adj* **gilt-edged market** mercato dei titoli di stato *nm* **gilt-edged security** titolo di stato *nm*, titolo di prim'ordine *nm*

**gilts** *npl* titoli di stato *nmpl*

**giveaway** *n* articolo in omaggio *nm*, omaggio *nm*

**global** *adj* globale *adj* **global economy** economia globale *nf* **global market** mercato globale *nm* **global marketing** commercializzazione globale *nf*, marketing globale *nm*

**globalization** *n* globalizzazione *nf*

**GMT (Greenwich Mean Time)** *abbr* ora di Greenwich *nf*

**gnome** *n* **the Gnomes of Zurich** gli gnomi di Zurigo *nmpl*

**GNP (Gross National Product)** *abbr* PNL (Prodotto Nazionale Lordo) *abbr*

**go-slow** *n* (strike) sciopero bianco *nm*

**going** *adj* corrente *adj* **going concern** azienda avviata *nf*

**gold** 1. *adj* **gold bullion** verghe auree *nfpl*, lingotti d'oro *nmpl* **gold coin** moneta d'oro *nf* **gold market** mercato dell'oro *nm* **gold reserves** riserve auree *nfpl* **gold standard** sistema monetario standard *nm* 2. *n* oro *nm*

**golden** *adj* **golden handcuffs** manette d'oro *nfpl* **golden handshake** liquidazione *nf*, buonuscita *nf* **golden**

**hello** premio d'ingaggio *nm* **golden parachute** paracadute d'oro *nm*

**goods** *npl* merci *nfpl*, beni *nmpl* **goods on approval** merci soggette a verifica *nfpl* **bulk goods** merci alla rinfusa *nfpl*, merci in massa *nfpl* **goods on consignment** merci in conto deposito *nfpl* **domestic goods** merci nazionali *nfpl* **export goods** merci d'esportazione *nfpl* **import goods** merci d'importazione *nfpl* **goods in process** semilavorati *nmpl* **goods in progress** semilavorati *nmpl* **goods transport** trasporto merci *nm*

**goodwill** *n* avviamento *nm*

**govern** *vb* governare *vb*, amministrare *vb*

**government** *n* governo *nm* **government body** ente statale *nm* **government bond** titolo di stato *nm* **government enterprise** impresa statale *nf* **government loan** prestito pubblico *nm* **government policy** politica statale *nf* **government sector** settore pubblico *nm* **government security** titolo di stato *nm* **government subsidy** sovvenzione statale *nf*

**graduate 1.** *n* (of university) laureato *nm*, laureata *nf* **2.** *vb* conferire la laurea *vb*, laurearsi *vb*

**grant 1.** *n* (of a patent) concessione *nf*, assegnazione *nf* **regional grant** sovvenzione regionale *nf* **2.** *vb* concedere *vb*

**graphics** *npl* **computer graphics** grafica computerizzata *nf*

**gratuity** *n* gratifica *nf*, (tip) mancia *nf*

**green** *adj* **green card** carta verde *nf* **green currency** valuta verde *nf* **green pound** sterlina verde *nf*

**Greenwich** *n* **Greenwich Mean Time (GMT)** ora di Greenwich *nf*

**grievance** *n* vertenza *nf*

**gross** *adj* lordo *adj* **gross amount** ammontare lordo *nm*, somma lorda *nf* **gross domestic product (GDP)** prodotto interno lordo (PIL) *nm* **gross interest** interesse lordo *nm* **gross investment** investimento lordo *nm* **gross loss** perdita lorda *nf* **gross margin** margine lordo *nm* **gross national product (GNP)** prodotto nazionale lordo (PNL) *nm* **gross negligence** negligenza grave *nf*, colpa grave *nf* **gross output** prodotto lordo *nm* **gross sales** fatturato lordo *nm* **gross weight** peso lordo *nm*

**group** *n* **group insurance** assicurazione collettiva *nf* **group of countries** gruppo di nazioni *nm* **group travel** viaggio in gruppo *nm*

**growth** *n* crescita *nf* **annual growth rate** tasso annuo di crescita *nm* **economic growth** crescita economica *nf* **export-led growth** crescita indotta dalle esportazioni *nf* **market growth** crescita del mercato *nf* **growth rate** tasso di crescita *nf* **sales growth** aumento delle vendite *nm* **growth strategy** strategia di sviluppo *nf*

**guarantee** *n* garanzia *nf* **quality guarantee** garanzia di qualità *nf*

**guarantor** *n* garante *nm*, mallevadore *nm*

**guest** *n* **guest worker** lavoratore ospite *nm*

**guild** *n* gilda *nf*

**guilder** *n* gulden *nm*, fiorino olandese *nm*

**h** *abbr* (hour) ora *nf*

**half** *n* metà *nf*, mezzo *adj* **half-an-hour** mezz'ora *nf* **half-board** mezza pensione *nf* **half-pay** mezza paga *nf* **half-price** a metà prezzo *adv* **to reduce sth by half** dimezzare *vb* **half-year** semestre *nm*

**hall** *n* **exhibition hall** sala d'esposizione *nf*

**hallmark** *n* marchio ufficiale di saggio *nm*, marchio di garanzia *nm*

**halt** *vb* (inflation) arrestare *vb*

**halve** *vb* dimezzare *vb*

**hand** *n* **in hand** in corso *adv* **to hand** a portata di mano

**hand over** *vb* consegnare *vb*

**handbook** *n* manuale *nm*

**handle** *vb* (deal) trattare *vb*, occuparsi di *vb* (money) gestire *vb* trattare *vb* **handle with care** Attenzione!

**handling** *n* **handling charges** spese di approntamento *nfpl* **data handling** gestione dei dati *nf*

**handmade** *adj* fatto a mano *adj*

**handshake** *n* stretta di mano *nf*

**handwritten** *adj* scritto a mano *adj*

**handy** *adj* a portata di mano *adv*, utile *adj*

**hang on** *vb* (wait) attendere *vb*, tener duro *vb* (on telephone) attendere *vb*

**hang together** *vb* (argument) essere coerente *vb*, essere ben congegnato *vb*

**hang up** *vb* (telephone) riattaccare *vb*

**harbour** *n* porto *nm* **harbour authorities** ente portuale *nm* **harbour dues** diritti di porto *nmpl* **harbour facilities** attrezzature portuali *nfpl* **harbour fees** diritti di porto *nmpl*

**hard** *adj* **hard bargain** affare a condizioni poco vantaggiose *nm* **hard cash** circolante *nm*, medio circolante *nm* **hard currency** valuta forte *nf* **hard disk** hard disk *nm* **hard-earned** guadagnato col sudore della fronte, guadagnato con fatica **hard-hit** colpito duramente **hard-line** linea dura *nf* **hard loan** prestito in valuta forte *nm* **hard news/information** notizie di prima pagina *nfpl* **hard price** prezzo alto *nm* **hard sell** hard sell (politica di vendite estremamente aggressiva) *nm* **the hard facts** fatti incontrovertibili *nmpl*, la realtà nuda e cruda *nf* **hard-working** laborioso *adj*, operoso *adj*

**hardware** (computer) hardware *nm*

**haul** *n* **long-haul** distanza lunga *nf*, tirata *nf* **short-haul** breve distanza *nf*

**haulage** *n* **road haulage, freight** (US) costo di trasporto *nm* **haulage company** vettore *nm*

**haulier** *n* vettore a contratto *nm*

**hazard** *n* pericolo *nm* **natural hazard** pericolo naturale *nm* **occupational hazard** rischio professionale *nm*

**hazardous** *adj* pericoloso *adj*

**head 1.** *adj* **head accountant** ragioniere capo *nm* **head office** sede centrale *nf* **2.** *n* **at the head of** alla testa di *prep*, a capo di *prep* **head of department** direttore di reparto *nm*, capufficio *nm* **head of government** capo di governo *nm* **per head** pro capite *adv* **to be head of** dirigere *vb*, essere a capo di *vb* **3.** *vb* (department) dirigere *vb*

**head for** *vb* dirigersi a *vb*

**headed** *adj* **headed notepaper** carta intestata *nf*

**heading** *n* intestazione *nf*

**headquarters** *n* quartiere generale *nm*

**headway** *n* progresso *nm* **to make headway** fare progressi *vb*

**health** *n* **health benefits** sussidio di malattia *nm* **health care industry** industria assistenziale medica *nf* **health hazard** pericolo per la salute *nm* **industrial health** igiene del lavoro *nf* **health insurance** assicurazione contro le malattie *nf* **Ministry of Health** Ministero della Sanità *nm*

**healthy** *adj* (finances) prospero *adj*

**heavy** *adj* **heavy-duty** per servizio pesante *adj* **heavy goods vehicle** veicolo per merci pesanti *nm* **heavy industry** industria pesante *nf* **heavy trading** intensa attività di borsa *nf* **heavy user** gran consumatore *nm*

**hedge** *n* **hedge against inflation** protezione antinflazionistica *nf*, hedging *nm* **hedge clause (US)** clausola di protezione *nf*

**hidden** *adj* **hidden assets** attività occulta *nf* **hidden defect** vizio occulto *nm*

**hierarchy** *n* gerarchia *nf* **data hierarchy** gerarchia dei dati *nf* **hierarchy of needs** gerarchia dei bisogni *nf*

**high** *adj* **high-class** di prim'ordine *adj* **higher bid** offerta più alta *nf* **high finance** alta finanza *nf* **high-grade** di qualità superiore *adj* **high-income** alto reddito *nm* **high-level** ad alto livello **high-powered** potente *adj*, dinamico *adj* **high-priced** a prezzo alto *adj* **high-ranking** altolocato *adj* **high-risk** ad alto rischio *adj* **high season** alta stagione *nf* **high-tech** high-tech *nf*, tecnologia avanzata *nf*

**hire 1.** *adj* **hire charges** canoni di nolo *nmpl*, canoni di fitto *nmpl* **hire contract** contratto di nolo *nm* **hire purchase** vendita con pagamento rateale *nf* **2.** *n* nolo *nm* **for hire** da nolo *adj*, libero *adj* **3.** *vb* (person) noleggiare *vb*

**history** *n* **employment/work history** impiego precedente *nm*, occupazione precedente *nf*

**hit** *vb* **hit-or-miss** casuale *adj* **to hit the headlines** fare notizia *vb* **to hit the market** essere lanciato sul mercato *vb* **to be hard hit by** essere duramente colpiti da *vb*

**HO (head office)** *abbr* sede centrale *nf*

**hoard** *vb* accumulare *vb*

**hold 1.** *adj* **hold area** stiva *nf* **on hold** (on phone) attendere *vb*, essere in linea *vb* **2.** *vb* **to hold a meeting** tenere una riunione *vb* **to hold sth as security** tenere come garanzia *vb* **to hold sb liable** tenere responsabile *vb* **to hold the line** (on phone) restare in linea *vb* **to hold sb responsible** considerare qualcuno responsabile di qualcosa *vb*

**hold back** *vb* (not release) trattenere *vb*

**hold on** *vb* (on phone) attendere *vb*

**hold over** *vb* (to next period) rinviare *vb*

**hold up** *vb* (delay) ostruire *vb*, ostacolare *vb* (withstand scrutiny) reggere *vb*, mostrarsi valido *vb*

**holder** *n* titolare *nm*, detentore *nm*, possessore *nm* **joint holder** titolare congiunto *nm* **licence holder** licenziatario *nm* **office holder** che ricopre una carica *adj*, ricoprente una carica *adj* **policy holder** assicurato *nm*, detentore di polizza *nm*

**holding 1.** *adj* **holding company** holding

*nf*, società finanziaria *nf* **2.** *n* partecipazione *nf* **foreign exchange holdings** riserve valutarie *nfpl* **majority/ minority holding** partecipazione di maggioranza/di minoranza *nf* **to have holdings** possedere titoli *vb*, possedere pacchetti azionari *vb*

**holdup** *n* arresto *nm*, interruzione *nf*

**holiday, vacation** (US) *n* **bank holiday (GB)** festa civile osservata dalle banche *nf* **on holiday** in ferie *adv* **holiday pay** retribuzione per le ferie *nf* **tax holiday** periodo di esenzione fiscale *nm*

**home** *adj* **home address** recapito personale *nm* **home buyer** compratore nazionale *nm* **home country** paese d'origine *nm*, patria *nf* **home delivery** consegna a domicilio *nf* **home industry** industria nazionale *nf* **home loan** mutuo edilizio *nm* **home market** mercato interno *nm* **home owner** proprietario d'abitazione *nm* **home sales** vendite sul mercato nazionale *nfpl* **home service** servizio a domicilio *nm* **home shopping** home shopping *nm*, spese da casa *nfpl*

**honorary** *adj* onorario *adj*

**horizontal** *adj* **horizontal analysis** analisi orizzontale *nf* **horizontal integration** integrazione orizzontale *nf*

**host** *n* ospite *nm*, ospitante *nm* **host country** nazione ospitante *nf*

**hot** *adj* **hot line** linea calda *nf*, linea diretta *nf* **hot money** capitali vaganti *nmpl*, moneta calda *nf*, denaro scottante *nm* **hot seat** carica di grande responsabilità *nf* **to be in hot demand** essere richiestissimi *vb*

**hotel** *n* albergo *nm* **hotel accommodation** alloggio in albergo *nm*, camere d'albergo *nfpl* **hotel chain** catena alberghiera *nf* **five-star hotel** albergo cinque stelle *nm* **hotel industry/trade** industria alberghiera *nf* **hotel management** direzione dell'albergo *nf*, gestione alberghiera *nf* **to run a hotel** gestire un albergo *vb*

**hour** *n* **after hours** dopo l'orario di chiusura **business hours** ore d'ufficio *nfpl* **busy hours (US)** ore di attività intensa *nfpl* **fixed hours** ore fisse *nfpl* **office hours** orario d'ufficio *nm* **per hour** ad ora, per ogni ora **per hour output** produzione oraria *nf*

**hourly** *adj* **hourly-paid work** lavoro retribuito con paga oraria *nm* **hourly rate** paga oraria *nf* **hourly workers** lavoratori retribuiti a ore *nmpl*

**house** *n* **clearing house** stanza di compensazione *nf* **house duty (US)** imposta sugli immobili *nf* **house journal/ magazine** giornale aziendale *nm* **mail-order house** casa di vendita per corrispondenza *nf* **packing house (US)** impresa di confezionamento *nf* **house prices** prezzi delle case *nmpl*, prezzi degli immobili *nmpl* **publishing house** casa editrice *nf* **house sale** vendita di una casa *nf* **house telephone** telefono interno *nm*

**household** *n* nucleo familiare *nm* **household expenditure** spesa del nucleo familiare *nf* **household goods** articoli casalinghi *nmpl* **household survey** indagine sui nuclei familiari *nf*

**householder** *n* capofamiglia *nmf*

**housewares (US)** *npl* articoli casalinghi *nmpl*

**housing** *n* **housing estate, tenement** (US) complesso urbano *nm*, quartiere *nm* **housing industry** industria dell'edilizia abitativa *nf* **housing project** progetto edilizio *nm* **housing scheme** piano edilizio *nm*

**hull** *n* scafo *nm* **hull insurance** assicurazione sullo scafo *nf*

**human** *adj* umano *adj* **human relations** relazioni umane *nfpl* **human resource management (HRM)** gestione delle risorse umane *nf* **human resources** risorse umane *nfpl*

**hundred** *adj* cento *adj* **one hundred per cent** cento per cento *nm*

**hydroelectricity** *n* energia idroelettrica *nf*

**hype** *n* pubblicità stravagante *nf*, pubblicità sensazionalistica *nf*

**hyperinflation** *n* iperinflazione *nf*

**hypermarket** *n* ipermercato *nm*

**hypothesis** *n* ipotesi *nf*

**idle** *adj* inattivo *adj* **idle capacity** capacità inutilizzata *nf*

**illegal** *adj* illegale *adj*, illecito *adj*

**implication** *n* **this will have implications for our sales** questo avrà conseguenze sulle nostre vendite

**import** **1.** *adj* **import agent** agente importatore *nm* **import barrier** barriera doganale sull'importazione *nf* **import control** controllo sulle importazioni *nm* **import department** reparto importazione *nm*, ufficio importazione *nm* **import duty** dazio d'importazione *nm* **import licence** licenza d'importazione *nf* **import office**

ufficio importazioni *nm* **import quota** contingente d'importazione *nm* **import restrictions** restrizioni delle importazioni *nfpl* **import surplus** eccedenza delle importazioni *nf* **2.** *n* importazione *nf* **imports** *npl* importazioni *nfpl*, articoli d'importazione *nmpl* **3.** *vb* importare *vb*

**importation** *n* importazione *nf*

**importer** *n* importatore *nm*

**importing** *adj* **importing country** paese importatore *nm*

**impose** *vb* **to impose a tax** imporre un'imposta *vb*, imporre un dazio *vb* **to impose restrictions** imporre restrizioni *vb*

**imposition** *n* (of tax) imposta *nf*, imposizione *nf*

**impound** *vb* confiscare *vb*, sequestrare *vb*

**imprint** *n* **to take an imprint** (credit card) fare un'impronta *vb*

**improve** *vb* migliorare *vb* **we must improve our performance** dobbiamo migliorare la nostra performance

**inadequate** *adj* inadeguato *adj*, insufficiente *adj*

**incentive** *n* incentivo *nm*

**incidental** *adj* **incidental expenses** spese occasionali *nfpl*

**include** *vb* **our price includes delivery** nel nostro prezzo è compresa la consegna **taxes are included** le imposte sono comprese, i dazi sono compresi

**inclusive** *adj* **inclusive of tax and delivery costs** dazi e costi di consegna inclusi, inclusivo di dazi e costi di consegna **the prices quoted are inclusive** i prezzi citati sono complessivi

**income** *n* reddito *nm* **gross income** reddito lordo *nm* **net income** reddito netto *nm* **private income** reddito personale *nm* **income tax** imposta sul reddito *nf*

**inconvenience** *n* inconveniente *nm*, svantaggio *nm*

**inconvenient** *adj* sconveniente *adj*, importuno *adj*

**increase** **1.** *n* **increase in the cost of living** aumento del carovita *nm* **price increase** aumento dei prezzi *nm* **wage increase** aumento salariale *nm* **2.** *vb* (prices, taxes) aumentare *vb*

**incur** *vb* (expenses) sostenere *vb*, subire *vb*

**indebted** *adj* indebitato *adj*, (thankful) grato *adj*

**indemnify** *vb* indennizzare *vb*, risarcire *vb*

**indemnity** *n* indennità *nf*, risarcimento *nm* **indemnity insurance** assicurazione contro i danni *nf*

**index** *n* indice *nm* **cost of living index** indice del costo della vita *nm* **growth index** indice di crescita *nm* **price index** indice dei prezzi *nm* **share index** indice azionario *nm*

**indicate** *vb* indicare *vb*

**indication** *n* indicazione *nf*

**indirect** *adj* indiretto *adj* **indirect cost** costo indiretto *nm* **indirect expenses** spese indirette *nfpl* **indirect tax** imposta indiretta *nf*

**industrial** *adj* industriale *adj* **industrial accident** infortunio sul lavoro *nm* **industrial arbitration** arbitrato industriale *nm* **industrial democracy** democrazia industriale *nf* **industrial dispute** disputa industriale *nf* **industrial expansion** espansione industriale *nf* **industrial region** regione industriale *nf* **industrial relations** relazioni industriali *nfpl* **industrial tribunal** tribunale industriale *nm* **industrial union** sindacato industriale *nm*

**industry** *n* industria *nf*

**inefficient** *adj* inefficiente *adj*

**inferior** *adj* (goods) scadente *adj*

**inflation** *n* inflazione *nf* **rate of inflation** tasso d'inflazione *nm*

**inflationary** *adj* inflazionistico *adj* **inflationary gap** scarto inflazionistico *nm* **inflationary spiral** spirale inflazionistica *nf*

**inform** *vb* informare *vb*

**information** **1.** *adj* **information desk** ufficio informazioni *nm*, banco informazioni *nm* **information management** gestione delle informazioni *nf* **information office** ufficio informazioni *nm* **information processing** elaborazione di informazioni *nf* **information retrieval** reperimento di informazioni *nm* **information storage** memorizzazione di informazioni *nf* **information systems** sistema informativo *nf* **information technology (IT)** informatica *nf*, tecnologia dell'informazione *nf* **2.** *n* informazione *nf*

**infrastructure** *n* infrastruttura *nf*

**inherit** *vb* ereditare *vb*

**inheritance** *n* eredità *nf* **inheritance laws** leggi sulle successioni *nfpl*

**inhouse** *adj* **inhouse training** addestramento sul posto di lavoro *nm*

**injunction** *n* ingiunzione *nf* **to take out an injunction** richiedere l'emissione di un'ingiunzione *vb*

**inland** *adj* interno *adj*, nazionale *adj* **the**

**Inland Revenue, The Internal Revenue Service (IRS)** (US) fisco *nm*, erario *nm*
**insider** *n* chi ha accesso ad informazioni riservate *nm*, membro *nm* **insider dealing, insider trading** (US) insider dealing *nm*
**insist on** *vb* insistere su *vb*
**insolvency** *n* insolvenza *nf*
**insolvent** *adj* insolvente *adj*
**inspect** *vb* ispezionare *vb*, controllare *vb*
**inspection** *n* ispezione *nf*
**inspector** *n* ispettore *nm* **customs inspector** doganiere *nm*
**instability** *n* instabilità *nf*
**install, instal** (US) *vb* installare *vb*, insediare *vb*
**installation** *n* installazione *nf*
**installment, instalment** (US) *n* rata *nf*
**institute** *n* istituto *nm*
**institution** *n* istituzione *nm* **credit institution** istituto di credito *nm*
**instruction** *n* istruzione *nf* **instruction book** manuale d'istruzioni *nm* **instruction sheet** scheda d'istruzioni *nf* **to follow instructions** seguire le istruzioni *vb*
**insurable** *adj* **insurable risk** rischio assicurabile *nm*
**insurance** 1. *adj* **insurance agent** agente di assicurazioni *nm* **insurance broker** broker di assicurazioni *nm* **insurance certificate** certificato di assicurazione *nm* **insurance company** compagnia di assicurazione *nf* **insurance contract** contratto di assicurazione *nm* **insurance fund** fondo di autoassicurazione *nm* **insurance policy** polizza di assicurazione *nf* **insurance premium** premio di assicurazione *nm* **insurance representative** agente d'assicurazioni *nm* **insurance salesperson** agente di assicurazioni *nm* **insurance underwriter** assicuratore *nm* 2. *n* assicurazione *nf* **car insurance** assicurazione auto *nf* **comprehensive insurance** assicurazione contro tutti i rischi *nf* **fire insurance** assicurazione contro l'incendio *nf* **National Insurance (GB)** assicurazioni sociali *nfpl* **third party insurance** assicurazione contro la responsabilità civile *nf* **to take out insurance** sottoscrivere una polizza assicurativa *vb* **unemployment insurance** assicurazione contro la disoccupazione *nf*
**insure** *vb* assicurare *vb*
**intangible** *adj* **intangible asset** attività immateriali *nfpl*
**intensive** *adj* intensivo *adj* **capital-intensive** ad uso intensivo di capitale **labour-intensive** ad uso intensivo di lavoro
**interest** *n* interesse *nm* **interest period** periodo d'interesse *nm* **interest rate** tasso d'interesse *nm* **to bear interest** fruttare interesse *vb*, generare interesse *vb* **to charge interest** caricare interessi *vb* **to pay interest** pagare gli interessi *vb*
**interest-bearing** fruttifero *adj*
**interest-free** senza interessi *adj*
**interface** *n* interfaccia *nf*
**interim** *adj* provvisorio *adj*, interinale *adj*
**intermediary** *adj* intermediario *adj*
**internal** *adj* **internal audit** revisione contabile interna *nf*, audit interno *nm* **internal auditor** revisore contabile interno *nm* **the Internal Revenue Service (IRS) (US)** Dipartimento delle imposte (US) *nm*
**international** *adj* internazionale *adj* **international agreement** accordo internazionale *nm* **international competition** concorrenza internazionale *nf* **International Date Line** linea del cambiamento di data *nf* **international organization** organizzazione internazionale *nf* **international trade** commercio internazionale *nm*
**intervene** *vb* intervenire *vb*
**intervention** *n* intervento *nm* **state intervention** intervento statale *nm*
**interview** 1. *n* colloquio *nm*, intervista *nf* **to attend for interview** presentarsi ad un colloquio *vb* **to hold an interview** fare un colloquio *vb*, intervistare *vb* **to invite sb to interview** invitare qualcuno *vb* 2. *vb* intervistare *vb*
**introduce** *vb* introdurre *vb*, presentare *vb*
**inventory** *n* inventario *nm* **inventory control** controllo del livello delle scorte *nm*
**invest** *vb* (money) investire *vb*
**investment** *n* investimento *nm* **investment adviser** consulente finanziario *nm* **investment portfolio** portafoglio titoli *nm* **investment programme, investment program** (US) programma degli investimenti *nm* **investment strategy** strategia degli investimenti *nf*
**investor** *n* investitore *nm*, risparmiatore *nm*
**invisible** *adj* **invisible exports**

esportazioni invisibili *nfpl* **invisible imports** importazioni invisibili *nfpl*
**invitation** *n* invito *nm*
**invite** *vb* invitare *vb*
**invoice** *n* fattura *nf* **duplicate invoice** copia della fattura *nf* **to issue an invoice** emettere una fattura *vb* **to settle an invoice** pagare una fattura *vb*
**irrecoverable** *adj* (loss) irrecuperabile *adj*
**irrevocable** *adj* irrevocabile *adj* **irrevocable letter of credit** lettera di credito irrevocabile *nf*
**issue 1.** *n* **bank of issue** banca di emissione *nf* **share issue, stock issue** (US) emissione azionaria *nf* **2.** *vb* emettere *vb*, rilasciare *vb* **to issue sb with sth** provvedere qualcuno di *vb*
**issuing** *adj* **issuing bank** banca emittente *nf*
**item** *n* articolo *nm*, voce *nf*
**itemize** *vb* specificare *vb* **itemized account** conto dettagliato *nm*
**itinerary** *n* itinerario *nm*
**jackpot** *n* successo strabiliante *nm*, monte premi *nm*
**jingle** *n* **advertising jingle** jingle *nm*, sigla musicale *nf*
**job** *n* **job analysis** analisi delle mansioni *nf* **job creation** creazione di posti di lavoro *nf* **job description** descrizione delle mansioni *nf* **job offer** offerta di lavoro *nf* **job rotation** rotazione delle mansioni *nf* **job satisfaction** soddisfazione nel lavoro *nf* **job shop** ufficio di collocamento (GB) *nm*
**jobber** *n* operatore di borsa *nm*
**Jobcentre (GB)** *n* ufficio di collocamento in Gran Bretagna *nm*
**jobless** *adj* disoccupato *adj* **the jobless** i disoccupati *nmpl*
**joint** *adj* congiunto *adj* **joint account** conto congiunto *nm*, conto a più firme *nm* **joint obligation** obbligazione solidale *nf* **joint ownership** comproprietà *nf* **joint responsibility** responsabilità collettiva *nf* **joint-stock company** società per azioni *nf* **joint venture** joint venture *nf*, impresa in partecipazione *nf*
**jointly** *adv* collettivamente *adv*, insieme *adv*
**journal** *n* giornale *nm*, libro giornale *nm*, periodico *nm*
**journalism** *n* giornalismo *nm*
**judicial** *adj* giudiziale *adj*
**junior** *adj* di secondo grado *adj*, più giovane *adj*, subalterno *adj*
**junk** *n* **junk bond** junk bond *nm*, obbligazione di rischio *nf*
**jurisdiction** *n* giurisdizione *nf*
**juror** *n* giurato *nm*
**jury** *n* giuria *nf*
**keen** *adj* (competition) vivace *adj* (price) conveniente *adj*
**keep** *vb* (goods) conservarsi *vb* **to keep an appointment** tenere un appuntamento *vb* **to keep the books** tenere la contabilità *vb* **to keep the business running** mandare avanti la baracca *vb*
**keep back** *vb* (money) trattenere soldi *vb*
**keep down** *vb* (prices) tener bassi i prezzi *vb*
**keep up with** *vb* (events) tenersi aggiornati *vb*
**key** *adj* **key currency** valuta chiave *nf* **key industry** industria chiave *nf* **key person** persona chiave *nf* **key question** domanda determinante *nf*, domanda chiave *nf*
**key in** *vb* inserire per mezzo di tastiera *vb*
**keyboard** *n* tastiera *nf*
**keynote** *adj* **keynote speech** discorso chiave *nm*
**keyword** *n* parola chiave *nf*
**kg** *abbr* kg (chilogrammo) *abbr (nm)*
**kill** *vb* **to kill a project** respingere un progetto *vb*, terminare un progetto *vb*, bocciare un progetto *vb*
**kilowatt** *n* chilowatt *nm*, kilowatt *nm*
**kind 1.** *adj* cortese *adj*, gentile *adj* **would you be so kind as to...** potreste ....... **2.** *n* natura *nf*
**king-size(d)** *adj* di misura superiore al normale
**kiosk** *n* (phone) cabina telefonica *nf*
**kit** *n* (equipment) kit *nm*, scatola di montaggio *nf*
**kite** *n* **kite mark (GB)** marchio apposto dalla British Standards Institution *nm*
**km, kilometer** (US) *abbr* km (chilometro) *abbr (nm)*
**knock** *vb* (disparage) denigrare *vb*, screditare *vb*
**knock down** *vb* (price) ribassare *vb*
**knock off*** *vb* (finish work) smontare dal lavoro *vb*
**knock-for-knock** *adj* **knock-for-knock agreement** accordo di indennizzo diretto *nm*
**knock-on** *adj* **knock-on effect** effetto a catena *nm*
**knockdown** *adj* **knockdown price** prezzo minimo *nm*, prezzo di liquidazione *nm*
**know-how** *n* know-how *nm*

**knowledge** *n* conoscenza *nf* **knowledge base** conoscenza di base *nf* **it is common knowledge** fatto noto a tutti *nm* **to have a thorough knowledge of sth** conoscere in profondità *vb* **to have a working knowledge of sth** essere pratico di *vb*, intendersi di *vb* **to my knowledge** per quanto mi risulta

**knowledgeable** *adj* bene informato *adj*

**known** *adj* **known facts** fatti noti *nmpl*

**krona** *n* (Swedish) corona svedese *nf*

**krone** *n* (Danish, Norwegian) corona norvegese *nf*, corona danese *nf*

**kudos** *n* prestigio *nm*

**kW** *abbr* kw (chilowatt) *abbr (nm)*

**kWh** *abbr* chilowattora *nm*

**label 1.** *n* etichetta *nf* **2.** *vb* etichettare *vb*

**labour, labor** (US) **1.** *adj* **labour costs** costi della manodopera *nmpl* **labour dispute** controversia sindacale *nf* **labour-intensive** ad uso intensivo di lavoro **labour law** legislazione del lavoro *nf* **labour market** mercato del lavoro *nm* **labour relations** relazioni industriali *nmpl* **2.** *n* lavoro *nm*, manodopera *nf*

**labourer** *n* manovale *nm*, bracciante *nm*

**lack** *n* mancanza *nf* **lack of investment** mancanza di investimenti *nf*

**land** *adj* **land purchase** acquisto di terreni *nm* **land reform** riforma fondiaria *nf* **land register** catasto *nm* **land tax** imposta fondiaria *nf* **land tribunal** tribunale con giurisdizione in materia di espropri *nm*

**landlord** *n* locatore *nm*, proprietario di immobile *nm*

**landowner** *n* proprietario terriero *nm*

**language** *n* lingua *nf*, linguaggio *nm* **language specialist** specialista linguistico *nm*

**large** *adj* **large-scale** su vasta scala *adv*

**launch 1.** *n* **product launch** lancio di un nuovo prodotto *nm* **2.** *vb* (product) lanciare *vb*

**law** *n* legge *nf* **business law** diritto commerciale *nm* **civil law** diritto civile *nm* **criminal law** diritto penale *nm* **international law** diritto internazionale *nm* **law of diminishing returns** legge dei rendimenti decrescenti *nf* **public law** diritto pubblico *nm*

**lawsuit** *n* causa *nf*, querela *nf*

**lay off** *vb* (workers) sospendere temporaneamente dal lavoro *vb*, licenziare *vb*

**LBO (leveraged buy-out)** *abbr* rilevamento di un'azienda con leverage *nm*

**leader** *n* **market leader** leader del mercato *nmf*

**leadership** *n* leadership *nf*, egemonia *nf*

**leading** *adj* **leading product** prodotto principale *nm*

**lease** *vb* dare in locazione *vb*

**leasehold** *n* possesso immobiliare *nm*

**leaseholder** *n* locatario *nm*

**leave 1.** *n* licenza *nf*, aspettativa *nf*, congedo *nm* **leave of absence** congedo *nm* **sick leave** congedo per malattia *nm* **to take leave** prendere congedo *vb* **to take leave of sb** accomiatarsi *vb* **2.** *vb* lasciare *vb* (resign from) dimettersi *vb*

**ledger** *n* libro mastro *nm* **bought ledger** partitario fornitori *nm* **ledger entry** voce contabile *nf*

**left** *adj* **left luggage** bagaglio depositato *nm* **left-luggage locker** deposito bagagli *nm* **left-luggage office** ufficio deposito bagagli *nm*

**legacy** *n* lascito *nm*

**legal** *adj* legale *adj* **legal tender** moneta a corso legale *nf* **to take legal action** intentare una causa *vb*

**legislate** *vb* promulgare leggi *vb*, legiferare *vb*

**legislation** *n* legislazione *nf* **to introduce legislation** presentare un progetto di legge *vb*

**lend** *vb* prestare *vb*, concedere in prestito *vb*, mutuare *vb*

**lender** *n* mutuante *nm*

**lessee** *n* locatario *nm*

**lessor** *n* locatore *nm*

**let** *vb* (property) dare in affitto *vb*, affittare *vb*

**letter** *n* **letter of application** domanda di sottoscrizione *nf*, domanda d'assunzione *nf*, domanda *nf* **letter of credit** lettera di credito *nf* **letter of introduction** lettera di presentazione *nf*

**letterhead** *n* foglio di carta intestata *nm*, intestazione *nf*

**level** *n* **level of employment** livello dell'occupazione *nm* **level of inflation** livello dell'inflazione *nm* **level of prices** livello dei prezzi *nm*

**levy** *vb* (tax) imporre *vb*, riscuotere *vb*

**liability** *n* responsabilità *nf*, passività *nf* **current liabilities** passività correnti *nfpl* **fixed liability** passività fissa *nf* **limited liability** responsabilità limitata *nf*

**liable** *adj* responsabile *adj*, passibile *adj*

**liable for damages** tenuto a risarcire i danni **liable for tax** soggetto a tassazione, soggetto a imposta
**libel** *n* pubblicazione diffamatoria *nf*, diffamazione *nf*, libello *nm*
**licence** *n* licenza *nf*, autorizzazione *nf* **licence fee** tassa di licenza *nf*
**license** *vb* autorizzare *vb*, dar licenza a *vb*
**licensee** *n* concessionario di licenza *nm*
**licensor** *n* concessore di licenza *nm*
**life** *n* **life assurance/insurance** assicurazione sulla vita *nf* **life member** iscritto a vita *adj*, membro a vita *nm*
**LIFO (last in first out)** *abbr* LIFO (ultimo entrato prima uscito) *abbr*
**limit** *n* limite *nm*, prezzo limite *nm* **credit limit** limite di credito *nm*
**limited** *adj* limitato *adj* **limited capital** capitale limitato *nm* **limited company** società a responsabilità limitata *nf*, società per azioni *nf* **limited liability** responsabilità limitata *nf* **limited partnership** società in accomandita *nf*
**line** *n* **assembly line** catena di montaggio *nf* **line management** la direzione di reparto *nf*, il line management *nm* **line manager** line manager *nm* **line of business** settore di attività *nm* **product line** linea di prodotti *nf*, classe di merci *nf*, gamma *nf*
**liquid** *adj* liquido *adj* **liquid assets** attività liquide *nfpl* **liquid capital** capitale liquido *nm*
**liquidate** *vb* liquidare *vb*, realizzare *vb*
**liquidation** *n* liquidazione *nf* **liquidation value** valore di liquidazione *nm*
**liquidity** *n* liquidità *nf*
**list** *n* listino *nm*, lista *nf*, elenco *nm* **listed share, listed stock** (US) titoli quotati in borsa *nmpl* **list price** prezzo di listino *nm*
**litigant** *n* parte in causa *nf*
**litigate** *vb* contestare *vb*, litigare *vb*
**litigation** *n* lite *nf*, causa *nf*
**load** 1. *n* carico *nm* 2. *vb* caricare *vb*
**loan** *n* prestito *nm*, mutuo *nm* **loan agreement** contratto di prestito *nm* **bank loan** prestito bancario *nm* **bridging loan, bridge loan** (US) prestito compensativo *nm* **personal loan** prestito personale *nm* **to grant a loan** concedere un prestito *vb* **to request a loan** richiedere un prestito *vb*
**local** *adj* locale *adj* **local taxes** imposte locali *nfpl*
**location** *n* ubicazione *nf*, localizzazione *nf*
**lockout** *n* (of strikers) serrata *nf*
**logistics** *npl* logistica *nf*
**Lombard Rate** *n* tasso lombard *nm*
**long** *adj* **long capital** capitale a lunga scadenza *nm* **long credit** credito a lunga scadenza *nm* **long deposit** deposito a lunga scadenza *nm* **long-distance** lontano *adj*, interurbano *adj* **long-range** a lungo termine *adj* **long-term** a lungo termine *adj* **long-term planning** pianificazione a lungo termine *nf*
**lose** *vb* (custom) perdere clienti *vb*
**loss** *n* perdita *nf* **financial loss** perdita finanziaria *nf* **gross loss** perdita lorda *nf* **loss leader** articolo civetta *nm* **net loss** perdita netta *nf* **loss of earnings** perdita di reddito *nf* **loss of job** perdita del lavoro *nf* **to minimise losses** minimizzare i danni *vb*
**lost-property** *adj* **lost-property office** ufficio oggetti smarriti *nm*
**lot** *n* (at auction) lotto *nm*, partita *nf*
**low** *adj* (price) basso *adj*
**lower** *vb* (price, interest rate) ridurre *vb*, abbassare *vb*
**lucrative** *adj* lucrativo *adj*
**luggage** *n* **excess luggage** bagaglio in eccedenza *nm* **luggage insurance** assicurazione per il bagaglio personale *nf*
**lump** *n* **lump sum settlement** pagamento in unica soluzione *nm*, pagamento forfettario *nm*
**luxury** *adj* **luxury goods** beni di lusso *nmpl* **luxury tax** imposta sui beni di lusso *nf*
**machine** 1. *n* macchina *nf* 2. *vb* fare a macchina *vb*, lavorare *vb*
**machinery** *n* macchinario *nm*, macchine *nfpl* **machinery of government** macchina dello Stato *nf*
**macroeconomics** *n* macroeconomia *nf*
**made** *adj* **made in France** fabbricato in Francia *prep*
**magazine** *n* (journal) periodico *nm*, rivista *nf*
**magnate** *n* magnate *nm*
**magnetic** *adj* **magnetic tape** (DP) nastro magnetico *nm*
**mail order** *n* ordinazione per corrispondenza *nf*
**mailing** *n* **mailing list** indirizzario *nm*
**main** *adj* principale *adj* **main office** ufficio centrale *nm* **main supplier** fornitore principale *nm*
**mainframe** *n* (DP) mainframe *nm*
**maintenance** *n* manutenzione *nf* **maintenance costs** costi di manutenzione *nmpl*
**major** *adj* maggiore *adj*, principale *adj*

**majority** *n* maggioranza *nf* **majority holding** azionariato di maggioranza *nm* **in the majority** nella maggior parte

**make** *vb* **to make a fortune** far fortuna *vb* **to make a living** guadagnarsi da vivere *vb* **to make money** far quattrini *vb*

**malingerer** *n* che si dà malato *adj*, che marca visita *adj*, lavativo *nm*

**mall** *n* **shopping mall** shopping mall *nm*, centro commerciale *nm*

**malpractice** *n* negligenza nell'esercizio professionale *nf*

**man-made** *adj* fatto dall'uomo *prep*

**manage** *vb* amministrare *vb*, dirigere *vb*

**management** **1.** *adj* **management buy-out** management buy-out *nm* **management consultant** consulente di direzione e organizzazione *nm* **management training** addestramento alla direzione *nm* **2.** *n* gestione *nf*, amministrazione *nf* **business management** direzione aziendale *nf* **management by objectives** direzione per obiettivi *nf* **financial management** gestione finanziaria *nf* **middle management** direzione a medio livello *nf* **personnel management** gestione del personale *nf* **top management** top management *nm*, alta direzione *nf*

**manager** *n* manager *nmf*

**manpower** *n* forza lavoro *nf*, manodopera *nf*

**manual** *adj* **manual worker** operaio *nm*

**manufacture** **1.** *n* fabbricazione *nf*, produzione *nf*, lavorazione *nf* **2.** *vb* fabbricare *vb*

**manufacturer** *n* produttore *nm*, fabbricante *nm*

**margin** *n* margine *nm* **profit margin** margine di profitto *nm*

**marginal** *adj* marginale *adj* **marginal cost** costo marginale *nm* **marginal revenue** ricavo marginale *nm*

**marine** **1.** *adj* marittimo *adj* **marine engineering** ingegneria marittima *nf* **marine insurance** assicurazione marittima *nf* **2.** *n* **merchant marine** marina mercantile *nf*

**mark** *n* **Deutsche Mark** marco tedesco *nm*

**mark down** *vb* (price) ribassare *vb*

**mark up** *vb* alzare il prezzo di *vb*

**markdown** *n* ribasso *nm*

**market** **1.** *adj* **market analysis** analisi di mercato *nf* **down-market** (product) (articolo) a basso prezzo destinato ad una clientela mediocre *adj* **market economy** economia di mercato *nf* **market forces** forze di mercato *nfpl* **market leader** leader del mercato *nmf* **market opportunity** opportunità di mercato *nf* **market price** prezzo di mercato *nm* **property/real estate (US) market** mercato immobiliare *nm* **market research** ricerca di mercato *nf* **market segmentation** segmentazione di un mercato *nf* **market share** quota di mercato *nf* **up-market** (product) esclusivo *adj*, selettivo *adj* **market value** valore di mercato *nm* **2.** *n* mercato *nm* **bear market** mercato al ribasso *nm* **black market** mercato nero *nm* **bond market** mercato delle obbligazioni *nm* **bull market** mercato al rialzo *nm* **buyer's market** mercato al ribasso *nm*, mercato del compratore *nm* **capital market** mercato finanziario *nm* **Common Market** Mercato Comune *nm* **domestic market** mercato nazionale *nm*, mercato interno *nm* **falling market** mercato tendente al ribasso *nm* **firm market** mercato stabile *nm*, mercato sostenuto *nm* **foreign market** mercato estero *nm* **futures market** mercato a termine *nm* **labour market** mercato del lavoro *nm* **money market** mercato monetario *nm* **retail market** mercato al dettaglio *nm* **seller's market** mercato al rialzo *nm*, mercato del venditore *nm* **stock market** mercato azionario *nm* **the bottom has fallen out of the market** Non c'è mercato per questo prodotto **to play the market** speculare in borsa *vb* **wholesale market** mercato all'ingrosso *nm* **3.** *vb* vendere *vb*, mettere in commercio *vb*

**marketable** *adj* commerciabile *adj*

**marketing** *n* marketing *nm* **marketing consultant** consulente di marketing *nmf* **marketing department** ufficio marketing *nm* **marketing director** direttore dell'ufficio marketing *nm*

**markup** *n* aumento *nm*, rialzo *nm*

**mart** *n* mercato *nm*

**mass** *adj* **mass marketing** marketing di massa *nm* **mass media** mass media *nmpl* **mass production** produzione di massa *nf*, produzione in serie *nf* **mass unemployment** disoccupazione di massa *nf*

**material** **1.** *adj* **material needs** bisogni materiali *nmpl* **2.** *n* **materials** materiali *nmpl* **building materials** materiali edili *nmpl* **raw materials** materie prime *nfpl*

**maternity** *n* **maternity leave** congedo per maternità *nm*
**matrix** *n* matrice *nf*
**mature** *vb* (business, economy) maturare *vb*, scadere *vb*
**maximise** *vb* massimizzare *vb*
**maximum** *adj* **maximum price** prezzo massimo *nm*
**MBA (Master of Business Administration)** *abbr* MBA (Master in amministrazione aziendale) *abbr*
**mean 1.** *adj* (average) medio *adj* **2.** *n* (average) media *nf* **means** *npl* mezzi *nmpl* **financial means** mezzi finanziari *nmpl* **to live beyond one's means** seguire un tenore di vita non conforme alle proprie possibilità **we do not have the means to...** non disponiamo dei mezzi per ...
**measure 1.** *n* misura *nf* **financial measure** misure finanziarie *nfpl* **safety measure** provvedimento di sicurezza *nm*, misura di sicurezza *nf* **2.** *vb* misurare *vb*
**mechanical** *adj* meccanico *adj* **mechanical engineering** ingegneria meccanica *nf*
**media** *n* mezzi pubblicitari *nmpl*
**median** *adj* mediano *adj*, di mezzo *adj*
**mediate** *vb* fare da mediatore *vb*, raggiungere un accordo tramite mediazione *vb*
**mediation** *n* mediazione *nf*
**mediator** *n* mediatore *nm*
**medical** *adj* medico *adj* **medical insurance** assicurazione contro le malattie *nf*, assicurazione malattie *nf*
**medium 1.** *adj* medio *adj* **medium-sized firm** media impresa *nf* **medium term** a medio termine *adv* **2.** *n* **advertising medium** veicolo pubblicitario *nm*
**meet** *vb* incontrare *vb*
**meeting** *n* incontro *nm*, riunione *nf*, assemblea *nf* **board meeting** riunione del consiglio di amministrazione *nf* **business meeting** riunione di lavoro *nf* **to hold a meeting** tenere una riunione *vb*
**megabyte** *n* megabyte *nm*
**member** *n* membro *nm*, socio *nm*, iscritto *nm* **Member of Parliament (MP) (GB)** deputato *nm* **Member of the European Parliament (MEP)** deputato del Parlamento Europeo *nm*, Eurodeputato *nmf*
**memo** *abbr* (= memorandum) memorandum *nm*
**memory** *n* (DP) memoria *nf* **memory capacity** capacità di memoria *nf*
**mercantile** *adj* mercantile *adj*
**merchandise** *vb* commerciare *vb*
**merchandizer** *n* merchandiser *nm*
**merchandizing** *n* merchandising *nm*
**merchant** *n* commerciante *nm* **merchant bank** banca mercantile *nf* **merchant navy, merchant marine** (US) marina mercantile *nf* **merchant ship** nave mercantile *nf*, mercantile *nm*
**merge** *vb* fondersi *vb*, incorporarsi *vb*
**merger** *n* incorporazione *nf*, merger *nm*
**merit** *n* **merit payment** salario a incentivo *nm*
**message** *n* messaggio *nm*
**messenger** *n* messaggero *nm*
**metal** *n* metallo *nm*
**meter** *n* contatore *nm*
**method** *n* **method of payment** metodo di pagamento *nm* **production method** metodo di produzione *nm*
**metre, meter** (US) *n* metro *nm* **cubic metre** metro cubo *nm* **square metre** metro quadro *nm*
**metric** *adj* metrico *adj*
**metrication** *n* conversione nel sistema metrico decimale *nf*
**metropolis** *n* metropoli *nf*
**microchip** *n* microchip *nm*, circuito integrato molto minaturizzato *nm*
**microcomputer** *n* microcomputer *nm*
**microeconomics** *n* microeconomia *nf*
**microfiche** *n* microscheda trasparente *nf*
**microprocessor** *n* microprocessore *nm*
**middle** *adj* **middle management** direzione a medio livello *nf* **middle manager** direttore di medio livello *nm*
**middleman** *n* intermediario *nm*
**migrant** *n* **migrant worker** lavoratore migratore *nm*
**mile** *n* miglio *nm* **nautical mile** miglio marino *nm*
**mileage** *n* indennità di percorso *nf*, distanza percorsa in miglia *nf*
**million** *n* milione *nm*
**millionaire** *n* milionario *nm*
**mine** *n* miniera *nf* **coal mine** miniera di carbone *nf*
**mineral** *n* minerale *nm*
**minimal** *adj* minimo *adj*
**minimum** *adj* **index-linked minimum wage** salario minimo indicizzato *nm* **minimum lending rate** tasso minimo di sconto *nm*
**mining** *n* attività mineraria *nf* **mining industry** industria mineraria *nf*
**minister** *n* ministro *nm*

**ministry** *n* ministero *nm*, dicastero *nm* **Ministry of Transport** Ministero dei trasporti *nm*
**minor** *adj* minore *adj*, di poca importanza *adj*
**minority** *n* minoranza *nf* **minority holding** azionariato di minoranza *nm* **in the minority** in minoranza
**mint** **1.** *n* zecca *nf* **2.** *vb* coniare *vb* **he/she mints money** conia monete
**minutes** *npl* **the minutes of the meeting** il verbale dell'assemblea *nm*
**misappropriation** *n* appropriazione indebita *nf*
**miscalculation** *n* errore di calcolo *nm*
**misconduct** *n* (bad management) cattiva amministrazione *nf*, cattiva condotta *nf*
**mishandling** *n* cattiva conduzione *nf*
**mismanagement** *n* cattiva gestione *nf*
**mistake** *n* errore *nm*, sbaglio *nm* **to make a mistake** commettere un errore *vb*, fare uno sbaglio *vb*
**mix** *n* **marketing mix** marketing mix *nm*, insieme degli elementi di marketing *nm* **product mix** mix dei prodotti *nm*
**mixed** *adj* **mixed economy** economia mista *nf*
**mode** *n* (method) modo *nm*, moda *nf*
**model** *n* (person) modello *nm*
**modem** *n* modem *nm*
**moderate** **1.** *adj* moderato *adj* **2.** *vb* moderare *vb*
**moderation** *n* moderazione *nf*
**modern** *adj* moderno *adj*
**modernization** *n* ammodernamento *nm*
**modernize** *vb* modernizzare *vb*
**module** *n* modulo *nm*
**monetarism** *n* monetarismo *nm*
**monetary** *adj* monetario *adj* **European Monetary System (EMS)** Sistema monetario europeo (SME) *nm* **International Monetary Fund (IMF)** Fondo monetario internazionale (FMI) *nm* **monetary policy** politica monetaria *nf*
**money** *n* **dear money** denaro caro *nm* **money market** mercato monetario *nm* **money order** vaglia postale *nm* **public money** denaro pubblico *nm* **money supply** offerta di moneta *nf* **to raise money** ottenere fondi *vb*, ottenere denaro liquido *vb* **money trader** broker *nm*
**moneymaking** *adj* (profitable) molto remunerativo *adj*
**monopoly** *n* monopolio *nm* **Monopolies and Mergers Commission** Commissione per i monopoli e le fusioni *nf*
**monthly** *adj* mensile *adj*
**moonlight*** *vb* svolgere contemporaneamente due professioni *vb*, avere un secondo lavoro *vb*
**moor** *vb* attraccare *vb*
**mooring** *n* ormeggio *nm* **mooring rights** diritti di ormeggio *nmpl*
**mortgage** *n* ipoteca *nf* **mortgage deed** contratto ipotecario *nm* **mortgage loan** prestito ipotecario *nm*
**mortgagee** *n* creditore ipotecario *nm*
**mortgagor** *n* debitore ipotecario *nm*
**motor** *n* **motor industry** industria automobilistica *nf*
**multilateral** *adj* multilaterale *adj*
**multinational** *adj* multinazionale *adj* **multinational corporation** multinazionale *nf*
**multiple** *adj* **multiple store** grande magazzino *nm*
**multiply** *vb* moltiplicare *vb*
**multipurpose** *adj* pluriuso *adj*, plurimpiego *adj*
**municipal** *adj* **municipal bonds** obbligazione municipale *nf*
**mutual** *adj* mutuo *adj*, reciproco *adj* **mutual fund (US)** fondo comune d'investimento a capitale variabile *nm*
**mutually** *adv* reciprocamente *adv*
**N/A (not applicable)** *abbr* non pertinente *adj*
**name** **1.** *n* **brand name** marchio di fabbrica *nm* **by name** di nome *adv* **named person** persona designata *nf* **full name** nome e cognome *nm & nm* **in the name of** in nome di *prep* **registered trade name** marchio depositato *nm* **2.** *vb* chiamare *vb*
**narrow** *adj* **narrow margin** margine stretto *nm* **narrow market** mercato languido *nm*
**nation** *n* nazione *nf*, stato *nm* **the United Nations** Nazioni Unite (ONU) *nfpl*
**national** *adj* **national debt** debito nazionale *nm* **national income** reddito nazionale *nm* **national insurance (NI) (GB)** assicurazioni sociali *nfpl* **national interest** interesse nazionale *nm* **National Bureau of Economic Research (US)** National Bureau of Economic Research, (organizzazione privata statunitense di ricerca)
**nationality** *n* nazionalità *nf*
**nationalization** *n* nazionalizzazione *nf*

**nationalize** *vb* nazionalizzare *vb* **nationalized industry** industria nazionalizzata *nf*

**nationwide** *adj* a carattere nazionale *adv*

**natural** *adj* **natural rate of increase** tasso naturale di crescita *nm* **natural resources** risorse naturali *nfpl*

**necessary** *adj* necessario *adj* **necessary qualifications** titoli necessari *nmpl*, qualifiche necessarie *nfpl*

**necessity** *n* (goods) necessità *nf*

**need** *n* **needs assessment** accertamento delle necessità *nm* **needs of industry** esigenze dell'industria *nfpl* **to be in need** aver bisogno di *vb*

**negative** *adj* **negative cash flow** cash flow negativo *nm* **negative feedback** feedback negativo *nm*, retroazione negativa *nf*

**negative (US)** *vb* respingere *vb*

**neglect** *adj* **neglect clause** clausola di negligenza *nf*

**negligence** *n* negligenza *nf* **negligence clause** clausola di negligenza *nf* **contributory negligence** concorso di colpa *nm* **gross negligence** colpa grave *nf*

**negligent** *adj* negligente *adj*

**negotiable** *adj* negoziabile *adj* **negotiable bill** cambiale trasferibile *nf* **negotiable cheque** assegno trasferibile *nm*

**negotiate** *vb* negoziare *vb*, contrattare *vb* **negotiated price** prezzo negoziato *nm*

**negotiating** *adj* **negotiating session** seduta di negoziazione *nf* **negotiating skills** abilità di contrattazione *nfpl*

**negotiation** *n* negoziazione *nf* **by negotiation** tramite negoziazione, in seguito a trattativa **to begin negotiations** intavolare trattative *vb*, iniziare le trattative *vb* **under negotiation** in fase di trattativa **wage negotiations** trattativa salariale *nf*

**negotiator** *n* negoziatore *nm*

**net, nett** 1. *adj* netto *adj* **net amount** ammontare netto *nm* **net assets** attività nette *nfpl* **net cost** costo netto *nm* **net earnings** utile netto di esercizio *nm* **net interest** interesse netto *nm* **net investment** investimento netto *nm* **net loss** perdita netta di esercizio *nf* **net price** prezzo netto *nm* **net proceeds** provento netto *nm* **net profit** utile di esercizio *nm* **net result** risultato netto *nm* **net sales** fatturato netto *nm* **net saving** risparmio netto *nm* **terms strictly net** condizioni di pagamento rigorosamente nette *nfpl* **net wage** salario netto *nm* **net weight** peso netto *nm* 2. *vb* ricavare *vb*, dare un utile netto di *vb*

**network** 1. *n* **banking network** rete bancaria *nf* **computer network** rete informatica *nf* **distribution network** rete di distribuzione *nf* 2. *vb* trasmettere *vb*

**neutral** *adj* neutrale *adj*

**new** *adj* **new account** nuovo conto *nm*, nuovo account *nm* **new business** nuova azienda *nf*, nuovi affari *nmpl* **new product** nuovo prodotto *nm* **new technology** nuova tecnologia *nf*

**newly** *adv* **newly-appointed** designato di recente **newly-industrialised** recentemente industrializzato *adj*

**news** *n* notizie *nfpl* **news agency** agenzia di stampa *nf* **bad news** brutte notizie *nfpl* **news bulletin** notiziario *nm*, giornale radio *nm* **news coverage** trattazione delle notizie *nf*, cronaca *nf* **financial news** notizie finanziarie *nfpl* **good news** buone notizie *nfpl*

**newsdealer (US)** *n* edicolante *nmf*

**newsletter** *n* bollettino *nm*, notiziario *nm*

**newspaper** *n* giornale *nm* **newspaper advertisement** pubblicità a mezzo stampa *nf* **daily newspaper** quotidiano *nm* **newspaper report** servizio giornalistico sulla stampa *nm*

**nil** *n* nulla *nf*, zero *nm* **nil profit** senza profitto

**no** *det* **no agents wanted** non si cercano agenti **no-claims bonus** sconto condizionato *nm* **no commercial value** senza valore commerciale

**nominal** *adj* nominale *adj* **nominal amount** somma nominale *nf* **nominal assets** attività nominali *nfpl* **nominal damages** danni nominali *nmpl* **nominal inflation** inflazione nominale *nf* **nominal price** prezzo nominale *nm* **nominal value** valore nominale *nm*, valore facciale *nm*

**nominate** *vb* nominare *vb* **nominate sb to a board/committee** designare *vb*, proporre la candidatura di qualcuno ad un comitato *vb*

**nomination** *n* nomina *nf*

**nominee** *n* intestatario *nm* **nominee shareholder** azionista prestanome *nmf*, azionista intestatario *nmf*

**non-acceptance** *n* mancata accettazione *nf*

**non-attendance** *n* assenza *nf*

**non-completion** *n* mancato perfezionamento *nm*

**non-contributory** *adj* non contributivo *adj*

**non-convertible** *adj* non convertibile *adj*
**non-delivery** *n* mancata consegna *nf*
**non-discriminatory** *adj* non discriminatorio *adj*
**non-essential** *adj* non essenziale *adj*
**non-interest-bearing** *adj* infruttifero *adj*
**non-intervention** *n* non intervento *nm*
**non-negotiable** *adj* non negoziabile *adj*
**non-payment** *n* mancato pagamento *nm*
**non-profitmaking** *adj* senza scopo di lucro
**non-returnable** *adj* non rimborsabile *adj*, non a rendere *adj*
**non-stop** *adj* ininterrotto *adj*
**non-transferable** *adj* non trasferibile *adj*
**norm** *n* norma *nf*, regola *nf*
**normal** *adj* **normal trading hours** orario d'apertura dei negozi *nm*, orario d'ufficio *nm*
**not** *adv* **not applicable** non pertinente *adj* **not available** non disponibile *adj* **not dated** non datato *adj*
**notary** *n* notaio *nmf*
**note** *n* **advice note** avviso *nm* **cover note** nota di copertura *nf* **credit note** nota di accredito *nf* **debit note** nota di addebito *nf* **delivery note** bolla di consegna *nf* **dispatch note** bollettino di spedizione *nm* **open note (US)** credito aperto in conto corrente *nm* **to compare notes** raffrontare idee con *vb* **to make a note of sth** prendere appunti su *vb*, annotare *vb*
**noteworthy** *adj* degno di nota *adj*
**notice** *n* **advance notice** preavviso *nm* **at short notice** con breve preavviso **final notice** ultimo avviso *nm* **notice period** termine di preavviso *nm* **term of notice** preavviso di licenziamento *nm* **to come to the notice of sb** apprendere *vb* **to give notice of sth** annunciare *vb*, comunicare *vb* **to take notice** osservare *vb*, notare *vb* **until further notice** fino a nuovo avviso
**notification** *n* notifica *nf*
**notify** *vb* notificare *vb*, avvisare *vb*
**null** *adj* **null and void** nullo e di nessun effetto *adj*, privo di valore legale *adj*
**number** *n* **account number** numero di conto *nm* **opposite number** equivalente *nmf*, corrispondente *nmf* **order number** numero d'ordine *nm*, numero dell'ordinativo *nm* **serial number** numero di serie *nm* **telephone number** numero di telefono *nm* **wrong number** numero sbagliato *nm*
**numeracy** *n* saper far di conto *nm*
**numerate** *adj* che sa far di conto *adj*
**numeric** *adj* **numeric-alphabetic** alfanumerico *adj* **numeric character** carattere numerico *nm*, cifra *nf*
**numerical** *adj* **numerical analysis** analisi numerica *nf*
**NYSE (New York Stock Exchange)** *abbr* Borsa Valori di New York *nf*
**object** *vb* opporsi a *vb*
**objection** *n* obiezione *nf* **to make/raise an objection** sollevare un'obiezione *vb*
**objective** *n* obiettivo *nm* **to reach an objective** raggiungere un obiettivo *vb*
**obligation** *n* obbligazione *nf*, impegno *nm* **to meet one's obligations** far fronte ai propri impegni *vb*
**obligatory** *adj* obbligatorio *adj*
**oblige** *vb* **to be obliged to do sth** essere obbligato a *vb*, dovere *vb*
**observation** *n* **under observation** sotto osservazione *adv*
**observe** *vb* **observe the rules** osservare le regole *vb*
**obsolescence** *n* obsolescenza *nf* **built-in obsolescence** obsolescenza automatica *nf*
**obsolete** *adj* obsoleto *adj*
**obtain** *vb* ottenere *vb* **to obtain credit** ottenere credito *vb*
**occupant** *n* affittuario *nm*, locatario *nm*
**occupation** *n* occupazione *nf*
**occupational** *adj* **occupational disease** malattia professionale *nf* **occupational hazard** rischio professionale *nm*
**occupier** *n* locatario *nm*, affittuario *nm*
**occupy** *vb* (premises) occupare *vb*
**off-the-job** *adj* **off-the-job training** addestramento fuori sede *nm*
**offence, offense** (US) *n* reato *nm*, trasgressione *nf*
**offer** *n* **firm offer** offerta ferma *nf* **offer in writing** offerta proposta per iscritto *nf* **offer subject to confirmation** offerta salvo conferma *nf* **offer valid until...** offerta valida fino a ... *nf*
**offeree** *n* destinatario *nm*
**offeror** *n* proponente *nmf*
**office** *n* ufficio *nm* **office equipment** attrezzatura di ufficio *nf* **office hours** orario di ufficio *nm* **office management** direzione di ufficio *nf* **office staff** personale di ufficio *nm* **to hold office** essere in carica *vb* **to resign from office** dimettersi da *vb*
**official** *n* ufficiale *adj* **official strike** sciopero ufficiale *nm*

**offshore** *adj* **offshore company** società offshore *nf*
**oil** *n* **oil industry** industria petrolifera *nf* **oil state** paese produttore di petrolio *nm*
**oilfield** *n* giacimento petrolifero *nm*
**oligopoly** *n* oligopolio *nm*, mercato oligopolistico *nm*
**ombudsman** *n* ombudsman *nm*, difensore civico *nm*
**on-line** *adj* on-line *adj*
**on-the-job** *adj* **on-the-job training** addestramento sul lavoro *nm*
**onus** *n* **the onus is on us to...** abbiamo l'obbligo di, abbiamo la responsabilità di
**open** 1. *adj* **open cheque** assegno aperto *nm*, assegno al portatore *nm* **open credit** credito in bianco *nm*, credito scoperto *nm* **open market** mercato aperto *nm* 2. *vb* **to open an account** aprire un conto *vb*
**open up** *vb* (market) aprire il mercato *vb*
**opening** *adj* **opening price** prezzo di apertura *nm* **opening times** orario d'apertura *nm*
**operate** *vb* **to operate a business** gestire un'impresa *vb*
**operating** *adj* **operating expenditure** spese di gestione *nfpl*, costi di esercizio *nmpl* **operating expenses** spese di gestione *nfpl*, costi di esercizio *nmpl* **operating income** utile di gestione *nm* **operating profit** utile di gestione *nm* **operating statement** conto economico operativo *nm*, conto profitti e perdite operativo *nm*
**operation** *n* (of business) operazione *nf*, conduzione *nf*, funzionamento *nm* (of machine) operazione *nf*, funzionamento *nm*
**operator** *n* operatore *nm*
**opportunity** *n* opportunità *nf*, occasione *nf* **market opportunities** opportunità del mercato *nfpl* **to seize an opportunity** cogliere l'occasione *vb*
**option** *n* opzione *nf*, alternativa *nf* **share option, stock option** (US) contratto a premio *nm* **options market** mercato a termine *nm* **option to buy** opzione di acquisto *nf* **option to cancel** opzione di annullamento *nf*
**optional** *adj* opzionale *adj*, facoltativo *adj*
**order** 1. *adj* **order book** libro ordinazioni *nm* **order form** buono d'ordine *nm*, modulo di ordinazione *nm* **order number** numero di ordine *nm* 2. *n* **pay to the order of...** pagare all'ordine di *vb* **to cancel an order** annullare un ordine *vb* **to place an order** ordinare *vb*
**ordinary** *adj* **ordinary general meeting** assemblea generale ordinaria *nf* **ordinary share, ordinary stock** (US) azione ordinaria *nf*
**organization** *n* organizzazione *nf*
**organize** *vb* organizzare *vb* **organized labour** (trade unions) lavoratori organizzati in sindacati *nmpl*
**origin** *n* (of a product) origine *nf* **country of origin** paese d'origine *nm* **statement of origin** dichiarazione di origine *nf*
**original** *adj* **original cost** costo originario *nm*
**outbid** *vb* offrire di più di *vb*
**outcome** *n* esito *nm*, risultato *nm*
**outgoings** *npl* esborsi *nmpl*
**outlay** *n* **capital outlay** spesa in conto capitale *nf*
**outlet** *n* **market outlet** punto di vendita *nm* **sales outlet** sbocco di vendita *nm*
**outlook** *n* **business outlook** prospettive commerciali *nfpl*
**output** *n* produzione *nf* **to increase output** incrementare la produzione *vb*
**outstanding** *adj* **outstanding amount** somma scoperta *nf*, ammontare in arretrato *nm* **outstanding debt** debiti insoluti *nmpl* **outstanding stock** capitale sociale in circolazione *nm*
**overcharge** *vb* fare prezzi troppo alti *vb*, far pagare troppo caro *vb* addebitare in più *vb*
**overdraft** *n* scoperto di conto *nm*, conto scoperto *nm* **to request an overdraft** richiedere uno scoperto di conto *vb*
**overdraw** *vb* andare allo scoperto *vb*, andare in rosso *vb* **overdrawn account** conto scoperto *nm*
**overdue** *adj* scaduto *adj*, in sospeso *adj*
**overhead** *adj* **overhead costs** costi comuni *nmpl*, costi generali *nmpl*
**overheads** *npl* costi comuni *nmpl*, spese comuni *nfpl*
**overheating** *n* surriscaldamento *nm*
**overload** *vb* sovraccaricare *vb*
**overlook** *vb* lasciarsi sfuggire *vb*
**overman** *vb* impiegare personale in soprannumero *vb* **overmanned** con eccesso di personale, con eccesso di manodopera
**overmanning** *n* (excess staff) eccesso di personale *nm*
**overnight** *adj* **overnight delivery** consegna il giorno dopo *nf*

**overpay** *vb* pagare troppo *vb*, remunerare eccessivamente *vb*
**overpayment** *n* pagamento eccessivo *nm*, remunerazione eccessiva *nf*
**overpopulation** *n* sovrappopolazione *nf*
**overproduce** *vb* sovrapprodurre *vb*
**overproduction** *n* sovrapproduzione *nf*
**overseas** *adj* estero *adj* **overseas market** mercato estero *nm* **overseas territory** territorio estero *nm* **overseas trade** commercio con l'estero *nm*
**oversell** *vb* vendere più di quanto si ha a disposizione *vb*
**oversight** *n* omissione *nf*, svista *nf* **due to an oversight** a causa di una svista, per sbaglio
**oversold** *adj* supervenduto *pp*
**oversubscribed** *adj* sottoscritto in eccesso *pp*
**oversupply** *vb* rifornire eccessivamente *vb*
**overtime** *n* straordinario *nm*
**overvalue** *vb* sopravvalutare *vb*
**overworked** *adj* con eccesso di lavoro *adj*, strapazzato *adj*
**owe** *vb* dovere *vb*, essere in debito di *vb*
**own** *vb* possedere *vb*
**owner** *n* proprietario *nm*, titolare *nmf*
**owner-occupier** *n* proprietario-occupante *nm*
**ownership** *n* proprietà *nf*
**pack** *vb* imballare *vb*
**package** *n* collo *nm*, pacco *nm* **package deal** pacchetto *nm* **package tour** viaggio tutto compreso *nm*
**packaging** *n* confezione *nf*, imballaggio *nm*
**packet** *n* pacco *nm*, pacchetto *nm*
**pallet** *n* pallet *nm*
**palletized** *adj* **palletized freight** trasporto pallettizzato *nm*
**paper** *n* **commercial paper** carta commerciale *nm* **paper loss** perdita nominale *nf* **paper profit** profitto nominale *nm*
**paperwork** *n* lavoro d'ufficio *nm*, documenti *nmpl*
**par** *n* **above par** sopra la pari **below par** sotto la pari
**parent** *n* **parent company** società madre *nf*, società di controllo *nf*
**parity** *n* parità *nf*
**part** *n* (of a machine) parte *nf*, pezzo *nm* **part payment** pagamento parziale *nm*, acconto *nm* **part shipment** spedizione parziale *nf* **spare part** (for machine) parte di ricambio *nf*, ricambio *nm*
**part-time** *adj, adv* a tempo parziale *adj, adv*, part-time *adj, adv*
**participation** *n* **worker participation** partecipazione operaia *nf*
**partner** *n* socio *nm* **sleeping partner** socio non amministratore *nm*
**partnership** *n* società semplice *nf*, società di persone *nf* **trading partnership** società commerciale *nf*
**passenger** *n* passeggero *nm*
**patent** *n* brevetto *nm* **patented** brevettato *adj & pp*
**patronage** *n* clientela *nf*, patrocinio *nm*
**pattern** *n* **spending patterns** trend della spesa *nmpl*
**pay 1.** *n* (salary, wages) paga *nf*, retribuzione *nf*, remunerazione *nf* **equal pay** parità salariale *nf* **pay rise** aumento di paga *nm* **severance pay** indennità di licenziamento *nf* **unemployment pay** indennità di disoccupazione *nf* **2.** *vb* **paid holiday** vacanza pagata *nf*, ferie pagate *nfpl* **paid-up capital** capitale interamente versato *nm* **to pay an invoice** pagare una fattura *vb* **to pay by credit card** pagare con la carta di credito *vb* **to pay for a service** pagare un servizio *vb* **to pay in advance** pagare in anticipo *vb* **to pay in cash** pagare in contanti *vb*
**payable** *adj* **accounts payable** conto creditori diversi *nm*
**payee** *n* beneficiario *nm*
**payer** *n* **prompt payer** pagatore puntuale *nm* **slow payer** pagatore lento *nm*
**payload** *n* (of vehicle) carico remunerativo *nm*, carico pagante *nm*
**payment** *n* pagamento *nm* **down payment** acconto *nm*
**payola (US)** *n* tangente *nf*, sottomano *nm*
**payroll** *n* ruolo paga *nm* **to be on the payroll** essere compreso nel ruolo paga *vb*
**peak 1.** *adj* **peak demand** domanda di punta *nf* **peak period** periodo di punta *nm* **2.** *n* valore massimo *nm*, punta *nf*
**pecuniary** *adj* **for pecuniary gain** per guadagno finanziario
**peddle** *vb* fare il venditore ambulante *vb*, spacciare *vb*
**peg** *vb* (prices) sostenere *vb*, stabilizzare *vb* **the HK dollar is pegged to the US dollar** il dollaro di Hong Kong è sostenuto rispetto al dollaro americano

**penetration** *n* **market penetration** penetrazione del mercato *nf*
**pension** *n* pensione *nf* **pension fund** fondo pensioni *nm* **retirement pension** pensione di vecchiaia *nf* **pension scheme** piano di pensionamento *nm*
**per** *prep* **per annum** all'anno *adv* **per capita** pro capite *adv* **per cent** per cento *adv*
**percentage** *n* percentuale *nf* **percentage of profit** percentuale di profitto *nf*
**performance** *n* performance *nf*, prestazione *nf* **performance appraisal** valutazione del personale *nf* **performance-related bonus** premio in funzione della performance *nm*
**period** *n* **cooling-off period** periodo di raffreddamento *nm* **period of grace** periodo di grazia *nm*
**peripheral** *adj* periferico *adj*
**perishable** *adj* **perishable goods** beni deperibili *nmpl*
**perk** *n* gratifica *nf*
**permanent** *adj* **permanent employment** impiego permanente *nm*
**permit** *n* permesso *nm*, autorizzazione *nf* **building permit** licenza edilizia *nf*
**perquisite** *n* (formal) gratifica *nf*
**person** *n* **third person** terzo *nm*
**personal** *adj* personale *adj*
**personnel** *n* **personnel department** ufficio del personale *nm* **personnel management** gestione del personale *nf*
**peseta** *n* peseta *nf*
**petrodollar** *n* petrodollaro *nm*
**petroleum** *n* **petroleum industry** industria petrolifera *nf*
**pharmaceutical** *adj* **pharmaceutical industry** industria farmaceutica *nf*
**phoney*** *adj* **phoney* company** società fittizia *nf*
**photocopier** *n* fotocopiatrice *nf*
**photocopy** 1. *n* fotocopia *nf*, copia fotostatica *nf* 2. *vb* fotocopiare *vb*
**pick up** *vb* (improve) riprendere vigore *vb*
**picket** *n* (strike) picchetto *nm*
**piecework** *n* cottimo *nm*, lavoro a cottimo *nm*
**pig iron** *n* ghisa di alto forno *nf*
**pilferage** *n* perdita per piccolo furto *nf*
**pilot** *n* **pilot plant** impianto pilota *nm* **pilot scheme** piano pilota *nm*
**pipeline** *n* oleodotto *nm*, gasdotto *nm*
**piracy** *n* (at sea) pirateria *nf* **software piracy** pirataggio *nm*, esecuzione non autorizzata di copie di software *nf*
**place** *vb* **to place an order** dare un'ordinazione *vb*
**plan** 1. *n* **economic plan** piano economico *nm* **plan of campaign** piano della campagna *nm* **to make plans** fare progetti *vb* 2. *vb* pianificare *vb* fare programmi *vb*, fare piani *vb* **planned economy** economia pianificata *nf* **planned obsolescence** obsolescenza programmata *nf*
**planning** *n* pianificazione *nf* **regional planning** pianificazione regionale *nf*
**plant** *n* (machinery) impianto *nm* **plant hire** locazione di impianto *nf* **plant manager** direttore degli impianti *nm*
**plastic** *n* **plastics industry** industria delle materie plastiche *nf*
**pledge** *n* pegno *nm*, garanzia *nf*
**plenary** *adj* (assembly, session) plenario *adj*
**plough back, plow back, to** (US) *vb* (profits) reinvestire *vb*
**point** *n* **point of sale** punto di vendita *nm*
**policy** *n* **insurance policy** polizza assicurativa *nf* **pricing policy** politica dei prezzi *nf*
**political** *adj* politico *adj*
**politics** *n* politica *nf*
**port** *n* porto *nm*
**portable** *adj* portatile *adj*
**portfolio** *n* **investment portfolio** portafoglio titoli *nm*
**post** 1. *n* (job) posto *nm*, impiego *nm* **post office** ufficio postale *nm* 2. *vb* imbucare *vb*
**postal** *adj* **postal services** servizi postali *nmpl*
**postdate** *vb* postdatare *vb*
**poste restante** *n* fermo posta *nm*
**poster** *n* (advertising) poster *nm*, manifesto *nm*
**postpone** *vb* posticipare *vb*, rimandare *vb*
**potential** *n* **sales potential** potenziale di vendita *nm*
**pound** *n* (weight) libbra *nf* **pound sterling** sterlina *nf*, lira sterlina *nf*
**power** *n* facoltà *nf*, capacità *nf*, potere *nm*, potenza *nf* **power of attorney** procura *nf*, atto di procura *nm*
**preference** *n* **community preference** preferenza comunitaria *nf*
**preferential** *adj* preferenziale *adj*, privilegiato *adj*
**premises** *npl* locali *nmpl* **office premises** locali adibiti a uffici *nmpl*

**premium** *n* premio *nm* **at a premium** sopra la pari
**prepayment** *n* pagamento anticipato *nm*
**president** *n* presidente *nm*
**press** *n* **press baron** barone della stampa *nm* **press conference** conferenza stampa *nf*
**price** *n* prezzo *nm* **market price** prezzo di mercato *nm* **stock exchange prices** prezzi di borsa *nmpl* **threshold price** prezzi di soglia *nmpl*
**pricing** *n* **pricing policy** politica di determinazione dei prezzi *nf*
**primary** *adj* **primary industry** industria primaria *nf*
**prime** *adj* **prime lending rate** tasso primario d'interesse ufficiale *nm*
**priority** *n* priorità *nf*
**private** *adj* **private sector** settore privato *nm*
**privatization** *n* privatizzazione *nf*
**privatize** *vb* privatizzare *vb*
**pro** **1.** *n* **pros and cons** pro e contro *nmpl* **2.** *prep* **pro rata** proporzionale *adj*
**probate** *n* copia autenticata di testamento *nf*
**proceeds** *npl* ricavo *nm*, proventi *nmpl*
**process** **1.** *n* processo *nm*, processo operativo *nm* **2.** *vb* lavorare *vb*
**produce** **1.** *n* prodotto *nm*, genere *nm* **2.** *vb* produrre *vb*
**producer** *n* produttore *nm*
**product** *n* prodotto *nm* **primary product** prodotto primario *nm*
**production** *n* produzione *nf* **production line** linea di lavorazione *nf*, linea di produzione *nf*
**productive** *adj* produttivo *adj*
**productivity** *n* produttività *nf* **productivity gains** incrementi della produttività *nmpl*
**profession** *n* professione *nf* **the professions** le libere professioni *nfpl*
**profit** *n* profitto *nm* **profit and loss** profitti e perdite *nmpl & nfpl* **profit margin** margine di profitto *nm* **net profit** profitto netto *nm*, utile di esercizio *nm* **operating profit** utile di gestione *nm* **profit-sharing scheme** piano di compartecipazione agli utili *nm* **to make a profit** registrare un profitto *vb*, guadagnare *vb*
**profitability** *n* redditività *nf*
**profiteer** *vb* affarista *nm*, speculatore *nm*
**program** *n* (DP) programma *nm*
**programmer** *n* (DP) programmatore *nm*
**programming** *n* (DP) programmazione *nf*
**progress** **1.** *n* progresso *nm* **2.** *vb* (research, project) procedere *vb*, avanzare *vb*
**project** *n* progetto *nm*
**promissory** *adj* **promissory note** pagherò *nm*, pagherò cambiario *nm*
**promote** *vb* promuovere *vb*
**promotion** *n* promozione *nf*
**promotional** *adj* promozionale *adj*, di sviluppo *adj* **promotional budget** budget promozionale *nm*
**prompt** *adj* sollecito *adj*, immediato *adj*
**property** *n* proprietà *nf*, patrimonio *nm* **property company** società immobiliare *nf* **property developer** sviluppatore di proprietà immobiliare *nm* **private property** proprietà privata *nf*
**proprietary** *adj* brevettato *adj* **proprietary brand** marca esclusiva *nf*
**proprietor** *n* proprietario *nm*, titolare *nm*
**prospect** *n* **future prospects** prospettive future *nfpl*
**prospectus** *n* prospetto *nm*, programma *nm*
**prosperous** *adj* prospero *adj*
**protectionism** *n* protezionismo *nm*
**protectionist** *adj* protezionista *adj*, protezionistico *adj*
**provide** *vb* (supply) fornire *vb*
**provision** *n* (stipulation) disposizione *nf*, norma *nf*
**proxy** *n* (power) delega *nf*
**public** *adj* pubblico *adj* **public company** società pubblica *nf*, società per azioni *nf* **public funds** fondi pubblici *nmpl* **public relations** relazioni pubbliche *nfpl* **public sector** settore pubblico *nm* **public service** servizio pubblico *nm*
**publicity** *n* pubblicità *nf*, propaganda *nf*
**publishing** *n* editoria *nf* **desk-top publishing** desk-top publishing *nm*
**purchase** **1.** *n* acquisto *nm*, compera *nf* **purchase price** prezzo d'acquisto *nm* **2.** *vb* acquistare *vb*, comprare *vb*
**purchasing** *n* **purchasing power** potere di acquisto *nm*
**pyramid** *n* **pyramid scheme** sistema di partecipazione piramidale *nm* **pyramid selling** pyramid selling *nm*, vendita piramidale *nf*
**qualification** *n* qualifica *nf*, titolo *nm* **academic qualification** titolo di studio *nm* **educational qualification** titolo di studio *nm* **professional qualification** qualifica professionale *nf*
**qualified** *adj* **qualified acceptance**

accettazione condizionata *nf* **qualified personnel** personale qualificato *nm*
**qualitative** *adj* qualitativo *adj*
**quality** *n* qualità *nf* **quality control** controllo della qualità *nm* **quality report** relazione sulla qualità *nf* **quality standard** standard di qualità *nm*
**quantitative** *adj* quantitativo *adj*
**quantity** *n* quantità *nf*, quantitativo *nm* **quantity discount** sconto di quantità *nm* **quantity theory of money** teoria quantitativa della moneta *nf*
**quarter** *n* (of year) trimestre *nm*
**quarterly** *adj* trimestrale *adj* **quarterly interest** interessi trimestrali *nmpl* **quarterly trade accounts** estratti conto trimestrali *nmpl*
**quasi-contract** *n* quasi-contratto *nm*
**quasi-income** *n* quasi-rendita *nf*
**quay** *n* banchina *nf*, molo *nm*
**quayage** *n* diritti di banchina *nmpl*
**questionnaire** *n* questionario *nm* **market research questionnaire** questionario di ricerca di mercato *nm*
**queue** *n* coda *nf*
**quick** *adj* **quick assets** attività di pronto realizzo *nfpl*
**quiet** *adj* **quiet market** mercato tranquillo *nm*
**quit** *vb* (resign) andarsene *vb*, cessare *vb*, abbandonare un impiego *vb*
**quittance** *n* saldo *nm*
**quorate** *adj* **quorate meeting** avente un quorum *adj*, avente un numero legale *adj*
**quorum** *n* numero legale *nm*, quorum *nm* **quorum of creditors** quorum di creditori *nm*
**quota** 1. *adj* **quota agreement** accordo di contingente *nm* **quota buying** criterio del riordino per quote *nm* **quota sampling** campionamento proporzionale *nm* **quota system** sistema del contingentamento *nm* 2. *n* quota *nf*, contingente *nm* **import quota** contingente d'importazione *nm* **sales quota** quota di vendite *nf*
**quotation** *n* (price) quotazione *nf*, preventivo *nm*
**quoted** *adj* **quoted company** società quotata in borsa *nf* **quoted investment** investimento in valori mobiliari *nm* **quoted share, quoted stocks** (US) azioni quotate in borsa *nfpl*
**racket** *n* racket *nm*, truffa *nf*
**racketeer** *n* truffatore *nm*
**racketeering** *n* attività illegali per estorcere denaro *nfpl*
**rag** *n* **the rag trade** (informal) industria della confezione *nf*, industria dell'abbigliamento *nf*
**rail** *n* **by rail** in treno, per ferrovia
**railway, railroad** (US) *n* ferrovie *nfpl*
**raise** *vb* (price, interest rate) aumentare *vb* (capital, loan) aumentare *vb*, rincarare *vb*
**RAM (random access memory)** *abbr* (DP) RAM (random access memory) *abbr*
**random** 1. *adj* **random selection** selezione casuale *nf* 2. *n* **at random** a casaccio, alla cieca
**range** *n* gamma *nf*
**rate** *n* **base rate** saggio base *nm* **rate of exchange** cambio *nm*, corso del cambio *nm* **rate of expansion** tasso di espansione *nm* **rate of growth** tasso di crescita *nm* **rate of inflation** tasso inflazionistico *nm* **rate of interest** tasso d'interesse *nm* **rate of investment** tasso di investimento *nm* **rate of return** tasso di rendimento *nm* **rates** (tax) imposte locali *nfpl*
**ratification** *n* ratifica *nf*
**ratify** *vb* ratificare *vb*
**ratio** *n* rapporto *nm*
**rationale** *n* base razionale *nf*, giustificazione logica *nf*
**rationalization** *n* razionalizzazione *nf* **rationalization measures** misure di razionalizzazione *nfpl*
**rationalize** *vb* razionalizzare *vb*, organizzare razionalmente *vb*
**raw** *adj* (unprocessed) greggio *adj*
**re** *prep* in relazione a *prep*, in riferimento a *prep*, oggetto *nm*
**re-elect** *vb* rieleggere *vb*
**re-election** *n* rielezione *nf*
**ready** *adj* **ready for despatch** pronto per la consegna *adj*
**real** *adj* **real estate** proprietà immobiliare *nf* **real price** prezzo reale *nm* **real time** tempo reale *nm* **real value** valore reale *nm* **real wages** salario reale *nm*
**realization** *n* **realization of assets** realizzo di attività *nm*
**realize** *vb* (profit) realizzare *vb*
**reallocate** *vb* (funds) ripartire *vb*, ridistribuire *vb*
**reallocation** *n* (of funds) ripartizione *nf*, ridistribuzione *nf*
**realtor (US)** *n* agente immobiliare *nm*
**reappoint** *vb* rinominare *vb*, rieleggere *vb*
**reappointment** *n* nuova nomina *nf*
**reasonable** *adj* (price) ragionevole *adj*

**rebate** *n* ribasso *nm*, rimborso *nm* **to grant a rebate** concedere un rimborso *vb*
**receipt** *n* **to acknowledge receipt** accusare ricevuta *vb* **to issue a receipt** rilasciare una ricevuta *vb*, emettere una ricevuta *vb*
**receive** *vb* ricevere *vb*
**receiver, administrator** (US) *n* (bankruptcy) curatore *nm*, amministratore giudiziale *nm*
**recession** *n* recessione economica *nf*
**recipient** *n* destinatario *nm*
**reciprocal** *adj* reciproco *adj*
**reclaimable** *adj* (materials) recuperabile *adj*
**recommend** *vb* raccomandare *vb*
**recommendation** *n* raccomandazione *nf*
**recompense** *n* ricompensa *nf*
**record** *n* registrazione *nf*, documentazione *nf*, trascrizione *nf* **according to our records** risulta dai dati a nostra disposizione
**recover** *vb* **to recover money from sb** ricuperare una somma di denaro da *vb*
**recovery** *n* (of debt) ricupero *nm* (economic) ripresa economica *nf*
**recruit** *vb* reclutare *vb*, assumere *vb*
**recruitment** *n* reclutamento *nm* **recruitment campaign** campagna di reclutamento *nf*, campagna di assunzione *nf*
**recyclable** *adj* riciclabile *adj*
**recycle** *vb* riciclare *vb*
**red** *adj* **red tape** burocrazia *nf* **to be in the red** essere in deficit *vb*, essere allo scoperto *vb*
**redeem** *vb* riscattare *vb*, ammortare *vb*
**redeemable** *adj* riscattabile *adj* **redeemable bond** obbligazione redimibile *nf*
**redemption** *n* riscatto *nm* **redemption fund** ammortamento *nm*, redenzione *nf*
**redirect** *vb* (mail) rispedire ad un nuovo indirizzo *vb*
**reduce** *vb* ridurre *vb* **at a greatly reduced price** ad un prezzo nettamente ridotto
**reduction** *n* riduzione *nf*
**redundancy** *n* esuberanza di personale *nf*
**redundant** *adj* esuberante *adj* **to make sb redundant** dichiarare esuberante *vb*
**refer** *vb* **we refer to our letter of...** in riferimento alla nostra lettera del .... **we refer you to our head office** vogliate consultare il nostro ufficio centrale
**referee** *n* arbitro *nm* **to act as referee** agire da referenza *vb*
**reference** *n* referenza *nf*, attestato *nm*, riferimento *nm* **credit reference** attestato di posizione creditizia *nm* **reference number** numero di riferimento *nm* **to take up a reference** richiedere una referenza *vb* **with reference to** in riferimento a *prep*
**referendum** *n* referendum *nm*
**reflation** *n* reflazione *nf*
**reflationary** *adj* reflazionistico *adj*
**reform** *n* riforma *nf* **currency reform** riforma monetaria *nf*
**refund** **1.** *n* rimborso *nm* **2.** *vb* rimborsare *vb*
**refundable** *adj* rimborsabile *adj*, risarcibile *adj*
**refurbish** *vb* mettere a nuovo *vb*
**refurbishment** *n* ammodernamento *nm*
**refusal** *n* rifiuto *nm*
**refuse** *vb* **to refuse a claim** respingere una richiesta d'indennizzo *vb* **to refuse goods** rifiutare merci *vb* **to refuse payment** rifiutare pagamento *vb*
**regard** *n* **with regard to...** riguardo a *prep*, in quanto a *prep*
**regarding** *prep* relativamente a *prep*, concernente *adj*
**regional** *adj* **regional office** ufficio regionale *nm*
**register** *n* registro *nm*
**registered** *adj* **registered bond** titolo nominativo *nm* **registered capital** capitale sociale nominale *nm* **registered company** società costituita mediante registrazione *nf* **registered letter** lettera raccomandata *nf* **registered mail** posta raccomandata *nf* **registered office** sede legale *nf*, sede sociale *nf* **registered share** azione nominativa *nf* **registered trademark** marchio depositato *nm*
**regret** *vb* **we regret to inform you that...** ci rincresce informarvi che ...
**regular** *adj* **regular customer** cliente abituale *nmf*
**regulation** *n* regolamento *nm*, direttiva *nf* **according to the regulations** secondo le regole
**reimburse** *vb* rimborsare *vb*
**reimbursement** *n* rimborso *nm*, risarcimento *nm*
**reimport** *vb* reimportare *vb*, importare di nuovo *vb*
**reimportation** *n* reimportazione *nf*
**reinsurance** *n* riassicurazione *nf*
**reinsure** *vb* riassicurare *vb*
**reject** *vb* (goods) scartare *vb*
**relation** *n* **business relations** rapporti di

affari *nmpl* **industrial relations** relazioni industriali *nfpl*
**relationship** *n* **working relationship** rapporto di lavoro *nm*
**relax** *vb* (restrictions) rilassare *vb*
**relevant** *adj* pertinente *adj*
**reliability** *n* affidabilità *nf*, attendibilità *nf*
**reliable** *adj* affidabile *adj*, attendibile *adj*
**relocate** *vb* trasferire *vb*
**relocation** *n* trasferimento *nm*
**remaining** *adj* (sum) rimanente *adj*
**reminder** *n* lettera di sollecito *nf*
**remittance** *n* rimessa *nf* **remittance advice** distinta di accompagnamento *nf*
**remunerate** *vb* remunerare *vb*
**remuneration** *n* remunerazione *nf*
**renew** *vb* (policy, contract) rinnovare *vb*
**renewable** *adj* rinnovabile *adj*
**rent** *vb* (house, office) affittare *vb*, dare in affitto *vb*, prendere in affitto *vb*
**rental** *n* canone di affitto *nm*
**repair** **1.** *n* **costs of repair** costi di riparazione *nmpl* **2.** *vb* riparare *vb*
**reparation** *n* riparazione *nf*
**repatriation** *n* rimpatrio *nm*
**repay** *vb* rimborsare *vb*
**repayment** *n* (of loan) restituzione (di un prestito) *nf*
**repeat** *adj* **repeat order** ordinazione ripetuta *nf*
**replace** *vb* sostituire *vb*
**replacement** *n* (person) sostituzione *nf*
**reply** *n* **in reply to your letter of...** in risposta alla vostra lettera del ...
**report** *n* rapporto *nm*, relazione *nf* **annual report** relazione annuale *nf* **to draw up a report** redigere una relazione *vb* **to submit/present a report** presentare una relazione *vb*
**repossess** *vb* riprendere possesso di *vb*
**repossession** *n* ripresa di possesso *nf*
**representative** *n* rappresentante *nm* **area representative** rappresentante di zona *nm* **sales representative** rappresentante di commercio *nm*, rappresentante di vendite *nm*
**repudiate** *vb* (contract) ripudiare *vb*
**reputation** *n* reputazione *nf* **to enjoy a good reputation** avere un buon nome *vb*
**request** *n* richiesta *nf* **request for payment** richiesta di pagamento *nf*
**requirement** *n* fabbisogno *nm*, esigenze *nfpl* **in accordance with your requirements** conformemente alle vostre esigenze **it is a requirement of the contract that...** secondo le disposizioni del contratto ...
**resale** *n* rivendita *nf*, dettaglio *nm*
**rescind** *vb* rescindere *vb*
**research** *n* ricerca *nf* **research and development (R&D)** ricerca e sviluppo (R&S) *nf & nm* **market research** ricerca di mercato *nf*
**reservation** *n* prenotazione *nf*, riserva *nf* **to make a reservation** fare una prenotazione *vb*
**reserve** **1.** *adj* **reserve currency** valuta di riserva *nf* **reserve stock** scorta di riserva *nf* **2.** *n* **currency reserve** riserva valutaria *nf* **to hold sth in reserve** tenere in riserva *vb* **3.** *vb* riservare *vb*, prenotare *vb*
**residual** *adj* residuo *adj*, residuale *adj*
**resign** *vb* rinunciare a *vb*, rassegnare le dimissioni *vb*, dimettersi *vb*
**resignation** *n* dimissioni *nf pl* **to hand in one's resignation** dare le dimissioni *vb*
**resolution** *n* (decision) delibera *nf* **to make a resolution** adottare una delibera *vb*, prendere una decisione *vb*
**resolve** *vb* (sort out) decidere *vb* **to resolve to do sth** decidere di fare qualcosa *vb*
**resort to** *vb* (have recourse) ricorrere a *vb*
**resources** *npl* risorse *nfpl*, mezzi *nmpl*
**respect** *n* **in respect of...** riguardo a *prep*
**response** *n* **in response to...** in risposta a *prep*
**responsibility** *n* **to take responsibility for sth** assumersi la responsabilità *vb*
**responsible** *adj* responsabile *adj*
**restrict** *vb* limitare *vb*, ridurre *vb*
**restriction** *n* limitazione *nf* **to impose restrictions on** imporre limitazioni a *vb*
**restrictive** *adj* restrittivo *adj* **restrictive practices** pratiche restrittive *nfpl*
**restructure** *vb* ristrutturare *vb*
**retail** *adj* **retail outlet** punto di vendita al dettaglio *nm* **retail price** prezzo al dettaglio *nm*, prezzo al minuto *nm* **retail sales tax** imposta sulle vendite al dettaglio *nf* **retail trade** commercio al dettaglio *nm*
**retain** *vb* trattenere *vb*, contenere *vb*
**retention** *n* trattenuta *nf* **retention of title** conservazione del titolo *nf*
**retire** *vb* andare in pensione *vb*
**retirement** *n* pensionamento *nm* **to take early retirement** andare in pensione anticipatamente *vb*
**retrain** *vb* riqualificare *vb*
**retraining** *n* riqualificazione *nf* **retraining**

**programme, retraining program** (US) programma di riqualificazione *nf*

**return** *n* **in return** in cambio di *prep* **return on capital** utile sul capitale *nm* **return on equity** rendimento del capitale netto *nm* **return on investment** utile sul capitale investito *nm* **return on sales** utile sulle vendite *nm* **returns** *npl* utili *nmpl*

**returnable** *adj* (deposit) restituibile *adj*

**revaluation** *n* (of currency) rivalutazione *nf*

**revalue** *vb* (currency) rivalutare *vb*

**revenue** *n* entrate *nfpl*, ricavi *nmpl*

**reverse** *vb* invertire *vb*

**revert** *vb* tornare *vb*

**revert to** *vb* tornare a *vb*

**revise** *vb* revisionare *vb*, ritoccare *vb*

**revocable** *adj* **revocable letter of credit** lettera di credito revocabile *nf*

**revoke** *vb* (offer) revocare *vb*, abrogare *vb* (licence) revocare *vb*

**right** *n* diritto *nm* **right of recourse** diritto di rivalsa *nm* **right of way** servitù di passaggio *nf* **rights issue** emissione riservata agli azionisti *nf* **sole rights** diritti esclusivi *nmpl* **the right to do sth** il diritto di fare qualcosa *nm* **the right to sth** il diritto a qualcosa *nm*

**rise, raise** (US) **1.** *n* aumento *nm*, rialzo *nm* **2.** *vb* aumentare *vb*

**risk 1.** *adj* **all-risks insurance** assicurazione contro tutti i rischi *nf* **risk analysis** analisi del rischio *nf* **risk assessment** perizia del rischio *nf* **risk capital** capitale di rischio *nm*, capitale azionario *nm* **risk management** gestione del rischio *nf* **2.** *n* rischio *nm* **at the buyer's risk** a rischio dell'acquirente **the policy covers the following risks...** la polizza copre i seguenti rischi

**road** *n* **by road** su strada *adv* **road haulage** trasporto su strada *nm* **road haulage company** vettore stradale *nm* **road traffic** circolazione stradale *nf* **road transport** trasporto su strada *nm*

**ROM (read only memory)** *n* ROM (read only memory) *abbr*

**Rome** *n* **the Treaty of Rome** Trattato di Roma *nm*

**room** *n* **room for manoeuvre** possibilità di manovra *nf & nfpl*

**royal** *adj* **the Royal Mint (GB)** Zecca reale britannica *nf*

**RSVP (répondez s'il vous plaît)** *abbr* è gradita una risposta

**run** *vb* (manage) condurre *vb*, dirigere *vb*, gestire *vb* **running costs** costi correnti *nmpl*

**run down** *vb* (stocks) ridurre *vb*

**run low** *vb* (stocks) diminuire le scorte *vb*

**rush** *adj* **rush hour** ora di punta *nf* **rush job** lavoro urgente *nm* **rush order** ordine urgente *nm*

**sack, fire*** (US) *vb* licenziare *vb*

**safe** *adj* sicuro *adj*

**safety** *n* **safety officer** responsabile dell'antifortunistica *nm*

**salary** *n* stipendio *nm*, retribuzione *nf*, salario *nm* **salary scale** scala retributiva *nf*

**sale 1.** *adj* **sales campaign** campagna di vendita *nf* **sales conference** conferenza del personale addetto alle vendite *nf* **sales department** reparto vendite *nm* **sales figures** ammontare delle vendite *nm* **sales forecast** previsione delle vendite *nf* **sales ledger** partitario vendite *nm* **sales management** management delle vendite *nm*, gestione delle vendite *nf* **2.** *n* vendita *nf*, smercio *nm*, saldo (end of season sale) *nm* **closing-down sale, closing-out sale** (US) svendita per cessazione di esercizio *nf* **export sales** vendite per esportazione *nfpl* **home sales** vendite sul mercato interno *nfpl*

**salesperson** *n* venditore *nm*

**salvage** *vb* salvare *vb*, ricuperare *vb*

**sample 1.** *n* campione *nm* **2.** *vb* campionare *vb*, distribuire *vb*, formare campioni *vb*

**sampling** *n* campionamento *nm*, campionatura *nf*

**sanction** *n* **trade sanctions** sanzioni commerciali *nfpl*

**savings** *npl* risparmi *nmpl* **savings bank** banca di risparmio *nf*, cassa di risparmio *nf*

**scab*** *n* crumiro *nm*

**scale** *n* scala *nf*

**scarcity** *n* scarsità *nf*, penuria *nf*

**schedule 1.** *n* programma *nm*, piano *nm*, allegato *nm* **2.** *vb* programmare *vb*

**scheme** *n* **pension scheme** piano di pensionamento *nm* **recovery scheme** programma di risanamento *nm*

**scrap** *n* (metal) rottami di ferro *nmpl*

**scrip** *n* buono frazionario *nm*

**SDRs (special drawing rights)** *abbr* diritti speciali di prelievo *nmpl*

**sea** *n* **by sea** via mare **sea freight** trasporto marittimo *nm*

**seal** 1. *n* sigillo *nm* 2. *vb* sigillare *vb* **sealed bid** offerta segreta *nf*

**season** *n* stagione *nf* **high season** alta stagione *nf* **low season** bassa stagione *nf*

**seasonal** *adj* stagionale *adj*

**SEC (Securities and Exchange Commission) (UK)** *abbr* SEC (Securities and Exchange Commission) (GB) *abbr*

**secondary** *adj* **secondary industry** industria secondaria *nf* **secondary market** mercato secondario *nm*

**secondment** *n* distaccamento *nm*

**secretary** *n* segretario *nm*, segretaria *nf* **executive secretary** segretario dirigenziale *nm*, segretario esecutivo *nm*

**sector** *n* settore *nm* **primary sector** settore primario *nm* **secondary sector** settore secondiario *nm* **tertiary sector** settore terziario *nm*

**secure** *adj* sicuro *adj*, garantito

**secured** *adj* **secured loan** mutuo garantito *nm*

**securities** *npl* **gilt-edged securities** titoli di stato *nmpl* **listed securities** titoli quotati in borsa *nmpl* **unlisted securities** titoli non quotati in borsa *nmpl*

**security** *n* sicurezza *nf*, garanzia **Social Security (GB)** previdenza sociale *nf*

**self-assessment** *n* autotassazione *nf*

**self-employed** *adj* autonomo *adj*, indipendente

**self-financing** *adj* autofinanziamento *nm*

**self-management** *n* autogestione *nf*

**self-sufficient** *adj* autosufficienza *adj*

**sell** 1. *n* **hard sell** hard sell *nm*, politica di vendite estremamente aggressiva *nf* **soft sell** soft sell *nm*, politica di vendita basata sulla persuasione *nf* 2. *vb* vendere *vb* **to sell sth at auction** vendere all'asta *vb* **to sell sth in bulk** vendere all'ingrosso *vb* **sell off** *vb* svendere *vb*, liquidare *vb* **to sell sth on credit** vendere a credito *vb* **to sell sth retail** vendere al dettaglio *vb* **this article sells well** questo articolo vende bene **sell up** *vb* mettere in liquidazione *vb* **to sell sth wholesale** vendere all'ingrosso *vb*

**seller** *n* venditore *nm*

**semi-skilled** *adj* semispecializzato *adj*

**send** *vb* spedire *vb*, inviare *vb*, mandare *vb* **send back** *vb* rispedire *vb*, rinviare *vb*

**sendee** *n* destinatario *nm*

**sender** *n* mittente *nm*

**senior** *adj* di primo grado *adj*, anziano *adj*, superiore *adj* **senior management** dirigenti di primo grado *nmpl*, senior management *nm*

**seniority** *n* anzianità di servizio *nf*

**service** *n* **after-sales service** servizio di assistenza *nm* **civil service** amministrazione pubblica *nf* **service included** servizio compreso *nm* **service industry** industria terziaria *nf* **National Health Service (GB)** Servizio sanitario nazionale (GB) *nm*

**set up** *vb* (company) avviare *vb*

**settle** *vb* (dispute) appianare (una lite) *vb* (account) saldare *vb*

**severance** *n* **severance pay** indennità di licenziamento *nf*

**shady*** *adj* (dealings) disonesto *adj*, equivoco

**share** 1. *n* azione *nf*, titolo azionario *nm* **a share in the profits** partecipazione ai profitti *nf* **market share** mercato finanziario *nm*, mercato dei titoli *nm* **ordinary share** azione ordinaria *nf* 2. *vb* **to share the responsibilities** condividere le responsabilità *vb*

**shareholder** *n* azionista *nm*, socio *nm*

**shark*** *n* imbroglione *nm*

**sharp** *adj* **sharp practice** pratica spregiudicata *nf*

**shift** *n* turno *nm* **the three-shift system** sistema a turni continui *nm* **shift work** lavoro a turni *nm*

**shipbuilding** *n* costruzioni navali *nfpl*

**shipment** *n* (consignment) spedizione *nf*

**shipper** *n* caricatore *nm*, mittente *nm*

**shipping** *n* **shipping agent** spedizioniere marittimo *nm* **shipping broker** spedizioniere *nm* **shipping line** linea di navigazione *nf*

**shipyard** *n* cantiere navale *nm*

**shirker*** *n* scansafatiche *nm*, imboscato *nm*

**shoddy*** *adj* scadente *adj*

**shop** *n* **shop assistant** commesso *nm*, commessa *nf* **closed shop** closed shop *nm* **shop steward** rappresentante sindacale *nm*, delegato di fabbrica *nm* **to shut up shop** (informal) chiudere bottega *vb*, sospendere ogni attività *vb* **to talk shop** (informal) parlare di lavoro *vb*

**shopping** *n* **shopping centre** shopping center *nm*, centro commerciale *nm*

**short** *adj* **short delivery** consegna in meno *nf* **to be on short time** lavorare a orario ridotto *vb*

**shortage** *n* carenza *nf*, ammanco *nm*, scarsità *nf*

**show** *n* (exhibition) mostra *nf*, esposizione *nf*
**showroom** *n* salone da esposizione *nm*, showroom *nf*
**shredder** *n* macchina distruggi documenti *nf*
**shrink** *vb* contrarre *vb*
**shrinkage** *n* **stock shrinkage** contrazione delle scorte *nf*
**shutdown** *n* fermata temporanea *nf*
**shuttle** *n* shuttle *nm*, navetta *nf*
**SIB (Securities and Investment Board) (GB)** *abbr* SIB *abbr*
**sick** *adj* **sick leave** congedo per malattia *nm*
**sickness** *n* **sickness benefit** sussidio di malattia *nm*
**sight** *n* **sight draft** tratta a vista *nf*
**sign** *vb* firmare *vb*
**signatory** *n* firmatario *nm*
**signature** *n* firma *nf*
**silent** *adj* **silent partner** socio non amministratore *nm*
**sinking** *adj* **sinking fund** fondo di ammortamento *nm*
**sit-in** *n* (strike) sit-in *nm*, raduno di protesta
**size** *n* dimensione *nf*
**skill** *n* abilità *nf*, capacità *nf*
**skilled** *n* (worker) operaio specializzato *nm*
**slackness** *n* (laxity) inerzia *nf*, inattività *nf*
**sliding** *adj* **sliding scale** scala mobile *nf*
**slogan** *n* slogan *nm*, motto pubblicitario
**slow down** *vb* rallentare *vb*
**slowdown** (economy) rallentamento *nm* (strike) sciopero bianco *nm*, sciopero di non collaborazione *nm*
**slump** **1.** *n* congiuntura bassa *nf* **2.** *vb* crollare *vb*, entrare in crisi *vb*
**slush** *adj* **slush fund** fondo nero *nm*, denaro destinato a tangenti *nm*
**small** *adj* **small ads** piccola pubblicità *nf* **small scale** su piccola scala
**smuggle** *vb* contrabbandare *vb*
**society** *n* **building society** società di credito edilizio *nf* **consumer society** società cooperativa di consumatori *nf*
**socio-economic** *adj* **socio-economic categories** categorie socioeconomiche *nfpl*
**software** *n* software *nm* **software package** pachetto software *nm*
**sole** *adj* **sole agent** esclusivista *nm*, agente esclusivo *nm*
**solicitor, lawyer** (US) *n* avvocato *nm*, procuratore legale *nm*
**solvency** *n* solvibilità *nf*
**solvent** *adj* solvibile *adj*
**source** *n* fonte *nf*, risorsa
**sourcing** *n* individuazione
**specialist** *n* specialista *nmf*
**speciality** *n* specialità *nf*
**specialize** *vb* specializzarsi *vb*
**specification** *n* specifica *nf*, capitolato *nm*
**specify** *vb* specificare *vb*
**speculate** *vb* speculare *vb*
**speculator** *n* speculatore *nm*
**spend** *vb* (time) trascorrere *vb* (money) spendere *vb*
**spending** *n* spesa *nf*
**spendthrift** *adj* scialacquatore *adj*, spendaccione *nm*
**sphere** *n* **sphere of activity** sfera di attività *nf*
**spin-off** *n* (product) succedaneo *adj*, spin-off *nm*
**split** **1.** *adj* **split division** divisione *nf* **2.** *vb* spaccarsi *vb*, aprirsi *vb* dividere *vb*
**spoilage** *n* deterioramento *nm*
**spoils** *npl* cariche *nfpl*, prede di guerra *nfpl*
**spokesperson** *n* portavoce *nmf*
**sponsor** *n* sponsor *nm*, patrocinatore *nm*
**sponsorship** *n* sponsorizzazione *nf*, patrocinio *nm*
**spot** *adj* **spot cash** pronti *nmpl* **spot market** mercato a pronti *nm* **spot price** prezzo a pronti *nm* **spot rate** tasso di cambio a pronti *nm*
**spread** *vb* (payments) distribuire *vb*
**spreadsheet** *n* spreadsheet *nm*, foglio elettronico *nm*
**squander** *vb* sperperare *vb*
**squeeze** **1.** *n* **credit squeeze** stretta creditizia *nf* **2.** *vb* (spending) stringere *vb*, restringere *vb*
**stable** *adj* (economy) stabile *adj*
**staff** *n* staff *nm*, personale *nm*
**staffing** *n* dotazione di personale *nf*
**stage** *n* **in stages** in varie fasi
**staged** *adj* **staged payments** pagamenti scaglionati *nmpl*
**stagger** *vb* (holidays, hours, shifts) scaglionare nel tempo *vb*
**stagnation** *n* ristagno *nm*
**stake** *n* posta *nf*, puntata *nf*
**stakeholder** *n* chi tiene le poste *nm*, partecipante *nmf*, *adj*
**stalemate** *n* punto morto *nm*, stallo *nm*
**standard** **1.** *adj* standard *adj*, modello *adj* **standard agreement** contratto tipo *nm* **2.** *n* **gold standard** sistema monetario

aureo *nm* **standard of living** tenore di vita *nm*
**standardization** *n* standardizzazione *nf*
**standardize** *vb* standardizzare *vb*
**standing** *adj* **standing charges** oneri fissi *nmpl* **standing order** commessa permanente *nf*
**staple** *adj* **staple commodities** prodotti principali *nmpl*
**start-up** *n* avviamento *nm* **start-up capital** capitale iniziale *nm*
**state** *n* **state-owned enterprises** aziende statali *nfpl*
**statement** *n* **bank statement** estratto conto *nm*
**statistics** *npl* statistica *nf*
**status** *n* **financial status** posizione finanziaria *nf* **status quo** status quo *nm*
**statute** *n* statuto *nm*, legge *nf*
**steel** *n* **steel industry** industria dell'acciaio *nf*
**sterling** *n* sterlina *nf*, lira sterlina *nf* **sterling area** area della sterlina *nf* **sterling balance** saldi in sterline *nmpl* **pound sterling** lira sterlina *nf*, sterlina *nf*
**stock, inventory** (US) *n* (goods) scorte *nfpl*, giacenze *nfpl*, stock *nm*, stoccaggio *n* **stock control** controllo del livello delle scorte *nm* **stock exchange** borsa valori *nf* **in stock** in stock *adv* **stock market** mercato dei titoli *nm* **out of stock** non in stock *adv* **stocks and shares** valori mobiliari *nmpl*
**stockbroker** *n* mediatore di borsa *nm*, stockbroker *nm*
**stockholder** *n* azionista *nm*, socio *nm*
**stocktaking** *n* inventario *nm*
**stoppage** *n* (strike) sospensione *nm*, sciopero *nm*
**storage** *n* **storage capacity** capacità di magazzinaggio *nf* **cold storage plant** magazzino refrigerato *nm*
**store** *n* (shop) negozio *nm*, grande magazzino *nm* **chain store** negozio a catena *nm*, grande magazzino a filiali multiple *nm* **department store** grande magazzino *nm*
**stowage** *n* stivaggio *nm*
**strategic** *adj* strategico *adj*
**strategy** *n* strategia *nf*
**stress** *n* **executive stress** executive stress *nm*
**strike** **1.** *n* sciopero *nm* **strike action** azione di sciopero *nf* **strike ballot** ballotaggio *nm* **wildcat strike** sciopero selvaggio *nm* **2.** *vb* scioperare *vb*
**strikebreaker** *n* crumiro *nm*
**striker** *n* scioperante *nm*
**subcontract** *vb* subappaltare *vb*
**subcontractor** *n* subappaltatore *nm*
**subordinate** *n* subordinato *nm*, subalterno *nm*
**subscribe** *vb* sottoscrivere *vb*, iscriversi *vb*
**subsidiary** *n* società consociata *nf*, società affiliata *nf*
**subsidize** *vb* sovvenzionare *vb*
**subsidy** *n* **state subsidy** sussidio statale *nm*, sovvenzione statale *nf*
**suburbs** *npl* periferia *nf* **outer suburbs** sobborghi e zone limitrofe
**supermarket** *n* supermercato *nm*, supermarket *nm*
**supertanker** *n* superpetroliera *nf*
**supertax** *n* supertassa *nf*, supertax *nf*, imposta sul reddito addizionale *nf*
**supervisor** *n* supervisore *nm*
**supervisory** *adj* **supervisory board** consiglio direttivo *nm*, consiglio di supervisione *nm*
**supplementary** *adj* supplementare *adj*, integrativo *adj*
**supplier** *n* fornitore *nm*
**supply** **1.** *n* offerta *nf*, fornitura *nf*, approvvigionamento *nm* **supply and demand** domanda e offerta *nf* **2.** *vb* fornire *vb*, rifornire *vb*, offrire *vb*
**surface** *n* **surface mail** posta ordinaria *nf*
**surplus** *n* eccedenza *nf*, surplus *nm* **budget surplus** avanzo di bilancio *nm* **trade surplus** saldo attivo *nm*
**surtax** *n* imposta addizionale *nf*
**survey** *n* **market research survey** inchiesta di mercato *nf*
**swap** **1.** *n* swap *nm*, riporto valutario *nm* **2.** *vb* scambiare *vb*
**sweetener*** *n* (bribe) tangente *nf*
**swindle*** *n* truffa *nf*, imbroglio *nm*
**swindler*** *n* imbroglione *nm*
**switchboard** *n* centralino *nm* **switchboard operator** centralinista *nmf*
**syndicate** *n* consorzio industriale *nm*, sindacato industriale *nm*
**synergy** *n* sinergia *nf*
**synthesis** *n* sintesi *nf*
**synthetic** *adj* sintetico *adj*, artificiale *adj*
**system** *n* sistema *nm*, metodo *nm* **expert system** sistema esperto *nm* **systems analyst** analista di sistemi *nm*, systems analyst *nm*
**table** *vb* (motion, paper) proporre *vb*
**tabulate** *vb* (data) disporre in tabelle *vb* **tabulated data** dati tabulati *nmpl*

**tacit** *adj* tacito *adj*, implicito *adj* **by tacit agreement** per tacito accordo

**tactic** *n* tattica *nf* **delaying tactics** tattiche dilazionatorie *nfpl* **selling tactics** tattiche di vendita *nfpl*

**tailor** *vb* (adapt) adattare *vb*, personalizzare *vb*

**take** *vb* **to take legal action** adire le vie legali *vb* **to take notes** prendere appunti *vb* **to take part in** partecipare a *vb* **to take the chair** presiedere *vb* **to take the lead** prendere il comando *vb* **to take one's time** volerci tempo *vb*, richiedere tempo *vb*

**take over** *vb* (company) rilevare *vb*, acquisire il controllo di *vb*

**takeover** *n* acquisizione di controllo *nf*

**takeup** *n* accaparramento *nm*

**takings** *npl* incassi *nmpl*

**talk** 1. *n* **sales talk** trattative di vendita *nfpl* 2. *vb* **to talk business** parlare d'affari *vb*, discutere di affari *vb*

**tally** 1. *n* riscontro *nm*, verifica *nf* 2. *vb* controllare *vb*, fare la spunta *vb*

**tally up** *vb* calcolare *vb*, contare *vb*

**tally with** corrispondere a *vb*

**tangible** *adj* **tangible asset** attività materiali *nfpl*

**tap** *vb* **to tap a market** sfruttare un mercato *vb*, utilizzare un mercato *vb* **to tap resources** sfruttare le risorse *vb*

**target** 1. *adj* **target date** data obiettivo *nf*, data traguardo *nf* **target market** mercato obiettivo *nm*, mercato traguardo *nm* 2. *n* obiettivo *nm*, traguardo *nm* **production target** obiettivo della produzione *nm*, produzione traguardo *nf* **sales target** obiettivo delle vendite *nm* **to set a target** stabilire un traguardo *vb*, stabilire un obiettivo *vb*

**targeted** *adj* **targeted campaign** campagna indirizzata a un settore specifico *nf*

**tariff** 1. *adj* **tariff barrier** barriera tariffaria *nf* **tariff negotiations** negoziati tariffari *nmpl*, contrattazioni tariffarie *nfpl* **tariff quota** contingente tariffario d'importazione *nm* **tariff reform** riforma tariffaria *nf* 2. *n* tariffa *nf*, tariffa doganale *nf* **to raise tariffs** riscuotere le tariffe *vb*, aumentare le tariffe *vb*

**task** *n* compito *nm*, funzioni *nfpl* **task management** direzione per funzioni *nf*, task management *nm*

**tax** 1. *adj* **tax allowance** sgravio d'imposta *nm*, detrazione d'imposta *nf* **tax claim** ricorso per rimborso di imposte *nm* **tax-deductible** detraibile *adj* **tax-free** esentasse *adj*, esente da imposte *adj* **tax liability** imposizione dell'onere fiscale *nf*, imponibilità *nf* **tax rate** aliquota d'imposta *nf* **tax year** anno fiscale *nm*, esercizio finanziario *nm* 2. *n* tassa *nf*, imposta *nf* **after tax** a netto di tasse, al netto di imposte **before tax** a lordo di imposte **capital gains tax** imposta sui redditi di capitale *nf* **direct tax** imposta diretta *nf* **income tax** imposta sul reddito *nf* **indirect tax** imposta indiretta *nf* **to levy taxes** esigere tributi *vb*, riscuotere tributi *vb*, stabilire imposizioni *vb* **value-added tax, sales tax** (US) imposta valore aggiunto (IVA) *nf*

**taxable** *adj* **taxable income** reddito imponibile *nm*

**taxation** *n* tassazione *nf* **corporate taxation** imposta sulle società *nf*

**taxpayer** *n* contribuente *nm*

**team** *n* **research team** équipe di ricerca *nf*

**technical** *adj* **technical director** direttore tecnico *nm*

**technician** *n* tecnico *nm*, perito *nm*

**technique** *n* **sales technique** tecnica di vendita *nf*

**technology** *n* tecnologia *nf* **information technology** informatica *nf*, tecnologie dell' informazione *nfpl* **technology transfer** trasferimento di tecnologia *nm*

**telebanking** *n* telebanking *nm*

**telecommunications** *npl* telecomunicazioni *nfpl*

**telecopier** *n* facsimile *nm*, telecopiatrice *nf*

**telefax** *n* fax *nm*, facsimile *nm*, telefax *nm*

**telephone** *n* telefono *nm* **telephone box, telephone booth** (US) cabina telefonica *nf* **telephone call** telefonata *nf*, chiamata *nf* **telephone directory** elenco telefonico *nm* **telephone number** numero telefonico *nm*, numero di telefono *nm*

**teleprocessing** *n* elaborazione a distanza *nf*, teleelaborazione *nf*, operazione telematica *nf*

**telesales** *npl* televendite *nfpl*

**televise** *vb* trasmettere per televisione *vb*, teletrasmettere *vb*

**teleworking** *n* lavoro a distanza *nm*

**telex** 1. *n* telex *nm* 2. *vb* (message) trasmettere un messaggio a mezzo telex *vb*, inviare un telex *vb*

**teller** *n* cassiere *nm*, cassiera *nf*

**temporary** *adj* provvisorio *adj*,

temporaneo *adj* **temporary employment** occupazione temporanea *nf*

**tenant** *n* locatario *nm*, inquilino *nm*, conduttore *nm*

**tend** *vb* **to tend toward** tendere a *vb*

**tendency** *n* tendenza *nf* **market tendencies** tendenze del mercato *nfpl*

**tender 1.** *adj* **tender offer** offerta pubblica di acquisizione *nf* **tender price** prezzo d'offerta di appalto *nm* **2.** *n* offerta di appalto *nf*, offerta di fornitura *nf* **sale by tender** vendita con gara di appalto *nf* **to lodge a tender** presentare un'offerta *vb* **to put sth out for tender** indire una gara d'appalto per *vb*

**tenderer** *n* offerente *nm*

**tendering** *n* licitazione *nf*

**tentative** *adj* **tentative offer** offerta provvisoria *nf* **tentative plan** piano provvisorio *nm*

**tenure** *n* possesso *nm*, occupazione *nf*

**term** *n* **at term** a termine, a scadenza **long term** a lungo termine **medium term** a medio termine **term of office** periodo di permanenza in carica *nm* **terms and conditions** condizioni *nfpl* **short term** a breve termine **terms of reference** termini di riferimento *nmpl* **terms of trade** termini di scambio *nmpl*

**terminal 1.** *adj* finale *adj* **terminal bonus** terminal bonus *nm* **terminal market** mercato a termine *nm* **2.** *n* **air terminal** terminal *nm* **computer terminal** periferica *nf*

**termination** *n* terminazione *nf*, rescissione *nf*, estinzione *nf* **termination date** scadenza *nf* **termination of employment** cessazione di impiego *nf*, licenziamento *nm*

**tertiary** *adj* **tertiary industry** settore terziario *nm*

**test** *n* **test case** causa legale che serve a creare un precedente *nf* **test data** test data *nmpl*, dati di prova *nmpl* **to put sth to the test** mettere a prova *vb* **to stand the test** reggere alla prova *vb*

**test-market** *vb* testare il mercato *vb*

**testimonial** *n* attestato di buona condotta *nm*, benservito *nm*, certificato di servizio *nm*

**textile** *n* **textile industry** industria tessile *nf*

**theory** *n* **in theory** in teoria, teoricamente *adv*

**third** *adj* **third party** terzi *nmpl* **third-party insurance** assicurazione sulla responsabilità civile *nf* **the Third World** il terzo mondo *nm*

**thirty** *adj* **Thirty-Share Index (GB)** indice delle azioni ordinarie del Financial Times *nm*

**thrash out** *vb* (agreement, policy) chiarire *vb*, scoprire *vb*

**three** *adj* **three-way split** divisione in tre parti *nf*

**threshold** *n* **tax threshold** scaglione fiscale *nm*, aliquota fiscale *nf*

**thrive** *vb* prosperare *vb*, crescere *vb*

**through** *prep* **to get through to sb** (phone) riuscire a comunicare con qualcuno *vb*, pervenire a qualcuno *vb* **to put sb through (to sb)** (phone) mettere in comunicazione *vb*, mettere in linea *vb*

**tick over** *vb* segnare il passo *vb*, ristagnare *vb*

**ticket** *n* (receipt) scontrino *nm*, foglio *nm*, cartellino *nm* (air, train, bus) biglietto *nm* **ticket agency** agenzia per la vendita di biglietti *nf* **ticket office** biglietteria *nf* **price ticket** cartellino del prezzo *nm*, prezzo del biglietto *nm* **return ticket, round-trip ticket** (US) biglietto di andata e ritorno *nm* **season ticket** abbonamento *nm*, tessera *nf* **single/one-way ticket** (rail/flight) biglietto di sola andata *nm*

**tide over** *vb* far fronte *vb*, superare *vb*

**tie up** *vb* (capital) immobilizzare *vb*

**tied** *adj* **tied loan** prestito vincolato *nm*

**tier** *n* **two-tier system** sistema a due livelli *nm*

**tight** *adj* **to be on a tight budget** avere un budget limitato *vb*

**time** *n* **time and a half** lavoro straordinario *nm* **double time** pagamento orario doppio *nm* **time frame** time frame *nm* **lead time** intervallo fra progettazione e produzione *nm*, intervallo fra ordinazione e conseguimento *nm* **time limit** limite di tempo *nm* **time management** gestione del tempo *nf*

**time-consuming** *adj* comportante una considerevole quantità di tempo *adj*

**time-saving** *adj* con risparmio di tempo

**timescale** *n* durata *nf*

**timeshare** *n* timeshare *nm*

**timetable** *n* orario *nm*

**timing** *n* tempestività *nf*, misurazione dei tempi *nf*

**tip** *n* (restaurant) mancia *nf* (suggestion) suggerimento *nm*, consiglio *nm* **market tip** informazione riservata sul mercato *nf*

**title** *n* (to goods) titolo *nm* **title deed** titolo di proprietà *nm*, istrumento *nm*
**token** *n* **token payment** anticipo *nm*, pagamento simbolico *nm* **token strike** sciopero dimostrativo *nm*
**toll** *n* pedaggio *nm*, tassa di transito *nf*
**ton** *n* tonnellata *nf* **metric ton** tonnellata metrica *nf*
**tone** *n* **dialling tone, dial tone** (US) (phone) segnale acustico di linea libera *nm*
**tonnage** *n* tonnellaggio *nm*, stazza *nf* **bill of tonnage** polizza di stazza *nf* **gross tonnage** tonnellaggio lordo *nm*, stazza lorda *nf* **net tonnage** tonnellaggio netto *nm*, stazza netta *nf*
**top** *adj* **top management** alta direzione *nf* **top prices** prezzi più alti *nmpl* **top priority** priorità assoluta *nf*
**top-level** *adj* a livello dirigenziale *adv*
**top-of-the-range** *adj* d'altissima qualità *adj*
**total** 1. *adj* totale *adj*, complessivo *adj* **total sales** vendite totali *nfpl* 2. *n* totale *nm* **the grand total** somma complessiva *nf*, totale generale *nm*
**tough** *adj* **tough competition** concorrenza spietata *nf*
**tour** *n* **tour of duty** viaggio di dovere *nm*
**tourism** *n* turismo *nm*
**tourist** *n* turista *nm* **the tourist trade** turismo *nm*
**town** *adj* **town centre** centro cittadino *nm* **town council** consiglio comunale *nm* **town hall** municipio *nm* **town planning** urbanistica *nf*
**TQM (Total Quality Management)** *abbr* TQM (gestione della qualità totale) *abbr*
**track** *n* **track record** performance *nf*, prestazione *nf*, conseguimenti *nmpl* **to be on the right track** essere sulla strada giusta *vb*
**trade** 1. *adj* **trade agreement** accordo commerciale *nm* **trade balance** bilancia commerciale *nf* **trade barrier** barriera commerciale *nf*, barriera al libero scambio *nf* **trade cycle** ciclo economico *nm* **trade directory** guida commerciale *nf* **trade fair** fiera commerciale *nf*, mostra commerciale *nf* **trade figures** statistiche commerciali *nfpl* **trade name** marchio di commercio *nm*, nome commerciale *nm* **trade price** prezzo al rivenditore *nm* **trade restrictions** restrizioni commerciali *nfpl* **trade secret** segreto commerciale *nm* **trade talks** negoziati commerciali *nmpl* **Trade Descriptions Act** Trade Descriptions Act *nf*, legge britannica per la protezione dei consumatori *nf* **Trades Union Congress** Confederazione sindacale britannica *nf* **trade union** sindacato *nm* 2. *n* commercio *nm*, trade *nm*, esercenti *nmpl* **balance of trade** bilancia commerciale *nf* **by trade** di mestiere **fair trade** reciprocità commerciale *nf* **foreign trade** commercio estero *nm* **retail trade** commercio al dettaglio *nm* **to be in the trade** (informal) essere del mestiere *vb* 3. *vb* commerciare *vb* **to trade as** (name) svolgere attività commerciale come *vb* **to trade with sb** essere clienti di *vb*, fare affari con *vb*
**trademark** *n* marchio di fabbrica *nm* **registered trademark** marchio depositato *nm*
**trader** *n* commerciante *nmf*, esercente *nmf*
**trading** *adj* **trading area** area commerciale *nf* **trading capital** capitale di esercizio *nm* **trading company** compagnia commerciale *nf*, trading company *nf*, trading *nf* **trading estate** zona industriale *nf* **trading loss** perdita di esercizio *nf* **trading margin** margine di utile *nm* **trading nation** nazione commerciale *nf* **trading partner** partner commerciale *nm* **trading standards** normative commerciali *nfpl* **Trading Standards Office (US)** Trading Standards Office *nm* **trading year** anno commerciale *nm*
**traffic** *n* **air traffic** traffico aereo *nm* **rail traffic** traffico ferroviario *nm* **road traffic** traffico stradale *nm* **sea traffic** traffico marittimo *nm*
**train** 1. *n* **goods train, freight train** (US) treno merci *nm* **passenger train** treno passeggeri *nm* 2. *vb* (staff) addestrare *vb*, istruire *vb*, formare *vb*
**trainee** *n* apprendista *nmf*, tirocinante *nmf* **trainee manager** manager tirocinante *nmf*
**training** *n* addestramento *nm*, formazione professionale *nf* **advanced training** addestramento avanzato *nm*, formazione professionale avanzata *nf* **training centre** centro di addestramento *nm*, centro di formazione professionale *nm* **training course** corso di addestramento *nm*
**transaction** *n* operazione commerciale *nf*, transazione *nf* **cash transaction**

operazione a pronti *nf* **transaction management** gestione delle transazioni *nf*

**transcribe** *vb* trascrivere *vb*, trasmettere *vb*

**transfer 1.** *adj* **transfer desk** (transport) banco transiti *nm* **transfer duty** imposta di bollo sui trasferimenti di titoli azionari *nf* **transfer lounge** (transport) sala trasbordi *nf* **transfer payments** trasferimenti *nmpl* **transfer price** prezzo di trasferimento *nm* **transfer tax** imposta sul trasferimento di titoli *nf* **transfer technology** trasferimento di tecnologie *nf* **2.** *n* **bank transfer** bonifico bancario *nm* **capital transfer** trasferimento di capitale *nm* **credit transfer** bonifico *nm* **3.** *vb* (call) trasferire *vb* (ownership) cedere la proprietà *vb*, trasferire *vb* (transport) fare un trasbordo *vb*, trasbordare *vb*

**transferable** *adj* trasferibile *adj*, cedibile *adj*

**transit 1.** *adj* **transit goods** merci in transito *nfpl* **transit lounge** (transport) sala transiti *nf* **transit passenger** (transport) passeggero in transito *nm* **2.** *n* transito *nm* **in transit** in transito, in viaggio **lost in transit** perso in viaggio

**transmit** *vb* trasmettere *vb*

**transnational** *adj* transnazionale *adj*

**transport 1.** *adj* **transport agent** spedizioniere *nm* **transport company** società di trasporti *nf* **2.** *n* **air transport** trasporto aereo *nm* **public transport** trasporti pubblici *nmpl* **rail transport** trasporto ferroviario *nm* **road transport** trasporto stradale *nm*

**transportation** *n* trasporto *nm*

**transship** *vb* trasbordare *vb*

**travel 1.** *adj* **travel agency** agenzia di viaggi *nf* **travel insurance** assicurazione viaggi *nf* **2.** *n* **air travel** viaggio aereo *nm* **business travel** viaggio d'affari *nm*

**traveller, traveler** (US) *n* viaggiatore *nm* **traveller's cheque, traveler's check** (US) traveller's cheque *nm*, assegno turistico *nm*

**travelling, traveling** (US) *adj* **travelling expenses, travel expenses** (US) spese di missione *nfpl*, spese di viaggio *nfpl*

**treasurer** *n* **treasurer check (US)** assegno circolare *nm*, credenziale *nf* **company treasurer** tesoriere di impresa *nm*

**treasury** *n* **Treasury bill** buono del tesoro (BOT) *nm* **the Treasury** Tesoro *nm*, Ministero del tesoro *nm* **the Treasury Department (US)** Ministero del tesoro statunitense *nm*

**treaty** *n* trattato *nm*, accordo *nm* **commercial treaty** trattato commerciale *nm* **to make a treaty** raggiungere un accordo *vb*

**trend** *n* trend *nm*, tendenza *nf* **trend analysis** analisi di tendenza *nf* **current trend** trend attuale *nm* **economic trend** trend economico *nm* **market trend** trend del mercato *nm* **price trend** trend dei prezzi *nm* **to buck a trend** opporsi ad un trend *vb* **to set a trend** creare un trend *vb*

**trial 1.** *adj* **trial offer** offerta di prova *nf* **trial period** periodo di prova *nm* **2.** *n* **trial and error** tentativi *nmpl* **to carry out trials** effettuare prove *vb*

**tribunal** *n* **industrial tribunal** tribunale industriale *nm*

**trim** *vb* (investment) apportare tagli a *vb* (workforce) tagliare *vb*

**trimming** *n* **cost trimming** taglio delle spese *nm*, riassetto delle spese *nm*

**trip** *n* **business trip** viaggio d'affari *nm* **round trip** viaggio d'andata e ritorno *nm*

**triplicate** *n* **in triplicate** in triplice copia

**trust 1.** *adj* **trust agreement** negozio fiduciario *nm* **trust company** società fiduciaria *nf*, società di gestione del portafoglio *nf* **trust estate** proprietà tenuta in amministrazione fiduciaria *nf* **trust fund** fondo fiduciario *nm*, fondo comune d'investimento *nm* **2.** *n* **investment trust** società d'investimento *nf*, fondo comune d'investimento mobiliare *nm* **to hold sth in trust** avere l'amministrazione fiduciaria di *vb* **to set up a trust** istituire un fondo comune d'investimento *vb*, istituire un trust *vb* **to supply sth on trust** fornire a credito *vb* **unit trust** società d'investimento a capitale variabile *nf*, fondo aperto *nm*

**trustee** *n* fiduciario *nm*, amministratore fiduciario *nm* **trustee department** (bank) ufficio amministratori fiduciari *nm*

**trusteeship** *n* amministrazione fiduciaria *nf*

**try out** *vb* provare *vb*, mettere alla prova *vb*

**turn** *vb* (market) cambiare *vb*

**turn down** *vb* (offer) rifiutare un'offerta *vb*, declinare *vb*

**turn on** *vb* (machine) accendere *vb*

**turn out** *vb* (end) risultare *vb*, andare a finire *vb*

**turn over** *vb* consegnare *vb*, inoltrare *vb*, avere un volume d'affari di *vb*
**turn round, turn around** (US) *vb* (company) risanare *vb*
**turnabout** *n* inversione di tendenza *nf*, cambiamento repentino *nm*
**turning** *adj* **turning point** svolta *nf*
**turnover** *n* rotazione delle giacenze *nf*, giro d'affari *nm* **capital turnover** indice di rotazione del capitale *nm* **turnover rate** indice di rotazione *nm* **turnover ratio** indice di rotazione *nm* **turnover tax** imposta sugli affari *nf*
**twenty-four** *adj* **twenty-four-hour service** servizio continuo *nm*, servizio ininterrotto *nm*
**two** *adj* **two-speed** a due velocità **two-tier** doppio *adj*, duplice *adj*, a due livelli **two-way** a due direzioni, a due vie, a due sensi
**tycoon** *n* magnate *nm*, capitano d'industria *nm*
**type** 1. *n* **bold type** neretto *nm*, grassetto *nm* **italic type** carattere corsivo *nm* **large type** caratteri grandi *nm pl* **small type** caratteri piccoli *nm pl* 2. *vb* battere a macchina *vb*, dattilografare *vb*
**typewriter** *n* macchina da scrivere *nf*
**typing** *adj* **typing error** errore di battuta *nm*
**typist** *n* dattilografo *nm*, dattilografa *nf*
**ultimo** *adj* ultimo scorso *adv*, u.s. *abbr*
**unanimous** *adj* unanime *adj*
**uncleared** *adj* (customs) non sdoganato *adj* (cheque) assegno non passato alla stanza di compensazione *nm*, assegno non incassato *nm*
**unconditional** *adj* incondizionato *adj*, senza condizioni
**unconfirmed** *adj* non confermato *adj*
**undeclared** *adj* (goods) non dichiarato *adj*
**undercapitalized** *adj* sottocapitalizzato *adj*
**undercharge** *vb* addebitare in meno *vb*, far pagare meno *vb*
**undercut** *vb* vendere a prezzo inferiore a quello di *vb*
**underdeveloped** *adj* **underdeveloped country** paese sottosviluppato *nm*
**underemployed** *adj* sottoccupato *adj*
**underinsured** *adj* sottoassicurato *adj*
**underpay** *vb* retribuire inadeguatamente *vb*
**underpayment** *n* retribuzione inadeguata *nm*
**undersell** *vb* svendere *vb*, vendere sottocosto *vb*, vendere a un prezzo inferiore *vb*
**understanding** *n* intesa *nf*, accordo *nm*
**undersubscribed** *adj* non completamente sottoscritto *adj*
**undertake** *vb* assumere *vb*, assumersi l'impegno di *vb*
**undertaking** *n* impresa *nf*, impegno *nm*
**undervalue** *vb* svalutare *vb*, deprezzare *vb*, sottovalutare *vb*
**underwrite** *vb* (shares) sottoscrivere *vb* assicurare *vb* (risk) assumere un rischio *vb*
**underwriter** *n* sottoscrittore *nm*, assicuratore *nm*, finanziatore *nm*, società garante *nf*
**undischarged** *adj* (bankrupt) fallito non riabilitato *adj*
**unearned** *adj* **unearned income** risconto passivo *nm*, reddito di capitale *nm*, rendita *nf*
**unemployed** *adj* disoccupato *adj*
**unemployment** 1. *adj* **unemployment benefit** sussidio di disoccupazione *nm*, indennità di disoccupazione *nf* **unemployment insurance** assicurazione contro la disoccupazione *nf* 2. *n* disoccupazione *nf* **level of unemployment** livello della disoccupazione *nm* **rate of unemployment** tasso di disoccupazione *nm*
**unexpected** *adj* imprevisto *adj*
**unfair** *adj* **unfair dismissal** licenziamento iniquo *nm*
**unforeseen** *adj* **unforeseen circumstances** circostanze impreviste *nfpl*
**unification** *n* unificazione *nf*
**unilateral** *adj* (contract) unilaterale *adj*
**uninsurable** *adj* non assicurabile *adj*
**union** 1. *adj* **union membership** iscrizione al sindacato *nf*, iscritti al sindacato *nmpl* **union representative** sindacalista *nmf* 2. *n* **trade union, labor union** (US) sindacato *nm*
**unit** 1. *adj* **unit cost** costo unitario *nm* **unit price** prezzo unitario *nm* **unit trust** fondo comune d'investimento *nf* 2. *n* **unit of production** unità di produzione *nf*
**united** *adj* **United Nations** Nazioni Unite (ONU) *nfpl*
**unlimited** *adj* **unlimited company** società a responsabilità illimitata *nf*, società in nome collettivo *nf* **unlimited credit** credito illimitato *nm* **unlimited liability** responsabilità illimitata *nf*

**unload** *vb* scaricare *vb*
**unmarketable** *adj* invendibile *adj*, non commerciabile *adj*
**unofficial** *adj* **unofficial strike** sciopero spontaneo *nm*
**unpack** *vb* disimballare *vb*, disfare *vb*
**unpaid** *adj* **unpaid balance** saldo insoluto *nm*, saldo in sofferenza *nm* **unpaid bill** cambiale insoluta *nf*, sofferenza *nf* **unpaid cheque** assegno non onorato *nm*
**unprofessional** *adj* non professionale *adj*, scorretto *adj*
**unprofitable** *adj* non redditizio *adj*, non remunerativo *adj*
**unsaleable** *adj* invendibile *adj*
**unsatisfactory** *adj* insoddisfacente *adj*
**unsecured** *adj* **unsecured bond** obbligazione senza garanzia *nf* **unsecured credit** credito non garantito *nm*, credito in bianco *nm*
**unskilled** *adj* **unskilled worker** operaio non specializzato *nm*
**unsold** *adj* invenduto *adj*
**unsolicited** *adj* **unsolicited offer** offerta non sollecitata *nf*
**up-to-date** *adj* aggiornato *adj* **to bring sth up-to-date** aggiornare *vb*
**update** *vb* (records) aggiornare *vb*
**upgrade** *vb* (computer) potenziare *vb* migliorare *vb*, migliorare la qualità di *vb*, sostituire con un prodotto migliore *vb*
**upswing** *n* periodo di prosperità *nf*
**upturn** *n* ripresa *nf*
**upward** *adj, adv* verso l'alto *adv*
**urban** *adj* **urban renewal** bonifica urbana *nf* **urban sprawl** espansione urbana incontrollata *nf*
**urgency** *n* **a matter of urgency** una faccenda urgentissima *nf*
**urgent** *adj* urgente *adj*
**urgently** *adv* urgentemente *adv*
**usage** *n* **intensive usage** uso intenso *nm*
**use** *n* **to make use of sth** utilizzare *vb*
**user-friendly** *adj* user-friendly *adj*, amichevole per l'utente *adj*, facile da usare *adj*
**usury** *n* usura *nf*
**utility** *n* **marginal utility** utilità marginale *nf* **public utility** impresa di pubblici servizi *nf*
**utilization** *n* utilizzo *nm*, impiego *nm*
**utilize** *vb* utilizzare *vb*
**vacancy** *n* posto vacante *nm*
**vacant** *adj* vacante *adj*, libero *adj*, sfitto *adj*
**valid** *adj* valido *adj*
**validate** *vb* convalidare *vb*, omologare *vb*
**validity** *n* validità *nf*
**valuable** *adj* prezioso *adj*, di valore *adj*
**valuation** *n* valutazione *nf*, determinazione del valore *nf*, stima *nf*
**value** *n* valore *nm* **face value** valore nominale *nm* **market value** valore di mercato *nm* **to gain value** acquisire valore *vb*, aumentare di valore *vb* **to get value for one's money** spendere bene il proprio denaro *vb* **to lose value** diminuire di valore *vb*
**variable** *adj* variabile *adj* **variable costs** costi variabili *nmpl*, costi di funzionamento *nmpl* **variable rate** tasso variabile *nm*
**variance** *n* **budget variance** scostamente dalle previsioni di budget *nm*
**VAT (value added tax)** *abbr* IVA (imposta valore aggiunto) *abbr*
**vendee** *n* acquirente *nmf*
**vending machine** *n* distributore automatico *nm*
**vendor** *n* venditore *nm*, fornitore *nm* **vendor capital** capitale del venditore *nm* **joint vendor** venditore congiunto *nm*, venditore in partecipazione *nm*
**verbatim** *adv* parola per parola, letteralmente *adv*
**vertical** *adj* **vertical integration** integrazione verticale *nf*
**vested** *adj* **vested interests** interessi acquisiti *nmpl* **vested rights** diritti acquisiti *nmpl*
**veto** **1.** *n* veto *nm* **2.** *vb* mettere il veto *vb*
**viability** *n* vitalità *nf*, attuabilità *nf*
**video** *n* video *nm* **video facilities** attrezzature video *nfpl*, mezzi video *nmpl*, impianti video *nmpl*
**viewer** *n* spettatore *nm*, telespettatore *nm*
**VIP (very important person)** *abbr* VIP (very important person) *abbr*
**visa** *n* visto *nm*
**visible** *adj* **visible exports** esportazioni visibili *nfpl*
**visit** **1.** *n* visita *nf* **2.** *vb* visitare *vb*
**visitor** *n* visitatore *nm*
**visual** *adj* **visual display unit (VDU)** VDU *nf*, visualizzatore *nm* **visual telephone** videotelefono *nm*
**vocational** *adj* attitudinale *adj*, professionale *adj*, vocazionale *adj*
**volatile** *adj* (prices) variabile *adj*, volubile *adj*, mutevole *adj*
**volume** *n* **volume discount** sconto per volume *nm* **trading volume** volume delle contrattazioni *nm*

**voluntary** *adj* **to go into voluntary liquidation** mettersi in liquidazione volontaria *vb* **voluntary wage restraint** tregua salariale volontaria *nf*

**vote 1.** *n* **vote of no confidence** voto di sfiducia *nm* **vote of thanks** ringraziamento pubblico *nm* **2.** *vb* votare *vb*, dare il voto *vb*

**voting** *adj* **voting right** diritto di voto *nm*

**voucher** *n* buono *nm*, voucher *nm*

**wage 1.** *adj* **wage demand** richiesta di aumento salariale *nf* **wage earner** salariato *nm* **wage increase** aumento salariale *nm* **wage negotiations** trattative salariali *nfpl* **wage packet, salary package** (US) busta paga *nf* **wage policy** politica salariale *nf* **wage restraint** tregua salariale *nf*, pausa salariale *nf* **wage rise** aumento di salario *nm*, aumento salariale *nm* **wage(s) agreement** accordo salariale *nm* **wage(s) bill** conto degli aumenti salariali *nm* **wage scale** scala retributiva *nf*, scala dei salari *nf* **wage(s) claim** richiesta d'aumento salariale *nf* **wage(s) freeze** blocco dei salari *nm* **wage(s) settlement** accordo salariale *nm* **2.** *n* salario *nm* **average wage** salario medio *nm* **minimum wage** salario minimo *nm*, minimo salariale *nm* **net wage** salario netto *nm* **real wage** salario reale *nm* **starting wage** salario iniziale *nm* **3.** *vb* **to wage a campaign** intraprendere una campagna *vb*

**waiting** *adj* **waiting list** lista d'attesa *nf*

**waive** *vb* rinunciare a *vb*

**waiver** *n* rinuncia *nf*, abbandono *nm* **waiver clause** clausola di non pregiudizio *nf*, clausola di rinunzia *nf*

**wall** *n* **tariff wall** barriera tariffaria *nf* **to go to the wall** avere la peggio *vb*, fallire *vb*, far fiasco *vb* **Wall Street (US)** Wall Street (Borsa Valori di New York) *nf*

**war** *n* **price war** guerra dei prezzi *nf* **trade war** guerra commerciale *nf*

**warehouse** *n* magazzino *nm*, deposito *nm* **bonded warehouse** magazzino doganale *nm*

**warehousing** *n* immagazzinamento *nm*

**wares** *npl* merci *nfpl*, articoli *nmpl*

**warn** *vb* **to warn sb against doing sth** avvertire qualcuno di non fare qualcosa *vb*

**warning** *n* **due warning** debito avviso *nm* **warning sign** segnale di pericolo *nm* **without warning** senza preavviso

**warrant 1.** *n* garanzia *nf*, mandato *nm*, nota di pegno *nf*, certificato di diritto di opzione *nm* **warrant for payment** mandato di pagamento *nm* **2.** *vb* garantire *vb*

**warranty** *n* garanzia *nf* **under warranty** sotto garanzia

**wastage** *n* spreco *nm* **wastage rate** tasso di scarto *nm*

**waste 1.** *adj* **waste products** prodotti di scarto *nmpl*, rifiuti *nmpl* **2.** *n* **industrial waste** scarichi industriali *nmpl*, rifiuti industriali *nmpl* **waste of time** spreco di tempo *nm* **to go to waste** andare sprecato *vb* **3.** *vb* sprecare *vb*, perdere *vb*

**wasting** *adj* **wasting asset** risorsa soggetta a esaurimento *nf*, cespite ammortizzabile *nm*

**watch** *vb* **to watch developments** osservare gli sviluppi *vb*

**watchdog** *n* (fig.) organo di sorveglianza *nm* **watchdog committee** comitato di sorveglianza *nm*

**water down** *vb* mitigare *vb*, annacquare *vb*

**watered** *adj* **watered capital** capitale annacquato *nm* **watered stock** capitale azionario annacquato *nm*

**watertight** *adj* (fig.) perfetto *adj*, che non fa una grinza

**wave** *n* (of mergers, takeovers) ondata *nf*

**wavelength** *n* **to be on the same wavelength** essere in sintonia con qualcuno *vb*

**weaken** *vb* (market) indebolire *vb*

**wealth** *n* ricchezza *nf*, patrimonio *nm* **national wealth** patrimonio nazionale *nm* **wealth tax** imposta sul patrimonio *nf*

**week** *n* **twice a week** due volte alla settimana *adv* **working week** settimana lavorativa *nf*

**weekly** *adj* **weekly wages** paga settimanale *nf*

**weigh** *vb* **to weigh the pros and cons** soppesare il pro e il contro *vb*

**weight** *n* **dead weight** portata lorda *nf*, peso morto *nm* **excess weight** eccedenza di peso *nf* **gross weight** peso lordo *nm* **net weight** peso netto *nm* **weights and measures** pesi e misure *nmpl & nfpl*

**weighted** *adj* **weighted average** media ponderata *nf* **weighted index** indice ponderato *nm*

**weighting** *n* ponderazione *nf*

**weighty** *adj* grave *adj*, importante *adj*

**welfare 1.** *adj* **welfare benefits** sussidi

statali *nmpl* **welfare state** stato assistenziale *nm* **2.** *n* benessere *nm*, prosperità *nf*

**well-advised** *adj* avveduto *adj*

**well-informed** *adj* al corrente *adj*, bene informato *adj*

**well-known** *adj* rinomato *adj*

**well-made** *adj* ben fatto *adj*

**well-paid** *adj* ben pagato *adj*

**well-tried** *adj* provato *adj*, sicuro *adj*

**WEU (Western European Union)** *abbr* UEO (Unione dell'Europa occidentale) *abbr*

**white** *adj* **white-collar worker** colletti bianchi *nmpl*

**wholesale 1.** *adj* **wholesale price** prezzo all'ingrosso *nm* **wholesale trade** commercio all'ingrosso *nm* **2.** *n* **at/by wholesale** all'ingrosso *adv*

**wholesaler** *n* grossista *nm*

**wholly** *adv* **wholly-owned subsidiary** consociata controllata nella misura del 100 per cento

**wide-ranging** *adj* ad ampio raggio

**will** *n* testamento *nm*

**win** *vb* **win customers** guadagnarsi dei clienti *vb*, cattivarsi dei clienti *vb* **to win support** ottenere il sostegno *vb*

**wind up** *vb* liquidare *vb*

**windfall** *n* colpo di fortuna *nm*, guadagno inaspettato *nm* **windfall profit** sopravvenienza attiva *nf*, utile d'esercizio inatteso *nm*

**winding-up** *n* liquidazione *nf* **winding-up arrangements** procedure di liquidazione *nfpl* **winding-up order** ordine di liquidazione *nm*

**window** *n* **window of opportunity** spiraglio di opportunità *nm*

**withdraw** *vb* **to withdraw an offer** ritirare un'offerta *vb*

**withdrawal** *n* prelievo *nm* **withdrawal of funds** prelievo di fondi *nm*

**withhold** *vb* **to withhold a document** rifiutare di dare un documento *vb*, nascondere un documento *vb*

**withstand** *vb* resistere a *vb*, opporsi a *vb*

**witness 1.** *n* testimone *nm* **2.** *vb* testimoniare *vb* **to witness a signature** sottoscrivere l'apposizione di una firma come testimone *vb*

**word** *n* **to give one's word** dare la propria parola *vb* **to keep one's word** essere di parola *vb*

**word processing** word processing *nm*, elaborazione di testi *nf*

**word processor** word processor *nm*

**wording** *n* formulazione *nf*, dicitura *nf*

**work 1.** *adj* **work experience** esperienza di lavoro *nf* **work permit** permesso di lavoro *nm* **work schedule** programma di lavoro *nm* **work sharing** ripartizione del lavoro *nf* **work study** studio del lavoro *nm* **2.** *n* **casual work** lavoro avventizio *nm* **day off work** giornata libera *nf* **day's work** giornata di lavoro *nf* **factory work** lavoro di fabbrica *nm* **office work** lavoro d'ufficio *nm* **to be in work** avere un lavoro *vb* **to be out of work** essere disoccupato *vb* **to look for work** cercare lavoro *vb* **3.** *vb* lavorare *vb*, funzionare *vb* **to work to rule** fare lo sciopero bianco *nm* **to work unsocial hours** lavorare in orari scomodi *vb*

**workable** *adj* fattibile *adj*, operativo *adj*

**workaholic** *n* stacanovista *nm*, maniaco del lavoro *nm*, lavorodipendente *nm*

**workday (US)** *n* giornata lavorativa *nf*

**worker** *n* **casual worker** lavoratore avventizio *nm* **clerical worker** impiegato *nm* **worker-director** amministratore rappresentante i lavoratori *nm* **manual worker** operaio *nm*, manovale *nm* **worker participation** partecipazione operaia *nf* **skilled worker** lavoratore specializzato *nm* **unskilled worker** lavoratore non specializzato *nm*

**workforce** *n* forza lavoro *nf*

**working** *adj* **working agreement** accordo operativo *nm* **working area** area di lavoro *nf* **working capital** capitale netto di esercizio *nm* **working conditions** condizioni di lavoro *nfpl* **working environment** ambiente di lavoro *nm* **working hours** ore lavorative *nfpl* **working knowledge** conoscenza discreta *nf* **working language** lingua di lavoro *nf*, linguaggio di lavoro *nm* **working life** periodo di vita lavorativa *nm* **working majority** maggioranza effettiva *nf* **working model** modello funzionante *nm* **working paper** foglio di lavoro *nm* **working party** gruppo di lavoro *nm* **working population** popolazione attiva *nf* **working week (GB)** settimana lavorativa *nf*

**workload** *n* carico di lavoro *nm*

**workmate** *n* collega *nmf*

**workplace** *n* luogo di lavoro *nm*

**works** *n* stabilimento *nm*, fabbrica *nf* **public works programme (GB)** programma di lavori pubblici *nm* **works**

committee consiglio di fabbrica *nm* **works council** consiglio di gestione *nm* **works manager** direttore di stabilimento *nm*

**workshop** *n* officina *nf*, stabilimento *nm*

**workweek (US)** *n* settimana lavorativa *nf*

**world** 1. *adj* **world consumption** consumo globale *nm* **world exports** esportazioni globali *nfpl* **world fair** mostra mondiale *nf* **World Bank** Banca Mondiale *nf* **World Court** Corte Internazionale di Giustizia *nf* **2.** *n* mondo *nm* **the commercial world** mondo commerciale *nm*

**worldwide** *adj* su scala mondiale

**worth** *adj* **to be worth** valere *vb*

**wpm (words per minute)** *abbr* p/m (parole al minuto) *nfpl*

**wreck** *vb* mandare in rovina *vb*

**writ** *n* citazione in giudizio *nf*, querela *nf* **to issue a writ** emettere una citazione in giudizio *vb*, emettere una querela *vb*

**write down** *vb* (depreciation) svalutare *vb*

**write off** *vb* (debts) cancellare *vb*, stornare *vb* (vehicle) distruggere completamente *vb*, dichiarare non assicurabile *vb*

**write-off** *n* oggetto senza valore *nm*, perdita completa *nf*

**wrongful** *adj* **wrongful dismissal** licenziamento illecito *nm*

**xerox** *vb* fotocopiare *vb*

**Xerox (R)** *n* (machine) fotocopiatrice Xerox *nf*

**year** *n* **year-end dividend** dividendo di fine anno *nm* **year-end inventory** inventario di fine anno *nm* **financial year** anno finanziario *nm*, esercizio finanziario *nm* **fiscal year** anno finanziario *nm*, esercizio finanziario *nm* **tax year** anno fiscale *nm*

**yearly** *adj* **yearly income** reddito annuo *nm*

**yellow** *adj* **the Yellow pages (R) (GB)** le Pagine Gialle *nfpl*

**yen** *n* (currency) yen *nm* **yen bond** obbligazione in yen *nf*

**yield** 1. *adj* **yield curve** curva di rendimento *nf* **2.** *n* **yield on shares** rendita derivante da titoli azionari *nf* **3.** *vb* rendere *vb*

**young** *adj* **young economy** economia giovane *nf*

**zenith** *n* zenit *nm*, vertice *nm*

**zero** 1. *adj* **zero address** senza indirizzo **zero defect** senza difetti, assenza di difetti *nf* **zero growth** sviluppo zero *nm* **zero hour** l'ora zero *nf* **zero rate/rating** tasso zero *nm* **zero-rate taxation** tassazione a tasso zero *nf* **to be zero-rated for VAT** essere esenti dall'IVA *vb* **2.** *n* zero *nm* **below zero** sotto zero

**zip code (US)** *n* codice di avviamento postale statunitense *nm*

**zone** 1. *n* **currency zone** area valutaria *nf* **enterprise zone** enterprise zone *nf* **postal zone** zona postale *nf* **time zone** fuso orario *nm* **wage zone** zona salariale *nf*, categoria salariale *nf* **2.** *vb* suddividere in zone *vb*

**zoning** *n* suddivisione in zone *nf*